DEVELOPMENT OF A PRIMITIVE TRIBE

About the Author

Dr. Bhagyalaxmi Mahapatra having obtained her M.Sc. degree in Anthropology was awarded Ph.D. in the year 2004 by Berhampur University. Subsequently, she has pursued her research career on UGC and ICSSR, major sponsored projects on Self-Help Groups and Eco-tourism respectively. Now she is a Senior Fellow under Ministry of Culture.

Development of a Primitive Tribe

A Study of Didayis

Bhagyalaxmi Mahapatra

CONCEPT PUBLISHING COMPANY PVT. LTD.
NEW DELHI-110 059

ISBN-13 : 978-81-8069-782-1

First Published 2011

Published and Printed by

Concept
Since 1974

Concept Publishing Company Pvt. Ltd.

Regd. Office :

A/15-16, Commercial Block, Mohan Garden
New Delhi-110059 (India)
Phones : 25351460, 25351794, *Fax* : 091-11-25357109
Email : publishing@conceptpub.com
Website : www.conceptpub.com

Editorial Office :

H-13, Bali Nagar, New Delhi-110 015, India.

Cataloging in Publication Data--*Courtesy:* D.K. Agencies (P) Ltd. <docinfo@dkagencies.com>

Mahapatra, Bhagyalaxmi.

Development of a primitive tribes : a study of Didayis / Bhagyalaxmi Mahapatra.

p. cm.

Originally presented as the author's thesis (Ph. D.)--Berhampur University, 2004.
Includes bibliographical references (p.) and index.
ISBN 13: 9788180697821

1. Didayi (Indic people) 2. Malkangiri (India : District).--Social life and customs. 3. Malkangiri (India : District).--Economic conditions. 4. Didayi (Indic people)--Government policy--India--Malkangiri (District) 5. Rural development projects--India--Malkangiri (District) I. Title.

DDC 305.800954133 22

Dedicated to

My Mother

Dedicated to

My Mother

Foreword

Sixty years of independence have no doubt brought about a great many transformations in the Indian economy. The challenges before all the economic agents of the country are concerned with the issue of further strengthening our strength and remove our weakness. Certainly, we need an objective assessment of the past and a visionary perspective of the future. So far tribal development is concerned, it is quite imperative that the active participation of the people in the development programmes meant for them; since it is an important factor contributing to the success of the programmes.

Tribal development strategies have in fact proliferated since 1960 because of the interest of the Government and partly because of the rapid growth of awareness among the tribal leaders about the nature of their deprivation and entitlement. The Constituent Assembly of post-independent India accepted the tribal problem as an integral part of the development of the Indian people as a whole. The Article 46 lays down the safeguards for the Scheduled Castes and the Scheduled Tribes to protect them from the social injustice and all forms of exploitation. The Government launched Community Development Programmes (CDPs) and National Extension Service programmes (NES Blocks) from 1952 with a view to ameliorating the socio-economic conditions of the tribal and rural people. A more intense approach was adopted for tribal welfare through Special Multi-purpose Tribal Blocks (SMPT Blocks). Further, a special plan, called as "Tribal Sub Plan Strategy (TSP)" during Fifth Five Year Plan (1974) was evolved specially for the 75 PTGs of India. Under this plan Micro Projects were launched to cater the integrated needs of PTGs. In Orissa at present 17 Micro Projects have been operating for

12 PTGs out of which 13 Projects are within the scheduled areas. The Didayi is one amongst the 13 PTGs of Orissa and a Micro Project named as "Didayi Development Agency" (DDA) was established in the year 1986 at Kudumulugumma of Malkangiri district of Orissa.

The Didayi is indeed a little known Primitive Tribal Group of Orissa and is confined to Kondakamberu Mountain range and its foothills which constitutes the part of the Eastern Ghat Mountain Range. In fact the hill range is known as Didayi land. Their history claims that they were primarily leading a nomadic life within this confined area of hill range and valley of Machhkund river. Gradually, they settled down in hilltops, foothills and valleys. The construction of Balimela Hydel Project (1962) changed their lifestyle and habitat. The people settled in the valleys were displaced as their lands got submerged in the reservoir water. Most of them shifted to hill-top and some preferred to stay back at their own locality of river bank. A few availed the rehabilitation provisions of the government and settled. As a result, the geographical barrier had made them apparently alienated and are identified socio-culturally as plain, hill, cut off and Phulpadar rehabilitated Didayis on the basis of their geographical habitation.

Displacement has a definite after-impact on the people's social, cultural and economic identity which has become an instrumental factor for Dr. Bhagyalaxmi to take the Didayi for her doctoral research work. Apart from that Government's developmental intervention has been facilitating through the Micro Project since 1986. Under the Micro Project there are 37 villages covering three sectors: plain, hilltop and cut off. The DDA with an integrated approach, has been undertaking a series of developmental schemes with a view to bringing about socio-economic development of the people on a sustainable basis. This has also motivated the researcher to carry out an impact assessment study on the implemented schemes and programmes of the Micro Project. Righteously, she has selected 12 sample villages covering four from each sector: plain, hill-top and cut off, with a view to getting an overall impact of the Micro Project.

An assessment of any development programme has to be taken into account on the extent of success and failure achieved by various inputs invested in the different developmental programmes. On this angle the researcher has judiciously examined the ends and means of each programme of the DDA. An endeavour has been made by her to analyse the success and failure of the DDA programmes on the basis of seven guiding factors as stated by Bhowmick (1994 : 17) and Gaikwad (1991 : 10-11). While assessing the impact of the developmental programme, the researcher has compared the pre- and post-socio-economic impact of the respective programmes on the beneficiaries. As regards the expenditure pattern of the Micro Project is concerned, the least attention has been given on HRD which in fact needs utmost priority. The findings further reveal that the plain beneficiaries exhibit the utmost socio-economic impact in comparison to the other two sectors. The reasons behind the impact are mainly due to proximity and accessibility. Even many traditional customs and values have undergone a dramatic change by the forces of modernity. On the other hand, the hill dwellers have retained their traditional habits with negligible state of change. Because of the inaccessibility, lack of conscientisation and awareness, the desirable development is yet to be achieved. The cut off Didayis in a way, have lost their cultural identity because of their displacement and rehabilitation. They have even lost linguistic and socio-cultural identity owing to the influence of the Bengali refugees, Kondhs, Telugu businessmen and others. Furthermore, due to extreme inaccessibility, the government officials including the Micro Project employees find it very difficult to approach the households of cut off sector for rendering essential goods and services. As a result, they are the least beneficiaries of the targeted development scheme of the Government.

Dr. Bhagyalaxmi has rightly mentioned that infrastructure is the key to a community's economic, social and political development. While analyzing the individual scheme of the DDA, she has put forth findings and necessary suggestions which can be taken as a guiding resource for the Micro Project as well as for other development practitioners. True to the fact that major thrust are to be given on communication, education and health practices which are the key elements for the development and more pertinent to the Didayi tribe. The researcher has also highlighted about the Bengali Refugee's dominance in the area and their impact on the tribal people of the Malkangiri district of Orissa. She also suggests other researchers to carry out further extensive research work on core cultural values relating to land and forest in order to focus on Didayi identity. A reader will certainly find an unique blend of empirical authenticity with ground reality of developmental efforts.

23/12/07

Dr. Prasanata Kumar Mishra
Principal
J.K.B.K. College,
OMP Square, Cuttack (Orissa)

Preface

An important aspect of administrative evolution in India since independence has been the advent of development planning that contributed to a tremendous increase in contact between the functionaries connected with tribal development administration and the tribal people. During the post-independence period, the tribal development policies had been consistently modified on the guidelines of the National Planning Commission. However, since the desired benefits did not reach the Primitive Tribal Groups through the earlier programmes such as the Tribal Development Blocks and the Integrated Tribal Development Agencies, a special plan called as the Tribal Sub Plan Approach (TSP) was introduced during the Fifth Five Year Plan (1974-1979). Under TSP approach special development projects called as Micro Projects were launched to conceive, formulate and execute various programmes and schemes for all-round development of the PTGs with 500 to 1000 beneficiary households at grassroots level. The Micro Projects provide 100 per cent subsidy under individual family benefit oriented schemes. The project aims at the development of the core economic elements like agriculture, horticulture, soil conservation and animal husbandry and also facilitates infrastructure and human resource benefits. In Orissa, at present 17 Micro Projects have been operating for 13 PTGs out of which 13 Projects are within the scheduled areas. The Didayi is one amongst the 13 PTGs of Orissa and a Micro Project named as Didayi Development Agency (DDA) was established in the year 1986 at Kudumulugumma of Malkangiri district of Orissa.

The Didayi, one of the little known Primitive Tribal Groups of Orissa, is confined to Kondakamberu Mountain range of Eastern Ghat. In fact, the entire hill range is known as Didayi land which stretches along the valley of Machkund river. After construction of the Balimela Hydel Project in 1962, the people who settled in the valley regions were displaced. The displacement had compelled them to settle in four distinct regions : Plain, Hill, Cut off and Phulpadar rehabilitation colony. Eventually, the geographical barrier had made them socio-culturally distinct.

The study seeks to look at the after impact of displacement on the tribe as it has a definite impact on the peoples' social, cultural and economic identity. Apart from that the Micro Project has been implementing a number of development schemes and programmes with a view to providing assistance for integrated socio-economic development of the Didayi on sustainable basis under five major heads : Income generating schemes, Natural Resource Development, Human Resource Development, Infrastructure Development and Administrative facilities. The research study has analysed the effectiveness of these schemes by assessing their impact upon the socio-economic status of the people over a decade of functioning the Micro Project. At the same time, it figures out the success or failure of the implemented schemes and simultaneously, suggests a few recommendations for actions to be taken by the DDA for sustainable economic enhancement of the Primitive tribe.

The study also examines that how far a particular programme or scheme has been able to bring about sustainable development in harmony with the Didayi society and culture. Further, it seeks the core elements of their social identity on the basis of socio-cultural life and linguistic factors; so that information regarding the changing trends can be recorded.

It is hoped that the study will be a facilitating source for researchers, development practitioners and the planners.

I am grateful to the Chairman and Members of the Board of Governors of the Council of Analytical Tribal Studies who have granted permission for publication of the dissertation of my scholar.

31.12.09

P.C. Mohapatro
Director, COATS
Koraput

Acknowledgements

I convey my gratitude to Dr. P.C. Mohapatro, Director of C.O.A.T.S., Koraput, for publication of my doctoral thesis. Without his cooperation my book would not have seen the light today. I also express my deep sense of gratitude to my teacher Prof. K.K. Mahanti who has inspired me to publish the thesis.

I deem it my privilege to thank my teacher and research supervisor Dr. P.K. Mishra for the continued cooperation and untiring effort by him to make this work a success. My special thanks to Mrs. Nibedita Mishra, wife of Dr. P.K. Mishra who has been a source of inspiration throughout my doctoral work. I am also thankful to the Concept Publishing Company Pvt. Ltd. who readily agreed for publication of this study.

I am obliged to my father who despite his health problem, has rendered his untiring efforts for editing my thesis. My mother's blessings have inspired my work. I am also grateful to my in-laws for their supports.

I wish to record my greatest debt to my husband Col. L. Mahapatra without whose support I would not have endeavoured to fulfil my research passion. It is because of his inspiration I dared to venture into the inaccessible Naxalite affected areas of the Didayi habitat. Last but not least my son Lt. Chetan and daughter Akankshya have been a constant source of energy and enthusiasm throughout my research.

Bhagyalaxmi Mahapatra

Contents

List of Tables

List of Maps, Sketches, Graphs, Figures and Photographs

Maps

Sketches

Graphs

Figures

List of Photographs

List of Abbreviations

ADM	Administration
AH	Animal Husbandry
AIR	All India Radio
ANM	Assistant Nursing Midwife
APL	Above Poverty Line
BDO	Block Development Officer
BJD	Biju Janta Dal
BJP	Bhartiya Janta Party
BPL	Below Poverty Line
CAPS	Cluster Approach Pockets
CEP	Continuing Education Programme
CD Blocks	Community Development Blocks
CDP	Community Development Progammes
CGI	Corrugated Galvanised Iron
CM	Chief Minister
DDA	Didayi Development Agency
DP	District Panchayat
DRDA	District Rural Development Agency
DWACRA	Development of Women and Children of Rural Area
EAS	Employment Assurance Scheme
EDN	Education
EO	Extension Officer
EST	Establishment
Fd.Ast	Field Assistant
FYP	Financial Year Plan
GB	Governing Body
GoI	Government of India
GP	Gram Panchayat
HH	House Hold
HRD	Human Resource Development Scheme

HYV	High Yielding Variety
IADP	Integrated Area Development Project
ICDES	Integrated Child Development Services
IRDP	Integrated Rural Development Programme
ITDA	Integrated Tribal Development Agency
ITDP	Integrated Tribal Development Programme
JE	Junior Engineer
KPGBC	Koraput Panchabati Gramya Banks Cooperative
LAC	Livestock Aid Centre
LAMPS	Large sized Agricultural Multi-Purpose Society
LH pumps	Lift Hand Pumps
MADA	Modified Area Development Approach
ME	Middle Education
MFAL	Marginal Farmer and Agricultural Labourer
MLA	Members of Legislative Assembly
MNP	Minimum Needs Programme
MP	Member of Parliament
MPEWS	Multi-Purpose Education Workers Scheme
MSL	Mean Sea Level
NA	Not Available
NESP	National Extension Service Programme
NGO	Non-Governmental Organization
NOAPS	National Old Age Pension Scheme
NRD	Natural Resource Development
NREP	National Rural Employment Programme
OAPS	Old Age Pension Scheme
OREDA	Orissa Renewable Energy Development Agency
OTDP	Orissa Tribal Development Project
PD	Project Director
PDS	Public Distribution System
PLCE	Post Literacy Continuing Education
PM	Prime Minister
PTG	Primitive Tribal Group
PV	Photo Volt
RLEGP	Rural Landless Employment Guarantee Programme

RWSO	Rural Water Supply Organisation
SALT	Slopping Agricultural Land Technology
SASTC	Scheduled Areas and Scheduled Tribes Commission
SC	Scheduled Caste
SC & ST RTI	Scheduled Caste and Scheduled Tribe Research and Training Institute
SDO	Sub Divisional Officer
SFDA	Small Farmer Development Agency
SMPT Blocks	Special Multi-Purpose Tribal Blocks
Sr.Clk	Senior Clerk
ST	Scheduled Tribe
TD Blocks	Tribal Development Blocks
THRTI	Tribal and Harijan Research-cum-Training Institute
TRB	Tribal Research Bureau
TRYSEM	Training of Rural Youth for Self-Employment
TSP	Tribal Sub-Plan
TV	Television
UNESCO	United Nations Educational, Scientific and Cultural Organisation
UP	Upper Primary
VLW	Village Level Worker
WEO	Welfare Extension Officer
WHS	Water Harvesting Structure
WO	Welfare Officer

1

Introduction

India has a tribal population of 6,77,58,380 (1991 Census), constituting 9.5 per cent of the total population and is the second largest in the world. There are 427 tribes in India, mostly they are concentrated in the hilly and forest regions. There are about 250 Scheduled Tribe Communities, speaking of nearly 105 languages and 225 subsidiary languages. The Scheduled Tribes in India have been specified in 25 states and Union Territories, as per provisions contained in Article 342 of the Constitution of India. The Constitution provides a comprehensive framework, consisting various safeguards for protection of their interests. The provisions contained in Articles 15(4), 16(4), 19(5), 46, 164, 244, 244(A), 275, 330, 332, 335, 338, 342 and Fifth and Sixth Schedules of the Constitution, provide the guidelines for their welfare as well as protection against exploitation. All tribes have their distinct racial, linguistic, cultural and ethnic identities. In spite of these diversities they possess some striking similarities in their socio-economic-political ways of life. A tribal community is generally characterized by a small isolated group, confined to an area, having a village headman or a leader, maintaining their clan identity and kinship bonds.

Orissa is one of the largest tribal populated State, having 62 Scheduled tribal communities. The total population of them in Orissa is 70,32,214 constituting 22.21 per cent of the total population of 3,16,59,736 in 1991. At national level, Orissa comprises the second largest tribal population having more than one-tenth of the total tribal population in the country.

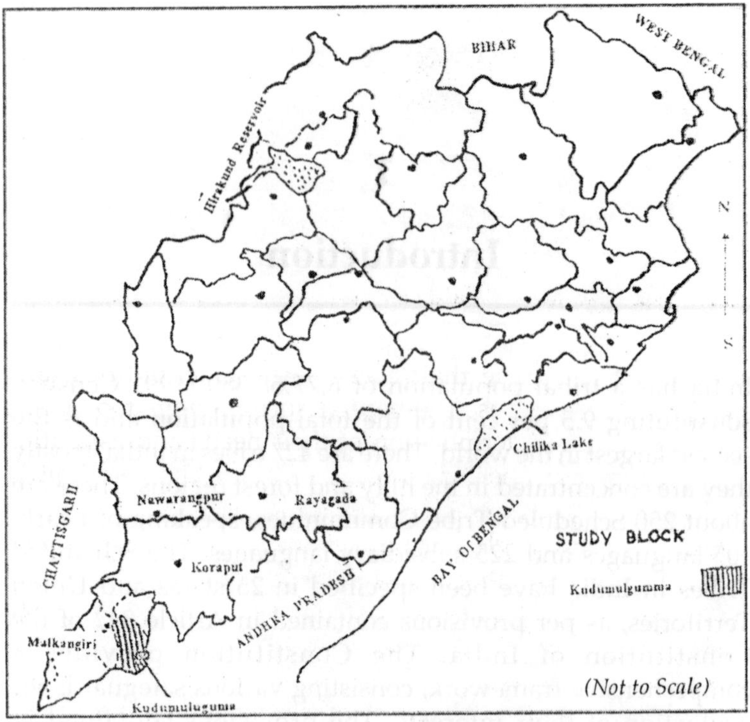

Map 1.1 : Map of Study Area in Orissa

The distribution of tribal population in different districts of the State is uneven. As per the 1991 Census, the districts of Malkangiri (2,46,000), Nowarangpur (4,68,000), Koraput (5,22,000), Rayagada (4,00,000), Gajapati (2,18,000), Nuapada (1,69,000) and Kandhamala (2,81,000) in southern Orissa and Mayurbhanj (10,91,000), Keonjhar (5,95,000) and Sundergarh (7,98,000) in the northern Orissa, have greater tribal concentration. Out of the 62 tribes of Orissa, 13 tribes have been identified as Primitive Tribal Groups (PTGs) and Didayi is one amongst them. They are exclusively confined to Malkangiri district, a southern part of undivided Koraput district. The location of study area in Orissa is given in Map 1.1.

According to a latest survey conducted in 1998, the Didayi population is 5,194. The Malkangiri district came into being on 2 October, 1992. It is predominantly a tribal dominated district having 12 types of tribes, viz. *Koya, Bonda, Paraja, Gadaba, Didayi, Bhumiya, Banjari, Santala, Dureuba, Kondha, Mafia,* and *Madua.* The total population of Malkangiri district is 4,21,917, out of which 2,46,214 (58%) constitute the tribal population as per 1991 Census.

The Problem

The primitive tribes usually live in secluded forest habitats. The local forest resources and the hilly environment indeed harmoniously shape their social, economic, political and religious way of lives. The natural surroundings too largely involved in the determination of their needs and aspiration for development. The Didayi is indeed a little known primitive Tribe of Orissa and is confined to *Kondakamberu Mountain Range* and its foothills, which forms part of the Eastern Ghat Mountain Range. They have been leading a peaceful and independent life almost divorced from the main stream prior to independence. It is said that initially they were leading a semi-nomadic life. Gradually, some of them are settled down in the plains and foothills and some are in the Machkund river valley. Settled cultivation became the primary occupation of the sedentary Didayi and the hill dwellers still continued food gathering with shifting cultivation. On construction of Balimela Hydel Project in 1962, the Didayi settled in valleys were displaced as their land got submerged with the Reservoir water. Most of them shifted to higher ridges (Hilltop) and some availing the rehabilitation scheme of Orissa Government shifted to newly established Rehabilitation Colonies. Since most of them could not sever their links with the natural surrounding, they preferred to stay at higher ground hugging to the water line. These people are apparently cut off from the main Didayi Land except having the only link of communication through the boat (*Ferry*) service. Their primary occupation now changed to settled and shifting cultivation.

Didayis were aware of the difficulties of becoming displaced and had protested against the construction of the Balimela Hydro Electric Project. The level of resentment can be perceived from the following reported extract : "No doubt it is a great shock to the people to hear that their homes, villages and fields which are so dear to them would be submerged under water. But the intensity of this feeling varies from community to community. Perhaps it shocked the Didayi to the maximum extent. They are the original inhabitants of this area and they are confined to this region chiefly. In their psyche, their region is the abode of their gods and the spirits of their ancestors which to them are inseparable and are a source of inspiration in their daily life. During interview many of the Didayi burst into tears which indicates the depth of their agony" (Adibasi, 1971-72 : 67).

They are extremely on the lower side of the development indicator and demonstrate a case of extreme deprivation. Due to the submersion of cultivable land and drastic degradation of environment associated with depletion of forest resources and reduction of land productivity, the Didayi suffered the worst economic disaster than other tribal communities since 1962. Lack of road communication to hilltop and cut off area has further compounded the problem. The major problems of the Didayi have been identified as poor economic status, very low educational level and poor health and hygienic condition (Socio-economic Survey, 1982-83, T.H.R.T.I.). Because of these factors, the Didayis are found to be isolated from the outside world and being less benefited by the impact of normal development programmes.

Joganath Shroff states "Particularly due to construction of the Chitrakonda Reservoir twenty thousand tribal people living in 151 villages covering 316 sq.km, adjoining Andhra Pradesh in Chitrakonda Tehsil and Kudumulugumma Block remain isolated from the rest of the district. Same is the case in respect of the group of villages lying on the other side of Jalaput Dam. No development worth the name has been taken up in this vast area which remains cut off due to lack of regular communication facilities. There is growing discontentment and frustration amongst the people of the area, which remains unapproachable. For no fault of theirs and due to irony of fate that instead of reaping the fruits of development, these are the victims of ill-conceived planning. This is a glaring instance of the worst effect of the major development projects on tribal life in the region" (Shroff, 1997 : 66).

"Anthropologists and Ethnologists like E.Thurston (1909), C.A. Henderson (1911), C.Von Furer-Haimendorf (1945) and Verrier Elwin (1950) have regarded the *Bondos* as members of a group of Austro-Asiatic tribes which had at some remote date migrated and settled in the wild Jeypore Hills. The *Bondos* themselves look upon their neighbouring tribes such as the *Gadba* and the Didayi as one family, the members of which eat together though for purpose of marriage, each tribe has become an endogamous unit. It was only when the tribal Sub-Plan came into operation at the beginning of the Fifth Five-Year Plan, a concerted attention was given to such primitive tribal communities for their development. As required under the new strategy for the development of the primitive communities, a special Micro Project was launched in the *Bondo* Hills in 1977 covering all the 31 *Bondo* villages including a few Didayi villages" (Patnaik, 1984 : 106-108).

'The *Bonda* Micro Project was registered under Societies Registration Act, 1860 in the month of May, 1977. In the process of functioning of *Bonda* Development Agency, the Government authorities took the notice of the pitiable plight of the Didayis in this area. On the recommendation and efforts of Scheduled Castes and Scheduled Tribes Research and Training Institute (SC & STRI), then known as Tribal and Harijan Research-cum-Training Institute (THRTI) Bhubaneswar, a Micro Project for the Didayi named Didayi Development Agency (DDA), was established at Kudumuluguma of Malkangiri District in the year 1986 after nine years gap of the establishment of the *Bondo* Development Agency though the Didayi tribe was in the same isolated state as the *Bondo* community. The DDA has carried out a number of schemes to alleviate their problems. Although, the DDA has made some tangible development, still a lot many to be achieved to ensure that Didayis move along the main stream, maintaining their distinct cultural tradition and ethnic identity.

The underlying implications of the study are to critically examine the specific empirical findings to identify the areas of weakness of development interventions and also to suggest the ways to improve human resource development as envisaged in the national policy and perspectives. The present study also seeks to critically evaluate the policies and programmes of Didayi Development Agency, assess their impact on the Didayi Community and simultaneously to propose a few suggestions for immediate action.

Conceptual Framework

Concept of Socio-economic Development

The concept of socio-economic development primarily revolves around Human Resource in conjunction and exploitation of the natural resources available in the special area without upsetting ecological balance. The need to view the economic and social development in a sustainable manner by enhancing the capacities of the people to use the material resources in such a manner that it will generate additional income and employment for further development.

Many Anthropologists and Sociologists like Montesquieu, E.B. Tylor, Morgan, Durkheim, Malinowski, Radcliffe-Brown, August Comte and many others have shared their valuable contribution in the way of the growth of the developmental theory. Therefore, development is a universal problem which has drawn the attention of the Third World or developing countries to the twin problems of nation-building and socio-economic progress. R.K. Sapru describes Third World or developing countries of Asia, Africa and Latin America as (a) they are relatively young; (b) they are confronted with similar development problems; (c) they are engaged in the development task of nation-building and socio-economic progress; (d) the per capita national income is less; (e) they are technologically less advanced; and (f) they are socially backward" (Upali, 1994 : 1).

The Indian concept of Human Resource Development places the people at the centre of development as the means and end of all development efforts and emphasizes economic growth along with self-reliance and social justice. That apart, it states that progress is measured by three factors—income, education and longevity.

Development designates a changing process that folds towards stage of advancement. The concept of development has always been a multi-directional, polygenous, poly-contextual and multi-dimensional. These encompass the facets like social, political, economic, religious and cultural. So, on the whole, the concept refers to both socio-economic development or progress with its complimentary but not with its contradistinction (Mohanti, *et al.*, 1996 : 3).

Undoubtedly, development is an active policy which refers to mature economy and self-sustaining growth and the related action pattern, will no doubt generate an increased productivity which in course of time will improve the quality of life, namely elevating the people from poverty to prosperity and opening up more employment opportunities, setting apart more leisure time by which their creative and philosophy can be reflected in finer things, diseases can be checked and ignorance can be removed, if the group is allowed to have a privileged life style (Bhowmik, 1993 : 12).

It is evident that development is a process of growth in the direction of nation building and socio-economic process. Development never will be and never can be defined to universal satisfaction (The Brandt Commission Report, 1979).

Economists and Social Anthropologists have described the 'developmental' phenomenon in several ways. It has been measured by a variety of indicators and the most widely used parameter is the per capita income. Higher the income often leads to higher per capita expenditure. Thus, per capita income and expenditure is treated as reasonably good index of economic development. In the present study, both the income and the expenditure are taken as the indicators for assessing development of the Didayi community. In addition to it, another important indicator 'Development Psyche' has been considered.

"Development psyche represents a process of inculcation of aspirations, building up of attitudes and the development of a forward looking, self-helping and action-oriented bent of mind. This 'development psyche' influences and in turn influenced by social change and economic transformation" (Arora, 1979 : XXIV). In other words, it is also known as 'development orientation' as it plays a significant role while formulating the developmental programmes, owing to the 'psyche' of the tribal community.

There has been a growing realization among the socio-economists as well as the social anthropologists that the economic problems of the tribal people and other backward communities are inter-linked with their social organization and cultural ethnicity. It has become a responsibility of all planners and thinkers to formulate the development schemes on the line of the socio-cultural values of the tribal community.

Development Models

The Tradition/Modernity Model of Modernization Theory

Parsons (1966), Eisenstadt (1966), Learner (1964) and Bauer (1981) expressed the view that modernization is primarily a cultural process that involves the adoption of values and attitudes suited to entrepreneurial ambitions, innovations, rationality and achievement orientation in place of the contrary values and life style of traditional society. Societies are at different stages of development according to the conditions they have institutionalized, for example, achievement rather than the aspiration is the basis for the allocation of reward. Thus the less developed societies are so because of the comparative absence of modern values-orientations. On the contrary, the Third World development is said to occur through both the diffusion of ideas and values from the West and through the 'logic of industrialism'.

The Model of Capitalist Underdevelopment

This model carries a number of versions of Marxist and Neo-Marxian analyses. This theory reflects the works of Frank,

Furtado and Cardoso, who argue that the Third World remains in a state of 'dependent underdevelopment' because its resources and surplus capital is exploited by other metropolitan developed States of Capitalist First World.

On the contrary, the Neo-Marxian articulationist such as Tylor, Alvi, and Wolpe argued that Third World underdevelopment can only be explained in terms of structural relationship between First World capitalism and non-capitalism systems in the Third World. Again this relationship or 'articulation' varies and determines the extent to which capitalism penetrates and displaces local economies. This articulation has cultural, political and economic effects within the Third World which are extremely varied. 'Dependency' is much too simplistic a notion to describe this state of affairs. However, Lipton, who although has accepted many of the argument advanced by both schools, criticized this model. He argued for an approach to development that cannot be placed neatly into the one or the other. He stressed on a self-reliant mass based on agriculture with an attendant industrial sector which many theorists regard as unworkable in the current global context.

The 'Alternative Development' Approach

This approach, represented by the work of Schumacher (1973), whose recommendations are based on an assessment of the current 'problems', associated with unrestrained industrialization. It also affected a number of theoretical and historical propositions about 'where we went wrong'. This approach offers an alternative to industrialization that would involve a significant de-industrialization of the mass production economies of today and the introduction of self-reliant, small scale technological system in the Third World.

However, the above three models offer very different diagnoses of the major problems and sources, that the world is facing today. In the present context, the modernization model approach is viewed to be more appropriate as it aims for the better productivity and better life.

India's Approach to Development

Fifty years of independence have no doubt brought about great many transformation in the Indian economy. The challenges before all the economic agents of the country are concerned with the issues of further strengthening our strengths and removing our weaknesses. Certainly, we need an objective assessment of the past and a visionary perspective of the future. India commenced its development process with the emphasis on industrialization, technology development and institution building in 1951 under the National Planning Commission headed by the first Prime Minister Pt. Jawaharlal Nehru. India has now undergone through Nine Five-Year Plans. It has been preparing annual plans those are integrated with the budgetary process. Every Five-year plan has a mid-term appraisal.

Despite improvements in several important criteria such as the state of the economy and role of the government, India continues to lag behind on the international competitiveness scale as per the rating of the Institute of Management Development (IMD) survey carried out in the year 1998. It is placed 41 out of 46 major national economic countries (Khadar, 1999 : 35-42).

"The target of development is the people. The purpose of development is to improve the quality of the life, first by assuring a level of sustenance acceptable to the people and second by increasing the choices they have for living their own lives up to their optimum expression. The people, one way or another must be involved in setting goals of any development programme for any particular place and for any particular time" (Jena, 987 : 20).

Chaturvedi and others indicated that development by itself does not yield satisfaction among people. People's satisfaction with development is related to their level of participation. Development which offers more scope for participation yields greater satisfaction to people. But the existing institutional structure of development offers little scope for people's participation. Citizen participation, although advocated and emphasized by Indian leadership, still remains to be integrated and incorporated in the institutional structure of development (Chaturvedi and Mitra, 1982).

There are four kinds of participation, according to Cohen and Uphoff, those are most relevant to rural development activities. They are : "(a) participation in decision-making; (b) participation in implementation; (c) participation in benefits; and (d) participation in evaluation." (Cohen and Uphoff 1977 : 7). Taking the above context in view, the present study requires to analyze the participation level between the Didayi people and the Micro Project activities.

It is again realised that People's participation in development can have varying degrees of success depending on the environmental context of the administrative system as well as the ability and willingness of the people actually participating in the decisional framework. When adequate attempts are made to enhance the willingness and the capacity of the people to participate in development process, utmost care is needed in selecting the most appropriate methods for channeling this participation spirit into effective action.

So far, tribal development is concerned, it is very much imperative that the active participation and involvement of the people in development programmes meant for them, is an important factor contributing to the success of the programmes. Bedi (1995 : 13) in his analytical study reveals that "Tribal development consists to be largely governmental programme at all levels such as policy formulation, planning, programme formulation, excellent monitoring and evaluation and public representatives and mostly non-concerned and even silent or even apathetic and passive participants." Thus, failing to generate active involvement of the tribal people in development programmes, the utilization of the service becomes minimal, ineffective and costly to operate. Therefore, it is necessary to understand the new strategies evolved to involve the tribal people themselves in the task of development.

"The United Nations Economic and Social Council has recommended that the Government should adopt participation as a basic policy measure in national development strategy. They should encourage the widest possible active participation of all individuals and national non-governmental organisations in development process in setting goals, formulating policies and implementing plans" (Sing, 1994 : 173).

All these studies corroborate the facts that the importance of people's participation in the process of development has been very much realised since the inception of development planning in India. It is also observed that there are inherent structural factors which favour mobilisation rather than participation. In such institutional framework development priorities are largely determined by centralised planning and their implementation becomes the responsibility of the field bureaucracy. In such situation it leads to mal-development in which people's participation gets confined to merely getting benefits. Thus, participation of people is seen largely in terms of receiving benefits. The participation of beneficiaries is so important factor in the socio-economic development of a tribal community that it cannot be overlooked so far as the present impact study is concerned.

Since the tribal development projects are designed to be more 'integrated' and aims at improving the quality of life for the tribal people, there is a great need to bring all development oriented components together. Bhowmick (1994 : 13) indicated that in order to achieve success in development, we shall have to consider the following aspects :

(i) The plans and the agencies formulating it as to whether they have an unbiased and clear idea about the culture of the people as well as their ecological setting, their history and tradition;
(ii) Understanding of the people with their culture entity, their image profile, mental make-up, along with their response to the developing or external situation. These should be well understood while formulating plan;
(iii) The implementing agency must be able to tackle the people during the development work, as also the government bureaucrats;
(iv) To keep provision for changing the plan or welfare programme, if found unsuitable or if it retards the growth; and

(v) To keep provision for regular monitoring with the help of experts in time and seeking from them constructive suggestions if needed.

The success of any development projects depends on the co-ordination of all the sectors, viz. the governmental machinery implementing agency and participation of the people. In this connection while evaluating a programme, it is utmost important not to ignore the role of the target group, their planning and implementation of the programme. No community ever likes to follow new administrative policies and programmes when imposed on them because of unawareness about the consequence. Hence, people's involvement is essential from the very beginning at grassroots level for any developmental planning process. This 'Bottom-up' approach is more effective than the usual 'Top-down' approach which has been a normal practice.

Keeping all the foregoing theoretical and empirical ideas in mind, the impact study aims at understanding the cultural values and practices of the Didayi people at first instance along with the ecology and environmental factors of the region. This study then makes an endeavour to analyze objectively various programmes, implemented by DDA for the overall development of the Didayi.

Tribal Development Strategies

Tribal development strategies have in fact proliferated since 1960 partly because of the interest of the government and partly because of the rapid growth of awareness among tribal leaders about their nature of deprivation and entitlement. However, it is felt that further to enhance this developmental achievement, definitely some planning from government side as well as the people's participation are necessary. On the whole, the developmental planning usually have a qualitative as well as a quantitative approach. Keeping in view the specific requirements of the various tribes *vis-à-vis* their culture and socio-economic status, following approaches have been evolved for development of tribal people in India.

Approaches to Tribal Development in Pre-Independence Period

Religious approach

Tribal people generally profess a religion which has been called animism. They are nature-worshippers. Their village deity is the ultimate religious supreme seat. Some sections of the tribal people have adopted Hindu religious faith after segregating themselves from the core group to enjoy higher social status compared to other fellow members. As a consequence, this process of the de-tribalisation brought about conversion of egalitarian tribal communities into segmented casteism. In the Pre-Independence period a major initiative was taken by Missionaries to assimilate tribal people into the religious fold of Christianity while undertaking Educational and Health Care activities free of cost. The process of conversion in later stages resulted into severe crises of tribal identity, ethnicity and integrity. The converted people find it difficult to adapt themselves to their newly acquired status and were debarred from attending social and religious ceremonial rites. Thus their harmonious community life was disrupted and jeopardized the integrated development of tribal life. This approach is proved to be counter-productive and seemed to be irrelevant.

Political approach

The British Government had tried to bring in tribal community under its administration by imposing stringent rules and regulations. Certain tribal groups did make strong protest specially in Bihar and Orissa. To diffuse the tribal tension, the government declared certain tribal concentrated areas as non-regulatory zones and simultaneously encouraged middlemen like zamindar, contractor, money-lenders to have a free reign over them. These people exploited the tribal groups, keeping them away from the mainstream. The benefit of administrative machinery and laws of the lands never reached them. They remain isolated and exploited by their own country men without any development in their respective areas. Till post-independence era, they were kept politically away from the mainstream.

Voluntary approach

A number of voluntary agencies like All India Backward Class Federation, Bharatiya Adim Jati Sevak Sangh, Bihar Adim Jati Seva Mandal, Indian Red Cross Society, Bharatiya Depressed Classes League, Orissa Adivasi Congress, etc. have initiated various reform movements in the tribal areas in order to raise the social awareness and the standard of living among the tribal people. It has been realised that though some breakthrough attempts have been successful in tribal pockets to certain extent still this approach has been found to be less effective due to lack of consistency and coordination from the concerned activists.

Anthropological approach

In 1939, Elwin advocated a plan to establish a sort of National Park of the tribal people and advised that their contact with the outside world need be reduced to the minimum. Again in 1941, he supported the idea of 'isolationism' to a great extent (Elwin, 1939 : 511-519). Ghurye was in favour of assimilation of tribal groups with Hindu communities but later pleaded for a national policy without disturbing their religious faiths. Other social anthropologists like Dube, Vidyarthi, Srinivas and Roy Burman opined that the tribal people should be brought into the fold of national mainstream.

Keeping in view the various recommendations, a national consensus has been evolved to formulate the strategy for the tribal development in their respective areas without disturbing their own ethnic identity so that education, health care, modern amenities, etc. could be availed by themselves without interruption and they would have the options to lead a better quality of life.

Strategies of Tribal Development after Independence

The primary objective of the government policy in regard to tribal people has been aimed at preserving tribal culture and social customs, safeguarding their traditional occupation, protecting them from all kind of exploitation while carrying out economic and social development in their area. Accordingly, suitable provisions have been made in the Constitution and socio-economic development is undertaken as an integral part of national development planning.

In the First Five Year Plan period as a part of community development movement, special multi-purpose tribal development projects were undertaken in the tribal areas. During Second Five Year Plan, establishment of Multi-purpose Tribal Blocks were initiated. The purpose of these blocks was to carry out social and economic activities for the Scheduled Tribes with the initiation of multifaceted programmes. During the Second Five Year Plan, only 43 Special Multi-Purpose Tribal (SMPT) Blocks were opened all over the country in the areas where tribal population concentration is more than 50 per cent in scheduled areas. The priorities were given on agriculture, cottage industry and forest cooperatives for rapid economic growth.

In the Third Five Year Plan period, the SMPT blocks were renamed as Tribal Development Blocks (TDBs) and were extended to areas with 66.6 per cent of tribal population. These TDBs usually covered about 200 square miles of area and a population of approximately 25,000 people. These Blocks also gave additional funds in comparison to CD Block which had a population size of 66,000 people. Emphasis was given on development of Economy, Education, Health, Housing and Communication in TD Block. By the end of the Third Five Year Plan, 480 Tribal Blocks were established. The same policy continued even during the Fourth Five Year Plan and more number of Tribal Development Blocks were established making a total of 504 TDBs in the country.

In addition to above measures, a few pilot projects with the aim of developing tribal areas by integrating various programmes implemented on general sector and tribal sector, were created. The funds available from various sources were channeled for the above integrated programmes. Thus six pilot projects were created in 1971-72. Locations of pilot projects in India are mentioned below :

(a) Andhra Pradesh - One in Srikakulam
(b) Bihar - One in Singhbhum
(c) Madhya Pradesh - Two in Bastar
(d) Orissa - Two. One each in Koraput and Ganjam.

Two more projects were created in Orissa during Fifth Five Year Plan, one in Keonjhar and other in Phulbani.

The study team on Tribal Development programmes by Shilu Ao Committee in 1969, indicated imbalance development in the Tribal communities. They also agreed with the views of Dhebar Commission in which he had identified four layers of tribals depending on their economic status. The lowest layer was very poor, primitive and in food gathering stage. It was recommended that utmost concern should be made towards this layer of Tribal population by the respective State Government. A separate scheme for education and economic uplifiment was made out of Central Funds.

However, following weaknesses have been noticed in the policies and programmes of tribal development :

(a) Lack of understanding of tribal way of life and their actual requirements.
(b) The programmes and policies were hardly need based.
(c) Inadequate funding for the programmes and the schemes to achieve any tangible results.

Therefore during Fifth Plan, the tribal development policy was reviewed and the Sector Authority is empowered to devise need based programmes and schemes in respect of specific tribal area. Two aspects were given emphasis, i.e. protection from exploitation and economic development. The plan is famous for its Tribal Sub Plan (TSP) and Integrated Tribal Development Projects (ITDP). Activities of different TDBs in an area were to be integrated and coordinated in the form of ITDPs/ITDAs (Integrated Tribal Development Agencies). At present, there are 194 ITDPs in the country. Since, the tribal populations are found to be concentrated in some area and dispersed in other areas, it was decided to have a focused developmental approach towards the concentrated area and only family oriented programmes for others. Tribal sub-plan was to be implemented in all scheduled areas/Blocks where at least 50 per cent of the population were tribal people. The resources were taken from concerned state plan, Central Ministry outlay, special Central assistance and institutional finance. Accordingly, Integrated Tribal Development Projects (ITDPs) were introduced, which formulate need based grassroots level plans for five years and were executed in phases as per the availability of funds from the above sources.

In the Sixth Plan (1980-1985), the concept of MADA (Modified Area Development Approach) whereby the areas (outside the ITDPs) having dispersed tribal population of at least 10,000 people or more but with at least 50 per cent of the tribal groups of that area, were included. In the Seventh Plan (1985-1990), the MADA was extended to the areas having even 5,000 tribal population and 249 MADA pockets were identified. In the Eighth Plan (1992-1996), MADA coverage have given to 252 pockets. 75 Primitive Tribal Groups (PTGs) have been identified till the end of this plan period. As per the Ministry of Welfare (Annual Report 1991-92) a national policy has been passed. Greater involvement of women, particularly in the area of preservation of ecology and tribal culture, the conservation of forests and land development is also envisaged (Vaid, 1996 : 8-10).

The Ninth Plan acknowledges the need for a National Tribal Policy. Accordingly, efforts will be made to formulate a comprehensive Tribal Policy with a special focus on the primitive tribes and displaced tribal people and their rehabilitation. The strategies are :

(a) Create an enabling environment that is conductive for the STs to exercise for their rights freely, enjoy their privileges and be able to lead a life with confidence and dignity.
(b) Adopt a three-pronged strategy of : (i) Social Empowerment; (ii) Economic Empowerment; and

(iii) Social Justice, in empowering this disadvantaged group.

(c) Ensure removal of disparities; eliminate exploitation and suppression and provide to the disadvantaged groups.

(d) Ensure the development benefit to reach the unreached through equitable distribution and with social justice.

(e) Ensuring participation of the STs in the process of planning not merely as the beneficiaries but to take part effectively in the formulation of the need-based progammes/projects, their implementation, supervision and monitoring.

(f) Accelerate the on-going process of improving the socio-economic status through effective implementation of various policies and programmes and thus bring them on par with the rest of the society.

Primitive Tribe

The large difference in the level of socio-economic development of various tribal communities had always become the important issues before the planners. There had been a constant effort to identify the most backward communities so that special programmes could be planned for their developmental sake. The Dhebar Commission (1961) had observed four different layers amongst the tribal people on the basis of several criteria like pre-agricultural pursuits, remote inhabitation, shifting cultivation, advanced agriculture system and modern ways of life. At the base layer, they identified a class of tribal people in extremely underdeveloped stage and recommended special provisions for them. These are : (a) it should be made the special concern of the State Governments and (b) the Chief Executive Officers with the task of implementing policies should be made responsible for the protection and development of the people. The Shilu Ao Team (1969) supported the view of the Dhebar Commission that the lowest layer needed the special concern. This Study Team prepared a list of backward tribal communities on the guidelines of Dhebar Commission, the Commissioner for Scheduled Castes and Scheduled Tribes and itself. However, the Study Team made the option for further addition or alterations for the classification of the PTGs. They suggested that the State Government and the Union Territories should undertake an objective study to find out the eco-cultural setting of the tribal communities as well as to evaluate the impact of the development programmes meant for them. Besides these, the separate schemes for imparting education and economic uplift of the most backward communities were to be carried out.

Characteristics of Primitive Tribes

The primitive tribes are found scattered throughout India. They inhabit in remote, inaccessible areas, almost cut off from the mainstream. Identification of the primitive groups is the most important exercise which needs great caution. A number of factors have to be taken into account while classifying a particular tribe under Primitive Group for the special beneficial programmes. Therefore, some of the criteria have been taken as an indicator for determining the primitive status of the tribal community. They are : (a) Pre-agricultural technology; (b) Stagnant or diminishing population; (c) Low level of literacy; (d) Distinctive linguistic and cultural traits; and (e) Low level of nutrition.

Strategy for Development of Primitive Tribal Groups

During the Fifth Five-Year Plan, the tribal development programmes were reviewed. The Ministry of Home Affairs issued guidelines for identification of primitive tribal groups as well as the preparation of project reports for their development on the guidelines of Shilu Ao Team. It also emphasized on the cent-per-cent financial support by the Ministry of Home Affairs.

In the new strategy of tribal development two concepts, viz. a prior stage of development and low level in the economic structure have been taken into account. Those groups which fall in the first category, have been grouped under primitive tribal communities while those in the second category are termed as the more backward tribal communities. It has clarified that the distinguishing feature of primitive tribal group programmes is that the individual family is to be considered as a distinct entity for the development programme. But in practice it was found to be difficult to lay down quantitative guidelines to identify the groups as they do not always qualify the criteria on the basis they have to be grouped under the PTGs status.

However, states have generally followed three norms to identify the PTGs. These are : (a) Pre-agricultural level of technology; (b) Low level of literacy; and (c) A stagnant and diminished population. On the basis of these criteria, 52 tribal communities have been identified as primitive till the end of 1979-80, with the population of 10 lakh. During the Sixth Plan period (1980-85) 20 tribal groups in addition were identified as Primitive raising the number to 72 with an estimated population of 15.34 lakh. During the Seventh Plan period, two more groups were added thus raising to 74 in 15 States and Union Territories. So far, 75 tribal communities are identified as the PTGs (Table 1.1), out of which 13 (17.57%) are found in Orissa, 12 (16.22%) in Andhra Pradesh, 9 (12.16%) in Bihar and one in the states of Rajasthan, Tripura, and Manipur (Table 1.1).

The Report of Working Group during Sixth Five-Year Plan period suggested few criteria on the basis of which the project reports for the primitive tribal groups should be finalised. The criteria are : (a) There should be a unique programme for each group; (b) The first phase of developmental plan should aim at conservation and reorganization of the traditional skills of the groups; (c) The second phase should spell out development programme; and (d) The programme must take into consideration of the ecosystem. The report also mentioned about the genetic diseases like sickle sell anemia, sexually transmitted diseases and the population decline among the primitive tribal groups.

The Working Group during the Seventh Five-Year Plan period emphasized on health care, nutrition and ecological

Table 1.1 : List of Identified Primitive Tribal Groups

Sl. No.	*Name of the State*	*Name of the primitive tribal groups*		
1.	Andhra Pradesh	1. Bondo-*Gadaba*	2. *Bondo* Poroja	3. Chenchu
		4. Dongria Khond	5. Gutob *Gadaba*	6. Khond Poraja
		7. Kolam	8. Konda Reddy	9. Konda Savaras
		10.Kutia Khond	11.Parengi Poroja	12.Thoti
2.	Bihar	13.Asurs	14.Birhor	15.Birjia
		16.Hill Kharia	17.Korvas	18.Mal Paharia
		19.Parhaiyas	20.Sauria Paharia	21.Savar
3.	Gujurat	22.Kathodi	23.Kotwalia	24.Padhar
		25.Siddi	26.Kolgha	
4.	Karnataka	27.Jenu Kuruba	28.Koraga	
5.	Kerala	29.Chola *Naikayan* (a section of Kottu *Naikayans*)		
		30.Kadar	31.Kattunayakan	32.Kurumbas
6.	Madhya Predesh	33. Abujh *Marias*	34.Baigas	35.Bharias
		36.Hill Korbas	37.Kamars	38.Saharias
7.	Maharashtra	39.Katkaria (Kathodia)	40.Kolam	41.*Maria* Gond
8.	Manipur	42.Marram Nagas		
9.	Orissa	43.Birhor	44.*Bondo*	45.Didayi
		46.*Dongaria*-Khond	47.Juangs	48.Hill Kharia
		49.Kutia Khond	50.Lanjia Sauras	51.Lodha
		52.Mankidia	53.Pauri Bhuyans	54.*Soura*
		55.Chuktia Bhunjia		
10.	Rajasthan	56.Seharias		
11.	Tamil Nadu	57.Kattu Nayakans	58.Kotas	59.Kurumbas
		60.Irulas	61.Paniyans	62.Todas
12.	Tripura	63.Reangs		
13.	Uttar Pradesh	64.Buxas	65.Rajis	
14.	West Bengal	66.Birhor	67.Lodhas	68.Totos
15.	A & N Islands	69.Onges	70.Great Andamanese	
		71.Jarvars	72.Sentenelese	73.Shompen

Source : Report of the Working Group on Development of Scheduled Tribes during Seventh Five-Year Plan, Government of India, Ministry of Home Affairs, New Delhi, December 1984.

study of the individual primitive tribal family. The Eighth Five-Year Plan aimed at the total development of the entire population. The priorities were given on primary education, adult literacy, health service and provision of minimum needs. The working group also recommended that the Central

Government should provide 100 per cent funding to the development projects of the PTGs. It also recommended the national awards for the government and non-governmental organizations for excellence in the field of development of PTGs.

The Ninth Plan acknowledges the need for a National Tribal Policy that gives a special focus on the primitive tribes and their rehabilitation. It adopts a three pronged strategy of : (a) Social empowerment; (b) Economic empowerment; and (c) Social justice, in empowering the PTGs.

During the Seventh Plan two more primitive tribes have been identified and thus the total number of primitive tribes in India is 74 and in Eighth Plan, one more is added, thus increasing to 75 PTGs (Vaid, 1996 : 10).

Micro Project

During the Fifth Five-Year Plan special development projects were taken up to fulfil the specific needs of the targeted PTGs since the desired benefits did not reach them through the programmes implemented by the Tribal Developmental Blocks (TDBs) and through the Integrated Tribal Dvelopmental Agencies (ITDAs). These new projects are known as the micro projects which are responsible to conceive, formulate and execute various programmes and schemes for all-round development of the PTGs at the grassroots level. Each micro project covers a specific PTG with 500 to 1000 beneficiary households. The projects take initiatives in the development of human resources as well as the natural resource in order to enhance their economic status in a sustainable manner. About 61,000 Scheduled Tribal people are covered under the schemes of micro projects.

The micro project provides 100 per cent subsidy for individual family benefit-oriented schemes. The project aims at the development of the core economic elements like agriculture, horticulture, soil conservation and animal husbandry. Also other infrastructure and human resource facilities like drinking water supply, health care and education are provided to a PTG.

Micro project functions as an autonomous body headed by a Project Officer who executes all the activities in accordance to ground realities. The officer is required to closely interact with the targeted tribal population, adequately investigate their needs and requirements, exchanges ideas and conceptualize necessary schemes and programmes for their development. He has to motivate and involve them in the ongoing developmental schemes. Therefore, the project plays a vital role for the development of poor tribal people. The people's participation in the developmental scheme is the bedrock of its success. The Micro project is staffed as per the typical requirement of the area.

In Orissa, at present 17 Micro Projects have been operating for 12 PTGs out of which 13 Projects are inside the Scheduled Areas (Table 1.2). Birhor is the only primitive tribal community for whom no separate Micro Project has been functioning as all the developmental endeavours are under the charge of the ITDA Bonai. The Micro Project for Didayi tribe established in the year 1986 was called Didayi Development Agency (DDA) and was initially located at Bayapada, a hill village. Due to inaccessibility of the village and some administrative inconvenience, the DDA is functioning at Kudumulgumma which is also a Block headquarters.

Scope of Study

The post-independence era witnessed a large number of development measures, policies and programmes focused on the overall development of the tribal areas. In spite of all the efforts, different tribal groups are living in differential stages of socio-economic standards. The primitive tribal groups are found to be most backward and in the lowest status of the socio-economic level. Out of 75 PTGs of India, 13 are in Orissa and Didayi is one among them. For their development, a Micro Project called 'Didayi Development Agency' (DDA) has been established in the year 1986.

In addition to the Community Development (CD) programmes, the Micro Project has also carried out various development schemes in the area, which undoubtedly has an

Table 1.2 : List of Micro Projects and their Location in Orissa

Sl. N.	*Year*	*District*	*Block*	*Name of Agency*	*Name of PTGs*
1.	1978-79	Anugul	Pallahara	Paudi Bhuyan Development Agency, Jamardihi	Paudi Bhuyan
2.	1993-94	Deogarh	Barkote	Paudi Bhuyan Development Agency, Rugudakudar	Paudi Bhuyan
3.	1978-79	Ganjam	Patrapur	Thumba Develop-ment Agency, Thumba	Lanjia Saora
4.	1994-95	Nuapada	Komna	Chuktna Bhunjia Devp Agency, Suna *Beda*	Chuktna Bhunjia
5.	1978-79	Sundar-garh	Bonia Luhanipard	Paudi Bhuyan Devp. Agency, Khuntagaon	Paudi Bhuyan
6.	1976-77	Malkangiri	Khairput	Bonda Devp. Agency, Mudulipada	Bonda
7.	1986-87	Malkangiri	Kudumul-gumma Khairput	Didayi Devp. Agency Kudumulgumma	Didayi
8.	1978-79	Rayagada	Bissam Cuttack Muniguda	Dongria *Kondha* Devp. Agency, Kurli	Dongria Kondha
9.	1987-88	Rayagada	K.Singpur	Dongria *Kondha* Devp. Agency Parsali	-Do-
10.	1984-85	Rayagada	Gunpur	Lanjia Saura Devp. Agency Puttasingi	Lanjia Saura
11.	1978-79	Gajapati	Gumma	Lanjia Saura Devp. Agency Seranga	-Do-
12.	1978-79	Gajapati	Mohana	Saura Devp. Agency Chandragiri	Saura
13.	1978-79	Phulbani	Tumidi-bandha	Kutia *Kondha* Devp. Agency Belghar	Kuia *Kondha*
14.	1986-87	Kalahandi	Th.Rampur Lanjigarh	Kutia Kandha Devp. Agency Lanjigarh	-Do-
15.	1978-79	Keonjhar	Bansapal	Juang Devp. Agency Gonasika	Juang
16.	1985-86	Mayur-bhanj	Suliapada Morda	Lodha Devp. Agency Morda	Lodha
17.	1986-87	Mayur-bhanj	Jashipur Karangia	Hillkharia and Mankidia Devp. Agency, Gudugudia	Hillkharia and Mankidia

Source : Chaudhury Bhagirathi, 1996 : 49.

impetus to the socio-economic growth of the Didayi community. However, the impact study of the DDA has not been carried out so far to analyze and see the efficacy of its activity, even after 12 years of its functioning.

The general objective of the study is to determine to what extent DDA is responsive to the needs of the people; whether DDA is aware of the feelings of the people and is how much helpful towards the targeted beneficiaries in making available the inputs. In other words, the study proposes to investigate the mutual cooperation and coordination between the officials and the people in designing and implementing programmes for achieving sustainable development.

On the basis of the foregoing analysis of the degree and dimensions of tribal development problems, a fresh study about the Didayi tribe of Orissa has become necessary with the specific objectives.

Objective of the Study

(a) To find out the core elements of the Didayi social-identity, defined and re-defined over-time.
(b) To understand the economic life of the Didayi in the context of their society.
(c) To analyse the impact of on-going government sponsored development activities through Block and the Micro Project for the Didayi.
(d) To identify the factors and causes of failure and success in the development projects and programmes.
(e) To understand the hopes and aspirations of the Didayi.
(f) To find out the alternate strategy to meet the expectations of Didayis.
(g) To assess the role of Non-Governmental Organizations (NGOs) in bringing the Didayi to the main stream, if any.

Methods of Study

The Didayi community is living in *Kondakamberu* hill and its foothill region of Malkangiri district in Orissa. On construction of Machkund reservoir for the Balimela Hydel Power Project, a number of Didayi villages in the Machkund river valley in the eastern part of the Kondakamberu foothills were submerged. Some of the villagers shifted to resettlement colonies and to hill-top villages. But most of them preferred to reside in the higher slopes—next to water line. These villages have been cut off from the main Didayi land.

Didayis are primarily dwelling in three distinct sectors of the region as under :

(a)	Western part of Plain foothill area of the Kondakamberu hill (The Plain Sector)	:	301 Households in five villages.
(b)	Kondakamberu hilltop area (The Hilltop Sector)	:	682 Households in 18 villages.
(c)	Eastern part of the foothills of the hill (The Cut off Sector)	:	302 Households in 14 villages.

Selection of Study Villages

In order to get wholesome view of socio-economic status of the Didayi inhabiting the three sectors of the Kondakamberu Hill Region, it was decided to take up the field study in select villages of all three sectors. A multi-staged random sampling method has been adopted in all phases of area selection from the level of district, block, GP to village informants. To obtain data from these sectors, 30 per cent villages in each sector have been selected as under :

(a) Plain Sector—Two (Oringi, Purunaguma)
(b) Hilltop Sector—Five (Bayapada, Suripada, Gangapada, Badakinyaguda and Ghising Beda)
(c) Cut off Sector—Five (Jantri, Totaguda, Dabuguda, Disariguda, Sanyasiguda)

Considering the size of the pupulation, concentration of ethnic group, literacy rate, physical distance as well as the linkage with the DDA, the above villages have been selected.

Techniques Adopted

During the study, emphasis were given to collect data from primary sources. Then relevant secondary data were obtained from various official sources including DDA. The techniques used for collection of data and information from the primary sources during the field study are conventional one such as participant and non-participant observations. Apart from these, structured and non-structured interview techniques were followed to elicit relevant data including group interviews. A very exhaustive schedule containing 50 questions was formulated to collect data regarding house pattern, dress, ornaments, marriage, family, sources of income and expenditure, political and impact aspects.

The information and first hand data necessary for the study were collected from twelve sample villages through rigorous field study for more than twelve months. During data collection each household of select villages was covered and the schedules and questionnaires were carefully canvassed. Help of local school teachers and interpreters were taken to have excellent communication with Didayi people. The researcher conducted formal interview and informal discussion with several officials and non-officials of the area to elicit information regarding the administrative process, procedures of seeking people's participation and problems which are encountered during the implementation of the programmes. The questionnaires were formulated prior to the interview after careful thinking and were filled during field study of the sample villages.

Selection of Informants

Selection of informant constitute a very important aspect of impact study as they tend to inform the explicit and implicit changes effectively through their subtle level of feeling, thinking and acting. Enough care was taken to identify the selective group on the basis of sex, age, occupation and involvement with DDA. The selective informants are broadly equal percentage (50) of males and females belonging to the following categories :

(a) School children (8-15 years)
(b) Village functionaries (traditional/modern)
(c) Beneficiaries (Male/Female : 16-40 years)
(d) Elderly persons (Male/Female : 41 and above)
(e) DDN Block Employee : 10

A very specific information collected from the various officials is given in Table 1.3. Data has also been collected from documentary sources like Records, Reports, Annual Action

Table 1.3 : Details of Officials Interviewed during Field Study

Sl. No.	*Name of the institution*	*Designation of person*	*Number of persons Interviewed*
1.	Block Office, Kudumulugumma	BDO, VLW, Extn. Officer	5 (Five)
2.	DDA, -do-	Project Officer, Extn. Officer, Junior Engnr. Non-formal School Teachers	9 (Nine)
3.	Tehsil Office, Chitrakonda	Revenue Inspector Record Room Incharge	2 (Two)
4.	T&RW Schools, Kudumulugumma Khairiput and Govind Palli.	Head Masters & Teachers	6 (Six)
5.	Forest Department and Social Forestry, Ballimela and Malkangiri.	DFO, Range Officers and Forester.	7 (Seven)
6.	Mini Bank, Kudumulugumma	Branch Manager	1 (One)
7.	ICDS Office, -do-	Supervisor and Anganwadi Worker	4 (Four)
8.	Child Labour School, Jantri and Kudumulugumma	Teacher	2 (Two)
9.	Primary School, (Edn. Dept.) Jantri & Kudumulugumma	Teacher	2 (Two)
10.	PHC, Kudumulugumma and Khairiput	Medical Officer	2 (Two)

Plans and Budgets of the Micro Project, since its inception (1986-1998). The land holding status in respect of Didayis of study villages have been obtained from Chitrokonda Tehsil Office Record Room. Besides the Five Year Plans and other documents of the Planning Commission, Census reports, the publications of Government of India, Gazette of Orissa and Koraput Gazette have been consulted for the study. Further, the available books, articles and research journals on the related subjects of the study are used to keep well abreast of the situation.

2

The Didayi

The Didayi, a little known primitive tribal group, is mainly confined to *Kondakamberu* hill region of Eastern Ghats which administratively comes under Kudumulgumma and Khairiput Blocks of Malkangiri district, Orissa. Some of them are also found in the adjoining areas under Sujanbeda police station of Andhra Pradesh. The history of Didayi claims that they were primarily leading a nomadic life. They were moving in search of food, fish and prey in the hill regions from Janbai to Machkund areas. Gradually, some of them started settled agrarian life in the Machkund river valley. Others followed nomadic life. On coming in contact with the other tribal groups of the region like *Kondh, Paraja, Gadaba,* and particularly with *Domb* (Scheduled Caste), they started making huts and slowly adapted to a settled life on the mountain tops and foothills of the *Kondakamberu* hill region. In the foothills and valleys, Didayis were practicing settled agriculture and fishing as their primary occupation. Whereas, the hill dwellers were busy in practicing shifting cultivation as well as hunting activities.

Didayi Land

Koraput district (Undivided)

The district of Koraput lies between 20°3′ and 17°50' north latitudes. The district Kalahandi of Orissa and Raipur district of Madhya Pradesh, are situated on the extreme north of it. On the west, the Bastar district of Madhya Pradesh and on the east, the districts of Srikakulam (Andhra Pradesh) and Ganjam

(Orissa), are situated. The entire district used to consist of five sub-divisions, namely Koraput, Nawrangpur, Malkangiri, Rayagada and Gunupur. On 2nd October, 1992, the district Koraput was sub-divided into 4 districts namely : Koraput, Malkangiri, Nawrangpur and Rayagada.

The Koraput district at present is having, 2 Sub-divisions, 7 Tehsils, 14 Community Development Blocks, and 20 Police Stations. There are 14 Tribal Blocks and 197 Gram Panchayats. It has a total population of 10,29,986, out of which Scheduled Caste (S.C.) and Scheduled Tribe (S.T.) are 1,38,000 (13.41%) and 5,22,000 (50.67%) respectively according to 1991 Census (Statistical Outline of Orissa, 1997 : 3-19).

Malkangiri District

Malkangiri was the sub-divisional headquarters of the undivided Koraput district. It had assumed the status of a district from 2nd October, 1992, consequent upon the recognisation of districts in the State by the late former Chief Minister Sh. Biju Patnaik. Being the southern most border district of Orissa, it is surrounded by Andhra Pradesh on south and east, while Madhya Pradesh on the west. On the north lie the Orissan districts like Koraput, Rayagada, Nawrangpur and Kalahandi (Map 2.1).

It is situated at a height of about 1000 ft. above the sea level, comprising an area of 6115.3 sq.km. which is 3.93 per cent of the total area of the State. Its total length from north to south is about 170 km. and its average breadth from east to west is about 90 km. The rivers like Tamasa, Sileru, Poteru, Satiguda and Saptadhara are flowing through the district.

Administrative Division

This district has one revenue sub-division, three tehsils, seven community development blocks, two urban-local bodies and eight police stations. There are 77 gram panchayats and 928 villages (Statistical Outline of Orissa, 1997 : 3-7), out of which 132 MV (Malkagiri Village) villages and 81 MFV (Malkangiri

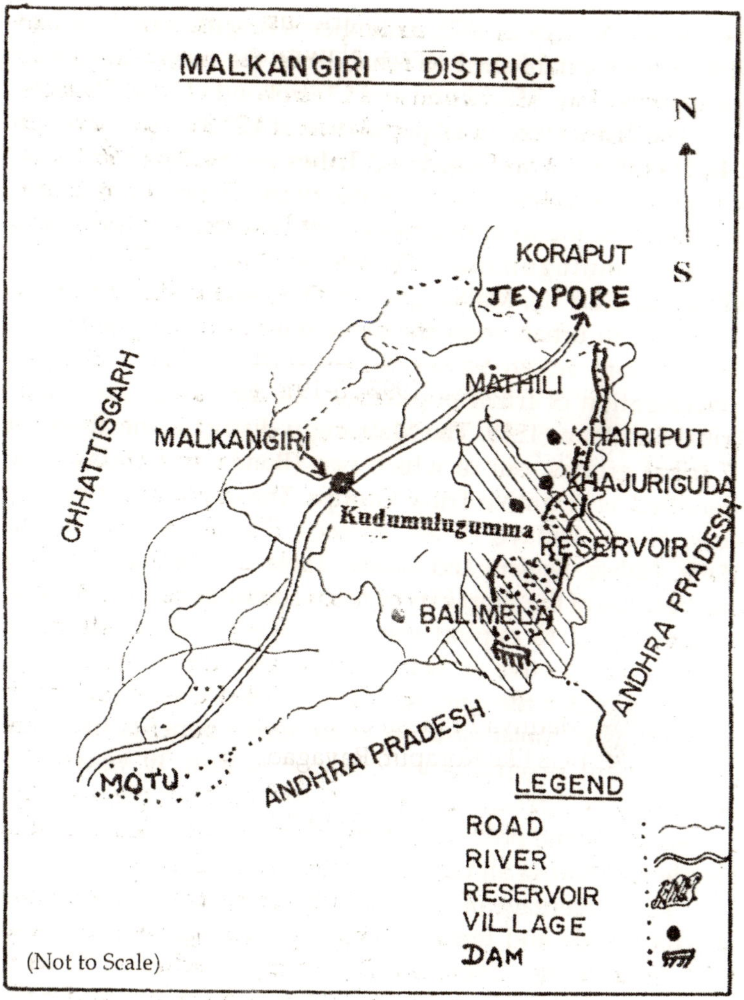

Map 2.1 : Map of Malkangiri District of Orissa

Forest Village) villages are exclusively occupied by over a lakh of refugees from East Bengal under the Dandakaranya Rehabilitation Project in a phased manner since 1961. It is often called as a district of numbers as the rehabilitated villages are named after numbers like MV-14,37,38 and MFV-4,14,65 etc. Some families of Srilankan refugees have also been settled in the district. As back as 1975, a number of Resettlement Colonies (RSCs) were established to rehabilitate the native displaced population of the Machkund and Chitrokonda Hydel Projects.

The district has a total population of 4,21,917, out of which 2,46,214 (58.36 %) are Scheduled Tribes and 84,208 (9.96 %) are Scheduled Castes. There more than 65 per cent tribal population is found in five blocks out of seven and the blocks are Kudumulugummaa (76.068 %), Mathili (74.948 %), Khairiput (72.7 %), Malkangiri (70.03 %) and Podia (65.38 %). However, in urban areas the percentage of tribal population varies from seven to seventeen only. Because of high concentration of tribal population, all the blocks are under Tribal Sub-Plan (TSP). The Malkangiri district is the abode of 17 tribal groups, out of which two (Bonda and Didayi) are identified as Primitive Tribal Groups. The important tribes are *Koya, Bonda,* Didayi, *Paraja, Parenga, Bhumia, Kondh, Santal, Matia, Halwa, Banjara* and *Gadba* (Table 2.1). It was reported that because of the simplicity of tribal communities, the Bengali refugees tend to exploit them in various ways. All these refugees irrespective of their original caste affiliation are now identified under the category of Scheduled Castes (SC) with the sub-caste *'Namasudra'* so as to derive benefits from the Government programmes. Though within 30 years, the Bengalis have prospered more than tribal people socially, economically and politically, they still view with the local tribal people for sharing all the development benefits.

The percentage of literacy in the district is only 16.3, out of which male and female literacy percentages are 12.5 and 4.32 respectively. There are 761 Primary Schools, 77 M.E. Schools, and 30 boy's and 3 Girl's High Schools run under the Education Department. Another 53 Sevashrams and 2 Kanyashrams are managed by the Tribal and Welfare Department, Government of Orissa.

There are two Irrigation Projects at Poteru and Satiguda. A Hydro Electric Project has been established at Balimela in the year 1956 and its Reservoir is situated at Chitrokonda.

Table 2.1 : Distribution of Scheduled Tribe of Malkangiri Distrist

S.No.	Name	Habitat/Place
1.	*Koya*	Malkangiri, Kalimela, Padia, Motu
2.	Banda	Mudlipada, Khairiput, Andrahal
3.	*Paraja*	Balimela, Somnathpur, Mathili, Jabaguda, Gobind-Pali, Chitrokunda, Sadasibpur
4.	Gadba	Pangam, Bhajaguda, Katameta.
5.	Didayi	Kudumulugumma, Khairiput
6.	*Bhumiyan*	Mathili, Sanaguma, Akur, Salim, Tentuligumma, Madupadar.
7.	*Banjari*	Gangala, Dengaguda.
8.	*Santal*	Malkangiri,M.V.—4, 2 & 3.
9.	*Duruba*	Tandapalli, Alur, Damaguda, Gandhipalli
10.	*Kondha*	Pimgam, Ganchoibalu, Kenduguda, Markapalli
11.	*Matia*	Luleru, Chaulamandi, Gobindpalli
12.	*Madua*	Kenduguda, Rangingudai, Tulenguda

Source : Nalla : 24.

The *Kondakamberu* hill range is the original land of the Didayi tribe and no other community used to inhabit the area. The *Kondakamberu* hill range is about 2000 to 3500 feet high from MSL and lies in the north east to south-west direction as part of the Eastern Ghat mountain ranges. The Machkund river flows along this range on which Machkund Hydel Project has been constructed close to the famous Duduma water-fall. Subsequently, this water flows along the *Kondakamberu* hill ranges into the Chitrakonda reservoir which is meant for Balimela Hydroelectric Power Project. This area is most inaccessible and is covered with thick forests. Most part of it is declared as Reserve forest and forms the southern part of Koraput district. The hill range overlooks the Malkangiri plains on to the west and descends sharply to the south to Machkund Valley, which separates border of Orissa and Andhra Pradesh. The Didayi have been inhabiting the area since time immemorial and this land stretches from Duduma water-fall to Machkund river valley, covering a distance of approximately 20 sq.km. In course of time, the Didayi preferred to give up the semi-nomadic life and settled down in the central part of

Kondakamberu range and Machkund river valley. Henceforth, the area is known as Didayi land.

During the pre-independence period, the hill range was administratively controlled by the Jeypore Zamindari of Visakhapatnam under Madras presidency. When Orissa was constituted as a separate province in 1936, the 'British' District of Koraput was formed designated as Agency tract. Jeypore became officially part of Koraput and was made a Partially Excluded Area under the Government of India Act, 1952. In practice it conveyed that a district as under the Agency tract or a Partially Excluded Area meant that arrangements could be made for the protection and development of the aboriginal population (Elwin, 1950 : 4-5).

Aparajita (1994 : 59) mentions that Jeypore estate was ultimately abolished from 29th December, 1952 *vide* Government notification No. 8231-R, under the provisions of the Orissa Estate Abolition Act, 1951 along with the other estates in the district.

Like most of the tribes of the undivided Koraput, Didayis too express their loyalty to Jeypore Zamindar (Raja) and some of them still claim legendary origin of their clan to be associated with Raja of Jeypore. Though, a majority of the tribal people of Koraput district in particular express a sense of negligence and deprivation since the Raja of Jeypore made a lot more development in the areas that now comes under Andhra Pradesh rather than the areas of Koraput district.

Prior to construction of Balimela Hydel Project, a research study was conducted to know the consequence of Didayi people in 1966 (Guha, 1968 : I). Their findings and recommendations have been discussed subsequently.

Flora and Fauna

The *Kondakamberu* range has deciduous forest with trees like *sal, sahja, bija, simili, tendu, kusum, bahada, amala, mahua,* tamarind, mango and jack-fruit. In addition to various kinds of broom stick grasses, *siali* creepers, bamboo, fern and medicinal plants are largely found in the hill and cut off sector forests. The forest around the villages like Chillipadar, Muduliguda, Naringjhola, Alingpada, Sanyasiguda has been declared as Reserved forest.

The wild animals, viz. leopard, bear, deer, barking deer, wild boar, elephant, monkey and porcupines, etc. dwell in the forest and often cause havoc by destroying the standing crops of the people. Even now the carnivorous animals occasionally venture into villages and create menace for their domesticated animals. The jungle is also infested with snakes like python, cobra and crates. Didayis take various precautionary measures. They make fence barricade around the hamlets, with a wooden door. Didayis pet the dogs, who guard their house premises and also the standing crops. Hill dwellers are seen with bow and arrow, spear on various traps in the hill track as well as near their crop field.

Origin of Didayi

It is said that the word 'Didayi' is derived from 'Dida', means the power or strength, on the basis of which their community has been recognized as Didayis since ancient times. As per their legend, in the long past a man had two sons and they were staying in *Kondakamberu* hill region. While the two sons were on hunting, they fought over a prey, got separated and started living in different areas. The progenies of these two sons came to be known as *'Bonda'* and 'Didayi' respectively.

The Didayi can be traced back to *'Munda* group' of the origin. As Kara (1999 : 2) shows the hereditary link of Didayi in Fig. 2.1.

This theory is further strengthened by the statements, made by Verrier Elwin when he states that "the myths of the origin of the Didayi from twelve *Gadaba* brothers being born on the bank of Godabari river subsequently came to Jeypore hill side in search of food and prey. Among them Didayi was one of the *Gadaba* brother. The eldest brother was a *Bhoj Gadaba*, next one was *Asura Gadaba* and the remaining brothers were *Kondh, Bonda,* Didayi, *Jhoria, Parenga, Dora Kondh, Holar, Pengu, Chileri* and *Maria*" (Elwin, 1950 : 2-3).

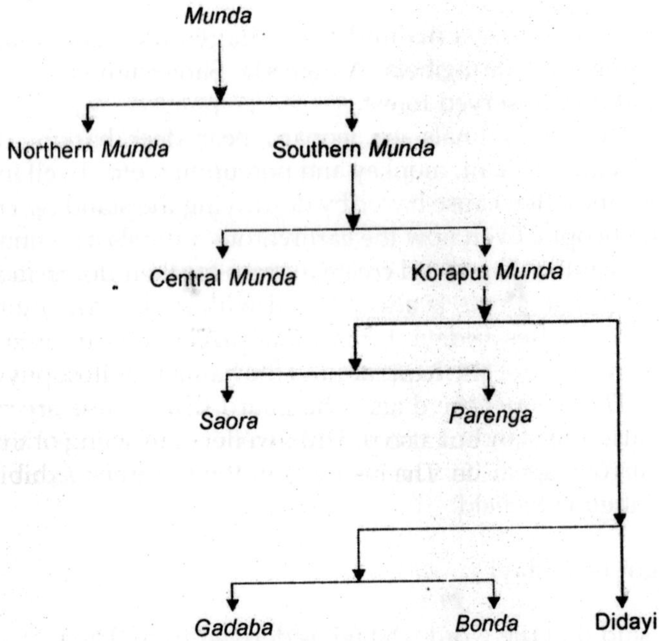

Fig. 2.1 : Origin Tree of Didayi Tribe

Sani Angra, an informant of Oringi village and also the president of the Didayi community, said that the ancient people (Adima Adhibasi) were all known as *Paraja* and subsequently they branched out to form seven tribal communities, viz. *"Kondha Paraja, Gadaba Paraja, Koya Paraja, Bonda Paraja, Jadia Paraja, Dimul Paraja* and *Parenga Paraja"*. He further stated that they all descend from a common parent, who was sent by the God *(Mahaprabhu)* when the Universe was still partly submerged in water. The God had sent a crow to help their parents to create a beautiful Mother, the Earth. Till today all these tribes are maintaining harmonious relationship amongst themselves as they trace their ancestry to a common apical ancestor.

The views expressed in the above-mentioned myths and legends relating to the origin of the Didayi seems quite mysterious, but from the folklores, it is evident that Didayis and other tribal groups of the neighbourhood are close kins and belonged to the descendants of a common ancestor.

Didayi Identity

Identity is usually a psychological self-conception of an ethnic group and can be viewed in a broad sense in terms of social identity, cultural identity and ethnic identity. Hence, ethnic identity of a community encompasses its culture, traditions, myth, beliefs, rituals, happiness, sorrows and philosophy of life, which are exclusive and unique to them. These are not only vital elements but also provide an understanding of their values and way of life. The Didayi as an ethnic group exhibit a distinct socio-cultural dignity, creativity, ingenuity, inherent skills and ideological values of their own. In spite of having cultural homogenous characteristics, the Didayi often, display certain differences in their physical characteristics, linguistic identity and socio-cultural pattern in respect to their settlements in three different areas, viz. plain, hill and cut off lands.

The Didayi have been further categorized on their own into four groups on the basis of their habitations and typical habits as under :

Plain Didayis : The Didayis living in the plain villages on the foothills are known as '*Jhadi*-Didayis,' which means their access is limited to fringes of jungle, having only shrubs and they are closer to the outer world.

Hill Didayis : They are known as '*Konglo*-Didayi' and '*Ghati Duar* Didayi' as they live on the mountain top and very stubborn in nature.

Cut-off Didayis : The Didayis living on the Machkund river valley and adjoining areas having been cut off from the main land due to the construction of reservoir, are known as '*Londia* Didayi'.' *Londia*' connotes isolation. Those who were separated and stayed in cut off area, are called '*Londia*' Didayi.

Phulpadar Didayi : The Didayis who had shifted to the rehabilitation colony from the Machkund Valley due to submerger of their lands in the reservoir, have been settled down at *Phulpadar* area. These Didayis are presently not being covered under the Micro Project, Didayi Development Agency (Map 2.2).

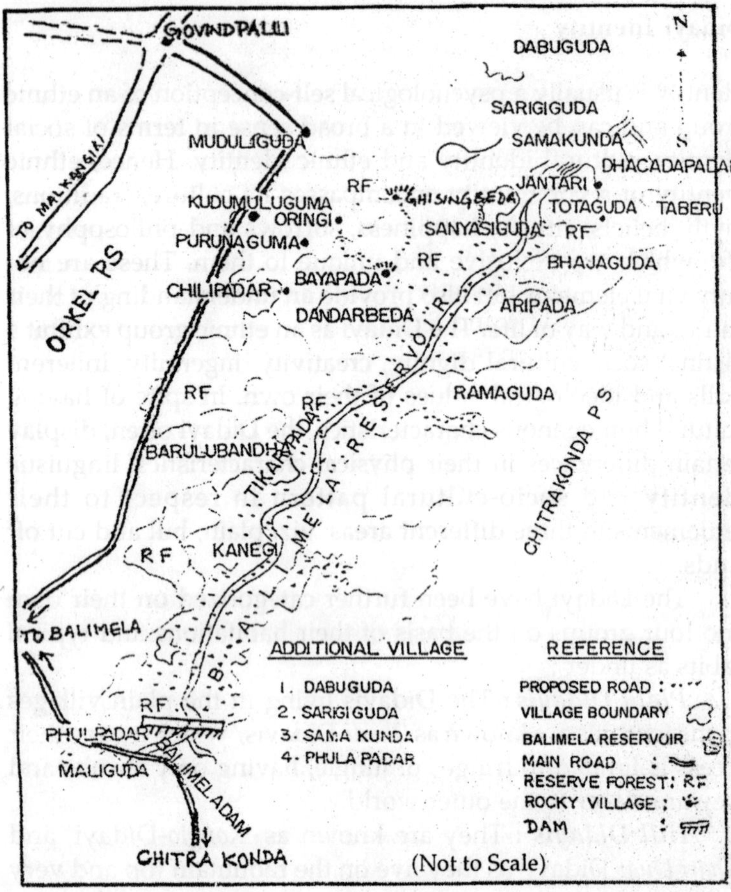

Map 2.2 : Area under the Micro Project

Population

Total population of the Didayi as per August 1998 census survey, conducted by the Micro Project is 5,194, constituting

2,531 males and 2,663 females. The Didayi population based on the census survey conducted since 1941 onwards, indicates that the Didayi population has increased by 19 per cent between 1941 and 1961. Subsequently, the population figure shows negative growth rate between 1961 and 1981. (Table 2.2 and Graph 2.1). This may be due to the displacement and disruption in their livelihood caused by the construction of Balimela Hydel Project as shown in Table 2.7. Furthermore, the population survey conducted by the Micro Project in 1994 and 1998, indicates that the growth has been reversed and population has increased by more than 125 per cent, taking 1981 census as base (Tables 2.2 and 2.3). The male population accounts for 48.72 per cent and female as 51.28 per cent of the total population (Table 2.4 and Fig. 2.2). It is also evident from the Table 2.4 that the female population is found to be 2.56 per cent more than the male population and the sex ratio is 1052 (Table 2.4). Furthermore, the plain villages constitute 1297 (24.97%) of the total Didayi population whereas the hilltop sector has a total population of 2740 (52.76%). Both the plain and the hilltop sectors possess a higher female ratio 1140 and 1074 respectively. Whereas, in cut off villages, male population accounts as 604 (52.21%) which is higher than female population status of 553 (47.79%) and also indicates a reverse sex ratio state of 915. However, the overall sex ratio is 1052 with a male population of 2531 (48.72%) and female as 2663 (51.28%).

Table 2.2 : Demographic Status of Didayi (1941-1998)

Sl. No.	Year of Census	Male	Female	Total	% of Pop. Growth
1.	1941	—	—	1661	—
2.	1961	962	1016	1978	19.08
3.	1971	1131	1033	2164	9.40
4.	1981	—	—	1977	–8.64
5.	1991	---	—	—	—
6.	*1994	2167	2293	4460	125.5
7.	*1998	2531	2663	5194	14.13

Note : * Indicates Survey by DDA, Kudumulugumma.

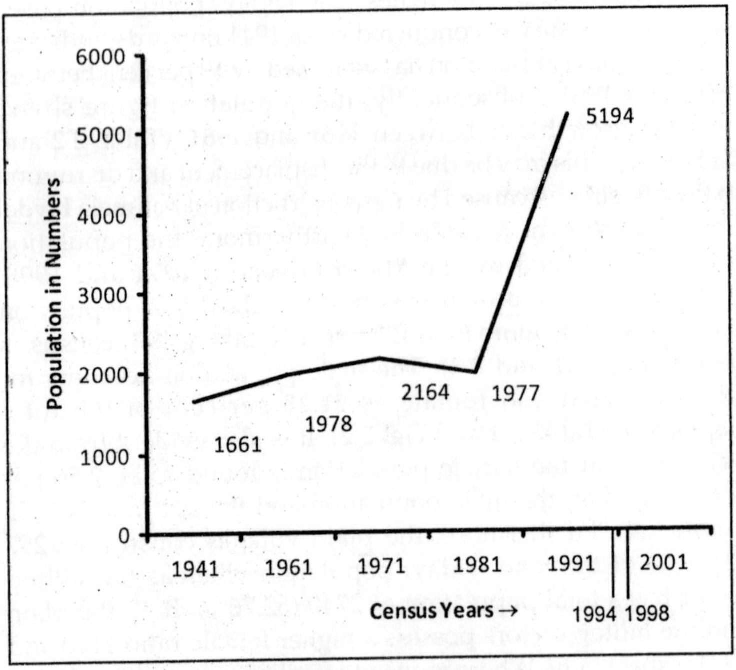

Graph 2.1 : Growth Rate of Didayi Population (1941-1998)

Table 2.3 : Didayi Population under DDA (1998)

Sl. No.	*Name of Village*	*No. of HH*	*Male*	*Female*	*Total*
Plain Sector					
Kudumulugumma—Block and GP					
1.	Purunagumma	37	71	85	156
2.	Chilipader	16	32	37	69
3.	Tikarpada	34	72	90	162
Khairiput—Block and Rasbeda GP.					
4.	Muduliguda (A)	92	184	200	384
5.	Oringi	122	247	279	526
		301	606 (46.72)	691 (53.28)	1297 (24.97)
Hill Sector					
Kudumulugumma—Block and Nakamamundi GP					
6.	Bayapada	37	69	87	156
7.	Suripada	22	41	50	104

Sl. No.	Name of Village	No. of H.H.	Male	Female	Total
8.	Gangapada	86	166	178	384
9.	Badankiaguda	64	117	107	224
10.	Bataguda	23	45	50	95
11.	Ghisingbeda	59	125	127	252
12.	Damodarbeda	83	176	189	365
13.	Bamaring	16	37	44	81
14.	Kaning	28	57	45	102
15.	Barlubandha	22	37	41	78
16.	Nilapari	26	49	47	96
17.	Karkaguda	46	77	80	157
18.	Amblibeda	60	116	137	253
19.	Anguruguda	19	32	46	78
20.	Tikaratada (B)	33	66	66	132
21.	Khajuriguda	25	42	63	105
22.	Naringijhola	27	58	49	107
23.	Muduliguda (B)	06	12	13	25
		682	1321 (48.21)	1419 (51.79)	2740 (52.76)
Cut off Sector					
Kudumulugumma—Block and Andarapalli GP					
24.	Orapadar	68	147	120	267
25.	Ramguda	4	11	9	20
26.	Kodigandhi	2	6	3	9
27.	Jantri	17	29	24	53
28.	Totaguda	16	29	24	53
29.	Maribeda	19	29	31	60
30.	Disariguda	13	27	25	52
31.	Sanyasiguda	6	9	11	20
32.	Kantamanjari	14	27	25	52
33.	Nadimanjari	21	40	41	81
34.	Dhakadpadar	40	92	81	173
35.	Dabuguda	30	57	59	116
36.	Taberu	39	86	78	164
37.	Anlingpada	13	15	22	37
		302	604 (52.21)	553 (47.79)	1157 (22.27)
	Total	1285	2531 (48.72)	2663 (51.28)	5194 (100)

Note : Figures in bracket indicate percentage.
Source : DDA, Kudumulugumma.

Table 2.4 : Distribution of Didayi Population (1998-99)

Sl. No.	Sector	No. of Male	No. of Female	Total No.of Population	% of G.Total	M/F
1.	Plain	606 (46.72)	691 (53.28)	**1297** (100)	 **(24.97)**	1140
2.	Hilltop	1321 (48.21)	1419 (51.79)	**2740** (100)	 **(52.76)**	1074
3.	Cut off	604 (52.21)	553 (47.79)	**1157** (100)	 **(22.27)**	915
		2531 (48.72)	2663 (51.28)	**5194** **(100)**		1052

Note : Figures in bracket indicate percentage.
Note : Figures in bold indicate the Gross percentage.

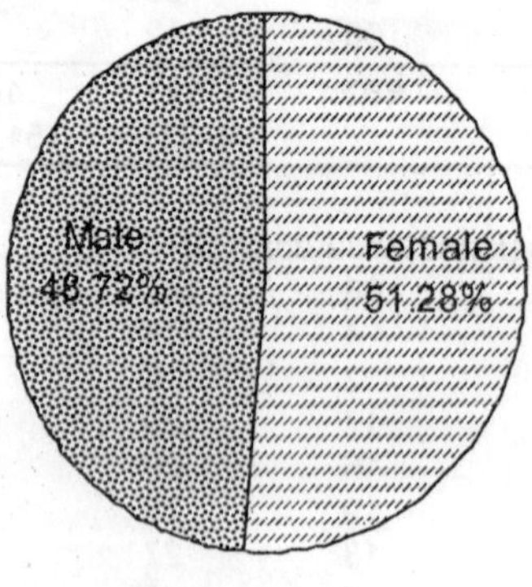

Fig. 2.2 : Male to Female Population Ratio in 1998

Physical Features

The Didayi of the respective areas, viz. plain, hill, cut off and the Phulpader, indicate a little distinctiveness in their physical features because of differential geographic set-up. The plain and the cut off Didayi are found to be weaker in body construction and lesser brownish in complexion than the Hill Didayi. On the contrary, Hill Didayis are well built, brown complexioned with traces of Mongolian eye fold and curly hair.

Linguistic Identity

The dialect is more or less similar to the dialects of the neighboring tribes, viz. *Bondo, Soura, Paraja* and *Gadba*. Since all of them claim mythical origin from the Godavari river, the influence of Dravidian linguistic style has been clearly marked in their language. Elwin (1950 : 2-3) suggests that the Didayi maintain a close linguistic affinity with the tribes descended fiom the Godavari river and the later tribes are *Parenga, Gadba* and *Bonda,* and to some extent with *Kondh.*

Guha's observation about the Didayi dialect is that "The Didayi speak a dialect that comes under the non-Khervari branch of the *Munda*-Kol group in the Austro Asiatic division of the Asiatic family. Hence, some characteristics, it is said to be close to the dialect of the *Boṅdo, Gadba, Saora, Juanga* and *Kharia,* etc. It, however, differs sharply from the dialect of the *Kondh,* who speak a Dravidian language. Thus linguistically, the Didayi are placed under the stratum of the Austro-Asiatic group of the tribes in the country." (Guha *et al.*, 1968 : 1-7).

In another study Mahanti (1982 : 1) states that the Didayi dialect, which comes closer to those of *Paraja, Gadba, Bonda, Soura* and *Juanga,* belongs to the Non-Kherwary branch of the *Munda*-Kol group under Austro-Asiatic branch of the Austro-Asiatic group of tribes in this country" (Mohanti, S.C, 1982, p. 1).

Haimendorf (1945 : 332) described both the Didayi and the Reddis, who are not only related through a common stock but are belonging to the stratum of primitive, semi-nomadic shifting cultivators. Both the Didayi and the Reddis are of nearly related stock. Both have now lost their original language but they have retained many of the essential features of their old economic and cultural life. There can be no doubt that they represent one of the few remnants of the culture and race, much more ancient than the Austro-Asiatic people.

However, it is observed that all Didayis do not speak same dialect. The Didayi dialect has four different accents because of their differential habitations. Those who are in plain areas, speak in a slow and steady manner with marked influence of

Oriya, Telugu, and Desia (mixed tribal language). Their dialect is known as *'Jagerla-Shong'*. The hill dwellers speak quite faster and their pronunciation differs from the former. In fact their language and style are considered as the original Didayi dialect, locally known as *'Bole-Shong'*. It is very interesting to mention that, the cut off Didayis have forgotten their original dialect. The village Jantri, Dabuguda etc. are using the mixed tribal and Oriya language (*Desihia Bhasa*). Even at home they are not using the mother tongue as they feel dignified to use other language. They are gradually losing their linguistic identity due to frequent interaction with Oriya, Telugu, Bengali refugee and other tribal people. Their dialect is locally known as *'Jagerla-Shong'*. The *'Phulpadar* Didayis' also use mixed form of dialect due to their regular contact with other communities in the rehabilitation colonies, whose dialect is known as *'Bole-Jung'*.

Few examples have been stated as follows :

	Items	*Plain*	*Hilltop*	*Cut off*
(a)	Aluminium anklet	pohari	panari	painiri/pohari
(b)	Nose ring	tandrum	julip	julup
(c)	Ear ring	nangu/nangula	nangu	nangul

Material Cultural Identity

Dress

Like language, dress pattern also reveals some of the cultural traits and identity of an ethnic group. The traditional dress of women is known as *'Kisalu'*, a self-woven unstitched clothing of bark fibres and thread. It is to be put on around the waist to cover the lower parts but the upper part is left uncovered. The traditional dress of man is known as *'Lengti'*, a piece of loin cloth put around a thread and the upper part remains uncovered (Photograph 2.1).

The married ladies wear the *sarees* in a particular way, so as to be distinguished from others. The one end of the cloth is either taken on the left or right shoulder, the other end is taken under the opposite armpit and is tied knot over the left or right shoulder. Usually the old ladies are seen putting on a long cotton cloth (*Pattai*) which may be either in white or red colour.

Normally, a Didayi lady of both plain and cut off sectors prefer to put on *sarees* with traditional style. But when they go outside, particularly to the weekly market and the Micro Project office, they use *sarees* and comb long hairs of the head quite attractively in the manner of neighbouring communities use to practise.

The Didayi of hilltop sector are relatively conservative with regard to dress. Only the young girls of some of the study villages like Bayapada and Suripada are seen in *sarees* like any moderate girl. The girls of interior most villages like Ghisingbeda, Gangapada and Badakinyaguda, clad *sarees* in the traditional way whether stay within the village or outside. However, it has been observed that the male and female folks seemed to be more conscious about their look, dress pattern, ornaments and hairstyle while posing for a photograph snap.

The male folks of three regions are still found with their traditional pieces of cloth (*lengti*) inside the villages. But among them some of the people prefer *'dhoti '* to *'lengti'* to wear even on normal days. The students and service holders are no more seen in their traditional dress. They normally put on shirt with trousers.

Hair Style

The Didayis use castor oil for nourishing head hair. It is because they grow castor in their kitchen garden. Both men and women are very particular in so far as combing is concerned. The married women are seen in hair knots. The unmarried girls are seen in both the traditional knots in addition to the modern hair style. However, a striking difference in the hair style among the women of the three sectors has been observed; ladies of the plain and the cut off areas do not decorate their knots with traditional ornaments like wooden small comb, sickle, and the metallic clips like that of hill women-folks (Photograph 2.2). The children below seven years are seen in the shaved heads in the study villages of three sectors.

Didayis of plain and cut off sectors generally need the services of the local barber. However, the hilltop people do not have the barber in their villages and they help each other for shaving and hair cutting. Customarily, the father himself does the shaving of his new born baby either on the tenth day or during the name giving ceremony.

Ornaments

Didayi women are fond of ornaments, made of silver, brass, copper and gold. The various ornaments, used by them are given in Table 2.5.

Table 2.5 : Ornaments of Didayis and the Local Terms

Sl. No.	*Body parts*	*Name of ornaments*	*Local terms*		
			Plain	*Hill*	*Cut-off*
1.	Arm	glass/metalic bangles	*gajula*	in all sectors	
		arm-lets	do not use	*gagarbala*	do not use.
2.	Ankle	aluminium anklet	*pohari*	*panri*	*pohari*
3.	Neck	blue bead necklace	*toha*	*toha*	do not use.
		Silver necklace	*rupa kangoli*	do not use	do not use
		yellow bead necklace	*sona Mali*	in all sectors	
4.	Nose	nose ring	*tandrumoo*	*julip*	julup
	Nasal septum	three types	*kagul, ludki,* dandi	*kagul, ludki,* dandi	do not use
5.	Ear	earrings	*nangu*	*nangu*	*nangul*
6.	Toe	toe rings	*tinangati*	*tinangati*	*tinangti*

There is subtle difference in their choices of putting on ornaments, as it has been observed among the Didayi living in three different sectors. The married ladies of plain wear glass/ metallic bangles, aluminium anklet (*pohari*), silver necklace (*rupa kungoli*), blue bead necklace (*toha*), yellow bead necklace (*sona mali*), nose ring (*tandrumoo*). Three types of rings the ladies use on nasal septum (*kagool, ludki* and *dandi*). The girls use bangles, silver necklace, yellow bead necklace (*sona mali*), blue bead necklace (*toha*). The male folks do not use any ornaments.

The females of cut off sector use a few ornaments viz. bangles, aluminium anklets (*pohari*), bead necklace and hair clips. They do not use nose rings. The males and children rarely put on any ornaments.

It is found that almost all Didayis of the hill sector put on ornaments irrespective of the age and sex. New borne babies, both boys and girls, customarily wear ear rings on their name giving ceremony. The father performs the rituals associated with this occasion. The unmarried girls use bangles, nose and ear rings, yellow bead necklace (*sona mali*), black and blue bead necklaces (*toha*). The married ladies wear ear rings (*nangu*), bangles, silver arm-lets (*limba*), brass arm-let (*gegar bala*), anklet wear (*panri*), toe rings (*tinangati*) and nose rings (*julupi*), other nasal ornaments (*chanakmunha*), decorative hair clips. Some of the traditional ornaments used by Didayi ladies are shown (Photograph 2.3).

In fact, significant change has been noticed in their dress patterns. In the plains, the girls are undergoing tailoring training and other kinds of skill-building training at DDA Kudumulugumma. They are seen with modest attire, indicating their nature of transformation towards modernity.

In the cut off sector, a lady Sarpanch of Totaguda village, Madhu Pangi was in her traditional wear and when approached for interviews and for a snap-shot, she along with her husband (village *Naik*) immediately accepted the proposal gladly. They took extra care to change over to modest wear. The woman clad in *saree* and blouse and the man with dhoti and shirt, posed for the photograph with wrist watch and a transistor (Photograph 2.2). This is a glaring inclination towards modernity in cut off villages but are incapable to afford costly modern gadgets because of low level of income. However, in the hill sector, the people are found to be in their simple traditional clothing and not much beyond that. The changes in interior areas are gradually penetrating to bring about a socio-cultural transformation in the Didayi society with regard to personal adoration and choice for low cost modern goods like wrist watch, transistor and some cosmetics. With advancement of time, the Didayis are also showing a clear sign of progress with regards to their material culture.

Household Assets

Didayis are self-content people. Their household assets consist of limited items of materials such as utensils, agricultural equipment, fishing implements and miscellaneous items which are either prepared by themselves or purchased from local markets. These are described as in succeeding manner.

Utensils

Utensils are of brass, aluminium and earthen types. Aluminium and brass utensils are used for cooking and carrying water from the water source. Earthen vessels and gourds are used for storing water.

Agricultural equipment

The agricultural implements are used for the settled and the shifting cultivation. They are plough (*cini*), long wooden handle of the plough, to be driven by the bullocks (*rirana*), spade (*korada*), wooden planks for levelling the ground (*pata*), spade with spikes (*insum*) and sickle (*hoes*) for cutting and clearing the podu lands. They also use axe (*malle*) for cutting the bushes to prepare the podu lands.

Besides these they themselves prepare grain storing baskets out of bamboo and leaves of *siali* creeper. The winnowing fan and the broom *(chun)* are used for husking the grains.

Fishing equipment

They use fishing net, conical bamboo basket and the fishing stick for catching the fish. The Didayi males of the cut off sector are found to be expert in the skill of weaving the fishing net.

Weapons

They use the weapons like bow and arrow, spear, axe, knife, and traps for hunting purposes. Themselves make the bow and arrow of bamboo. Generally, they carry an axe whenever they go to the forest. Various types of traps are used to capture the birds, rabbit, rat etc.

Miscellaneous items

For their day-to-day requirements various household items are used. They are: pounding stone (*tanka*), grinding stone for millet (*fininder*), cradle made of bamboo (*ajala*), earthen lamp (*batur*) and wooden cot. The modern amenities like radio, wrist watch, bicycle and tape recorder, etc. are found only among the plain (0.5%) and cut off (0.2%) villagers. Since there is no electricity in the area, television and other electrical appliances are not in use.

Food Habits

Mixed food is taken as the basic diet of the Didayi community. It is a combination of dietary form of millet, *suan* rice and some boiled vegetables. This staple diet is known as '*gruel*' or '*thuria*'. Their traditional cooking is mostly oil free and spice free except the salt, turmeric, and chilly. The cooking procedure is very simple and involves only boiling. The Didayi ladies pound the millet and rice as per the quantity required for the family everyday and cook afresh. A typical pounding stone (*tanka*) being, used by Didayi lady of the hill sector is given in Photograph 2.4. The communal feast is only prepared by the male folks, during the festival occasions.

They are all non-vegetarian and prefer beef. Didayis also eat goat, pig, chicken, wild bore, etc. Mostly, the animal is roasted with salt and turmeric paste. They use the cooking oil and the spices very rarely whenever they afford these items. They do not drink the milk but do not hesitate to take the milkbased tea. Guests are treated with a non-vegetarian food along with *salap* wine. The communal feast is prepared on special occasions like Chait festival, Push parva, funeral and marriage ceremony. They do not accept or give food and water to certain tribal and non-tribal groups because of communal restriction. The pattern of water and cooked food transaction among Didayi *vis-à-vis* other communities has shown in Table 2.6.

Table 2.6 : Inter-caste/Tribe Food Transaction System

Sl. No.	*Groups accept food from Didayi*	*Not accept food from Didayi*	*Didayi accept*	*Not accept*
1.	Kondh	Bhumia	Kondh	Harijan
2.	Bonda	Rana	Bhumia	Dambo
3.	Gadba	Gauda	Rana	Christians
4.	Harijan	Rauta	Bonda	—
5.	—	—	Gauda & Rauta	—

Liquor

Liquor is a part and parcel of tribal life. The alcohol is used in various socio-cultural and economic contexts of a tribe. As Verrier Elwin (1939 : 44) stated, "When our mouth is full of liquor say the Baiga, we talk like King. But when it is empty, we remember the money we had to borrow to pay for it." The statement holds good for the Didayi also.

Liquor seems to be an easily available source of entertainment for the tribal people. Didayis have strong inclination towards liquor and beverage. Liquor is associated with every phase of their life cycle rituals. A Didayi child of eight to ten days is given a sip of country liquor as a part of ritual. He continues to drink as part of his daily diet as well as on occasions of various festivals and rituals till end of his life. It is their conceptions that liquor gives them energy to cope with the hard and arduous life.

Types of Liquor

Generally, they take country liquor which includes *salap* wine, *mahula* liquor (a fermented and distilled juice of *mahula* flower) and *handia* (a fermented starch extracted out of mixed millets).

Salap liquor

A *salap* tree is a great economic asset to a Didayi. A *salap* tree generally after ten years continue to provide the wine for three to five years. Individual households are the owners of the *salap* tree and ownership succeeds to son after the death of the father. The ownership goes to his brother's son in case he has no son. There are more than fifteen *salap* trees found in and around the villages of plain and hilltop sector

Salap centre : In the hilltop villages, *salap* centres are found. *Salap* centres we located near the *salap* trees where all the villagers generally males assemble together to have the *salap* wine. It serves like a liquor bar where the owner of the tree provides the wine free of cost to all the assembled villagers at a particular time, that is about five a.m. to seven a.m. and four p.m. to six p.m. While consuming the free wine, the villagers have to follow certain restrictions that no one is allowed to drink more than five glasses at a time. He can only buy the extra liquor of any amount. The liquor is carried in a *'tumba'* which is a dried bottle gourd container.

A branch of *salap* tree is cut at the top end portion and an earthen pot for the collection of the wine is tied to it. A boy *(goti)* about 10 to 12 years whom the owner has kept for this purpose, collects the wine from the tree using certain techniques for climbing as well as descending. For this job, he only enjoys the drinks free of cost.

The plain and the cut off villages neither have the *salap* centres nor the system of free distribution of *salap* liquor. Liquor taking by the Didayi not of uniform pattern. Hill dwellers consume the drink after boiling the raw *salap* wine in an earthen pot. Whereas the plain and the cut off villagers consume the drink as it is available to them. Sometimes, they mix urea, chemicals and other locally available agents for getting more intoxicating effect.

***Economic benefit of Salap tree* :** On an average, a man gets Rs. 150 by selling *salap* liquor per day. A *salap* tree provides *salap* liquor worth more than Rs. 10,000 annually. Thus, the owner of the tree enjoys a special status in the village.

Mahula liquor (mahula saga/mahul a mapta)

Mahula liquor is the second favourite beverage of Didayis next to *salap*. It is only prepared in plain and cut off sectors. The villagers collect the *mahul* flower during the month of March and April. The flowers are allowed to dry up completely and stored in a bamboo basket or *siali* leaf basket for consumption throughout the year. Hilltop villagers buy the *mahul* flowers from the weekly markets because of the scarcity of *mahul* trees in the hill areas.

Preparation process : The *mahula* liquor is prepared by a simple distillation process after soaking *mahula* flowers with water inside a clay pot for two to three days. A glass of liquor costs about Rs. 3 to Rs. 4 depending on quality.

Bajara liquor

Since the *salap* tree dries up and *mahula* becomes scarce, the Didayis are forced to prepare the liquor out of *bajara* a type of millet generally available in the period of October to May months of a year.

The Didayis generally share liquor with other communities except Harijans particularly the *Dambas* for fear of pollution. Hill Didayis are more orthodox in this matter.

Smoking

Other than liquor, smoking seems to be a part and parcel of their life. Both male and female folk smoke a type of *bidi* roll called *'sunga'* which is prepared out of a locally grown tobacco rolled in a *tendu* or *siali* leaf. They always carry *bidi* rolls on their ear lobes or on the hair knots. Most of the kitchen garden of hill villagers grow tobacco plants whereas the cut off and plain villagers buy the leaves from the market. Generally, they smoke ten to twenty *bidis* per day.

Now-a-days many of them are seen chewing *'khaini'*, as this intoxicating item is easily available in the market.

Folk Dance and Music

Folk dance and music are the socio-cultural identity of any tribe. Didayi life cycle rituals are associated with folklore and music. They observe each festival with the folk dance and music depicting rhythm of their life. The sweeter the melody, the more vigorous and spirited is the folk dance. The folk dance (*demsa*) symbolises their cultural identity, community consciousness and feelings of broadness among themselves. The *demsa* marks a good coordination among themselves, associated with quick stepping with high pitch melody. They play various types of musical instruments in the ceremonial occasion. Every festival is observed with a pattern of folk dance and music. They are stated as follows :

	Name of the festival	Music and rhythms
(a)	Push parva	*Indardind* and *Terevilli*
(b)	Chaita parva	*Indarnde* and *Singphunhi*
(c)	Nandi/Lendi/Bandapana parva	*Wahtyayangwe*

Didayis have also added flavour through their songs and dances to programmes of All India Radio, Jeypore station in Koraput district.

Balimela Hydel Power Project and its Impact

Balimela Hydel Power Project started in the year 1962. The first unit was commissioned on August 14, 1973. Before the construction of the reservoir dam the Didayis were residing in Machkund valley between Duduma fall and Kondakamberu hill ranges within the area of 20 sq. mile constituting 26 villages. Since the valleys are proved to be fertile, the people took to agriculture as their main occupation.

Uma Guha and others (1968) expressed the concern about the Didayi. She stated that, "The research workers of the Tribal

Research Bureau of Orissa and some of the officials of Bhubaneswar, could hardly remember the Didayi tribe. They were under impression that the Didayi, if such a tribe did exist, must have been submerged by the Balimela Project already. However, Mr. Promod Singh, I.A.S., Secretary, Tribal and Rural Welfare Department, took great interest in our scheme and advised us to proceed to Koraput."

Surjit Sinha also states, "As a large part of their abode to be submerged under the Balimela Project and there was apprehension of their being scattered to other areas, it was considered urgent to study them. In February 1966, a team of the Anthropological Survey of India, under the leadership of Smt. U. Guha, was sent to the fieldwork among the Didayi" (Guha, 1968).

When the Balimela Project was proposed to be started, a list of 38 villages were provided to the staff of Tribal Research Bureau (TRB) for investigation, out of which there was chance of wholly submergence of eighteen villages lying within Machkund river valley. The report of TRB (1964), stated about the complete submergence of 18 villages and the rest of the villages to be wholly, partially or might not be submerged.

The State Tribal Research Bureau while preparing a planned rehabilitation scheme for the 18 villages out of 38 villages, those were going to be affected, were studied from various socio-economic viewpoints to know the people's attitude towards rehabilitation in a completely new environment. During the preparation of the report, the categories of villages were studied as under :

(i) Those affected villages which would be wholly submerged.
(ii) Villages might be partly submerged or not be submerged.
(iii) The third category of villages, are the new villages, which have not been included in the list of submerged villages (Adibasi, 1971 : 76).

The details of the Didayi villages, mentioned in the Survey Report (1964), are given Tables 2.7 and 2.8.

Table 2.7 : A List of Wholly Submerged Villages owing to Commissioning of Balimela Project

Sl. No.	*Village name*	*Total No. families*	*Population*	*Male*	*Female*
1.	Orapadar	21	58	28	30
2.	Sanyasiguda	16	66	31	35
3.	Totaguda	24	110	55	55
4.	Konangi	57	—	—	—
5.	Kenduguda	14	—	—	—
6.	Ladiguda	9	—	—	—
7.	Rava	1	—	—	—
8.	Mudliguda	4	—	—	—
9.	Siniguda	20	—	—	—
10.	Ramaguda	9	—	—	—
11.	Arapadar	14	—	—	—
	Total	189	234	—	—

Source : Survey Report 1964.

Table 2.8 : Caste/Tribe-wise Distribution of the New Villages

Sl. No.	*Village name*	*Total No. of families*	*No. of families belonging to other tribes*	*Didayi families*	*Total population*
1.	Amblibeda	38	13-*Kondh* 3-Gauda 1-*Rana* 2-Bonda	19	161
2.	Tikarpada	28	12-*Kondh* 2-Gadba 1-Lohar	13	137
3.	Bajaguda	26	2-Bonda	24	99
4.	Umruguda	7	7-Didayi	7	29
5.	Sanpansapadar	20	5-*Paraja* 13-Lohar	2	78
6.	Kenduguda (B)	44	26-*Paraja* 2-Gauda	16	298
	Total	163	82	81	802

Source : Survey Report 1964.

The strategy for rehabilitation

The eighteen villages which were under the category of the submergence, lay on either side of the river Machkund up to the Chitrakunda dam. Each village was situated around a streamlet, originated from the surrounding hills and fell into the river Machkund. There was no other conveyance available to reach the villages other than the foot-track ways. Out of these eighteen submerged category, only eleven Didayi inhabited villages were under the wholly submersion category. Under the category of the partially submersible villages (20), no Didayi village has been mentioned in the survey report. Besides these wholly or partially submerged villages, there were other thirty four villages, which are found to be situated in between the enlisted villages and have been categorized as 'New Villages'. The Didayi villages, viz. Amblibeda, Tikerpada, Jantri, Sanpandar, Bajaguda, Umuruguda, Kenduguda (B), were categorized under new villages (Adibasi, VII, XIII, 1971 : 89-99). These new villages accommodated 163 families having a total of 802 people. Out of total families, there were 81(49.7%) Didayi families. It is observed that the Didayi tribe of the valley have been affected mostly by the construction of Balimela Project. Besides these some of the Didayi populated villages in the valley were not figured in the list of rehabilitated villages, hence among them many are found missing as TRB report indicates (Table 2.8). It is ascertained that the population of these missing Didayi villages either have migrated to hilltop villages or to nearby cut off areas or else to the rehabilitated colony.

While going through all these accounts, it is revealed that the Didayi community has been worst affected compared to other community residing in the Chitrokonda valley.

Peoples' attitude towards resettlement

People usually maintain a specific value-orientation about the living space. They unanimously feel that human habitation is not only a home for the people, but also is the abode of their Gods, the spirits and their ancestors. It promotes a source of inspiration to them and is inseparable. The submersion of their villages and lands by the Chitrokonda reservoir had an adverse effect on their settled life. No doubt, it was a great shock to the tribal people affected by the project.

It is reported by Shroff (1997 : 66) that the displaced persons have not been provided alternative lands and common amenities. There is a great deal of resentment and remorse amongst the people of the area because they are cut off. For no fault of theirs and due to irony of fate that instead of reaping the fruits of development, these people are the victims of ill-conceived planning.

During the field study 15 cut off villagers between the age groups of 38-55, were interviewed to know their reaction with regard to displacement. Their statements are noted down.

Madhu Pangi, age-45, the lady Sarapanch of Totaguda village stated that her father could not get any compensation for want of genuine *pattas* of the lands, he possessed. It was a great shock to the family members and even now they have been cursing the action of the Government.

Sukra Bisoi, age-55 of village Jantri, is of the opinion that in their former villages they were reigning supreme in all respects over all communities but in newly relocated village, the Kondhs are in dominant position than the Didayi and it has bred discontentment among Didayi co-villagers.

Sukra Goluri, age-38 of village Disariguda has the resentment for not getting suitable Didayi grooms for their daughters in the limited Didayi inhabiting areas because of displacement. Hence, they are deprived forced to move to further community of Andhra region for marriage negotiation although they prefer to give marriage within their community.

It has been observed that a number of people are preferring neighbouring Andhra Pradesh markets of Chitrokonda of Orissa because of inconvenience of communication. It needs mention here that a person has to spend a night outside in addition to the extra expenditure towards the ferry service. Whereas a person going to the market of Andhra Pradesh can return on same day with all convenience. Hence, displacement has alienated them from their Didayi community, living across the Chitrokonda Reservoir.

Photograph 2.1 A Didayi man in traditional dress 'Lengti' (Hilltop village)

Photograph 2.2 : Lady Sarpanch and her husband with a transistor (Totaguda Cut off village)

Even, the relocated Didayi villagers resent for the ill-conceived planning of the State Government as there is no provision and basic amenities, provided to them. Thus, the rehabilitated people have suffered for the above reasons.

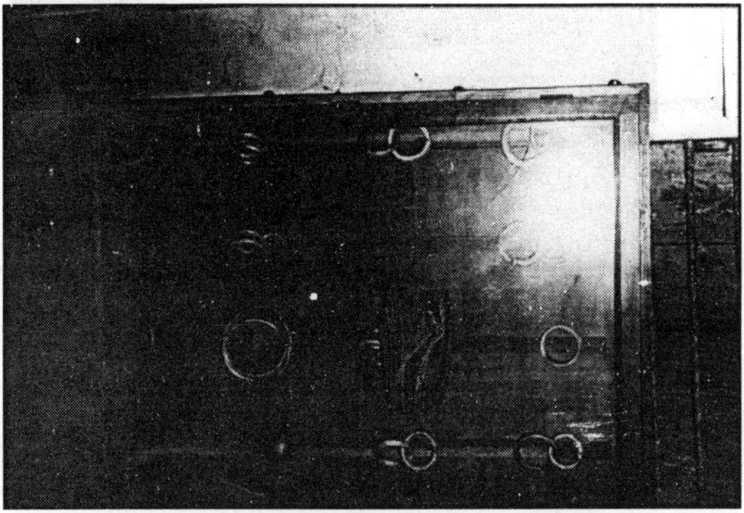

Photograph 2.3 : Traditional ornaments of Didayi women

Photograph 2.4 : A multipurpose pounding stone (Hilltop sector)

3

Study Villages

The Didayi, a less known PTGs, are confined to *Kondakamberu* range of Eastern Ghat. They have been living in thirty-seven (37) villages in three different land areas (Sectors), viz. the plains, hilltop and cut off. All these villages are found under four Gram Panchayats (GPs) and two CD Blocks. Out of thirty-seven villages, five are in plain sector, eighteen in hilltop sector and fourteen in cut off sector (Table 2.3). The plain villages are approachable and densely populated (24.97%). The villagers of the plain sector are settled agriculturists. The villages of the hilltop sector is highly populated (52.76%) and the practice of shifting cultivation is largely seen in the inaccessible parts of mountains. For the hilltop villagers shifting cultivation is the major source of income since they do not practise settled cultivation. Whereas, the cut off villages are thinly populated (22.27%) and people practise settled and shifting cultivation as well.

Out of 37 villages covered under Micro Project, 12 villages have been intensively studied during the months of March, May and October 1998-99, in different phases. The sample survey has covered 30 per cent of the total villages, with a view to gaining a holistic picture of the 'Tribe' as well as the impact of DDA (Didayi Development Agency) on them. The names of the villages selected for the study are as follows :

(a) Plain Sector—Two villages (Out of Five) : Purunagumal (*Kudumulugumma Block*) and Oring (*Khairiput Block*) .

(b) Hill Sector—Five villages (Out of eighteen) : Bayapada, Suripada, Gangapada, Badankiaguda and Ghisingbeda (*Kudumulugumma Block*)

(c) Cut off Sector—Five villages (Out of fourteen) : Jantri, Totaguda, Dabuguda, Disariguda and Sanyasiguda (*Kudumulgumma Block*).

The demographic feature of the study villages with different age groups is given in Table 3.1. It is evident from the table that the villages of hilltop sector are most densely populated (52.65%). The plain villages are also apparently populated (31.23%) than cut off villages (16.12%). The table also indicates that for 1000 males, the female population is 1123 which is higher than national level sex ratio (927).

Plain Didayis (2 Villages)

There are five plain villages, coming under the Micro Project. The three villages, viz. Purunaguma, Chilipadar and Tikarpada are under the Kudumulugumma Block, constituting the Kudumulugumma Gram Panchayat. The other two villages, Muduliguda and Oringi belong to Rasbeda G.P. of Khairiput Block. Out of three villages of Kudumulugumma G.P., the village Purunaguma has been selected for the sample study (Sketch Map 3.1). Firstly, it is approachable and just two kms away from the main road. Secondly, the only Girls High School of this locality, run by the Harijan and Tribal Welfare Department, is situated here. The village Oringi of Khairiput Block is taken as the second village for the study as it is the most populous village (Table 3.1) and also to assess the developmental impacts as it is being under the different Community Development Block of Khairiput.

Hill Didayis (5 Villages)

There are twenty-three hilltop villages, coming under the Nakamamundi G.P. of Kudumulugumma Block. The five villages, viz. Bayapada, Suripada, Gangapada, Badankiyaguda and Chisingbeda are taken as the study villages. Bayapada is the gateway village to the hilltop sector as one approaches this village after climbing the hill and passing through the Reserve Forest that begins from the Oringi plain village

Table 3.1 : Population of Study Villages with Different Age Groups

Sl. No.	Village	No. of HH	Age Groups (0-5) M	(0-5) F	(5-15) M	(5-15) F	(15-59) M	(15-59) F	(59 plus) M	(59 plus) F	Total
Plain Sector											
1.	Oringi	122	54	62	39	50	135	143	19	24	526
2.	Purunaguma	37	08	09	08	10	47	54	08	11	156
		159 (31.23)									682
Hilltop Sector											
1.	Bayapada	37	13	22	17	25	37	37	02	03	156
2.	Suripada	22	07	12	11	08	21	28	02	02	104
3.	Gangapada	86	37	39	28	32	85	89	16	18	384
4.	Badankiaguda	64	27	26	11	09	76	69	03	03	224
5.	Ghisingbeda	59	17	17	37	38	63	64	08	08	252
		268 (52.65)									1120
Cut Off Sector											
1.	Jantri	17	04	02	05	04	18	16	02	02	53
2.	Totaguda	16	05	03	05	04	17	16	02	01	53
3.	Dabuguda	30	08	10	15	11	32	35	02	03	116
4.	Disariguda	13	02	01	02	03	21	19	02	02	52
5.	Sanyasiguda	06	01	01	—	01	07	08	01	01	20
		82(16.12)									294
	Total	509 (100.00)	183	204	178	195	559	578	67	78	2096

Note : Figures in bracket indicate percentage.
Source : DDA survey, 1998.

(Sketch Map 3.2). Suripada is the adjacent village of Bayapada. The village Ghisingbeda is the farthest one and about 10 km from Bayapada village. The local people and the Micro Project staff discouraged us not to venture this village as the Didayi of Ghisingbeda are perceived as the most wild and ferocious people. In reality, it is not. The striking feature of the village is that there are small huts without perimeter fencing but there are huge stones and boulders which surround the village area. On the way of Ghisingbeda one has to come across the villages namely Bataguda and Badankiaguda. The village Gangapada is the most populous village among the hilltop villages where a DWCRA (Development of Women and Children in Rural Area) group has been operating since 1996. This village is four km away from the village Bayapada and is situated in the northern side of Bayapada (Route Sketch 3.1).

(NOT TO SCALE)

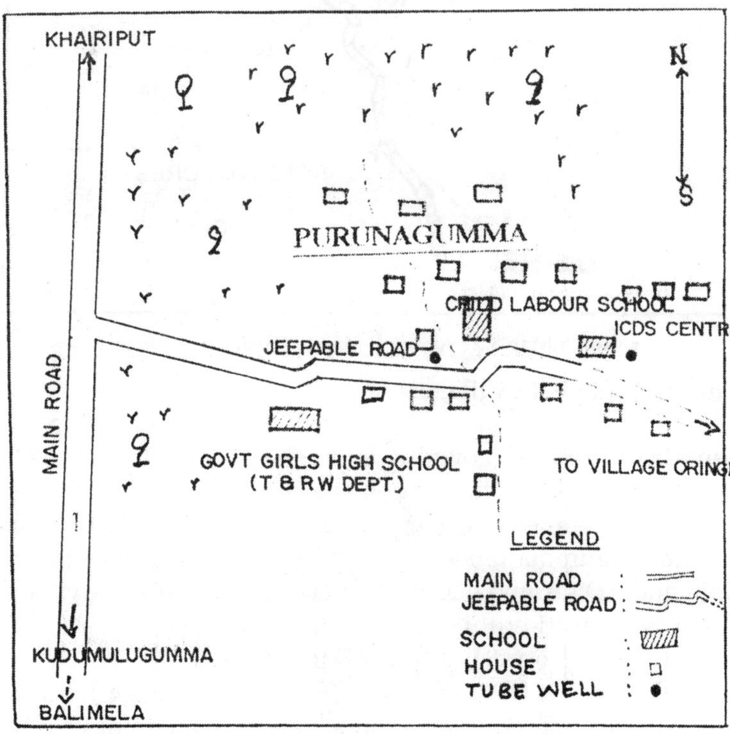

Sketch Map 3.1 : A Sketch Map of Purunaguma Village

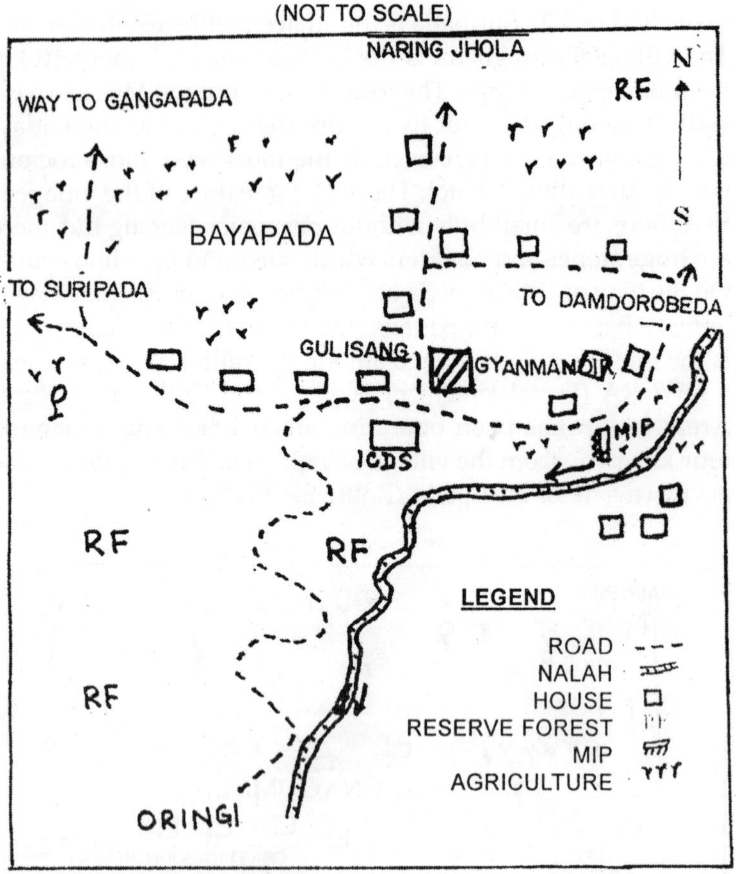

Sketch Map 3.2 : A Sketch Map of Bayapada Village

Cut off Didayis (5 Villages)

The Micro Project is covering fourteen cut off villages, out of which five villages have been selected as sample villages. Fourteen villages are coming under Andrapalli G.P. of Kudumulugumma Block. The five study villages are—Jantri, Dabuguda, Disariguda, Sanyasiguda and Totaguda. The village Jantri is a multi-ethnic village where majority are *Kondhs* (22HH) and rest are Didayis (17HH), Gadba (10HH), *Paraja* (18HH), *Rana* (12HH) and Dum (6HH). The village Jantri is the last ferry point of the cut off area. One Platoon of OSAPF

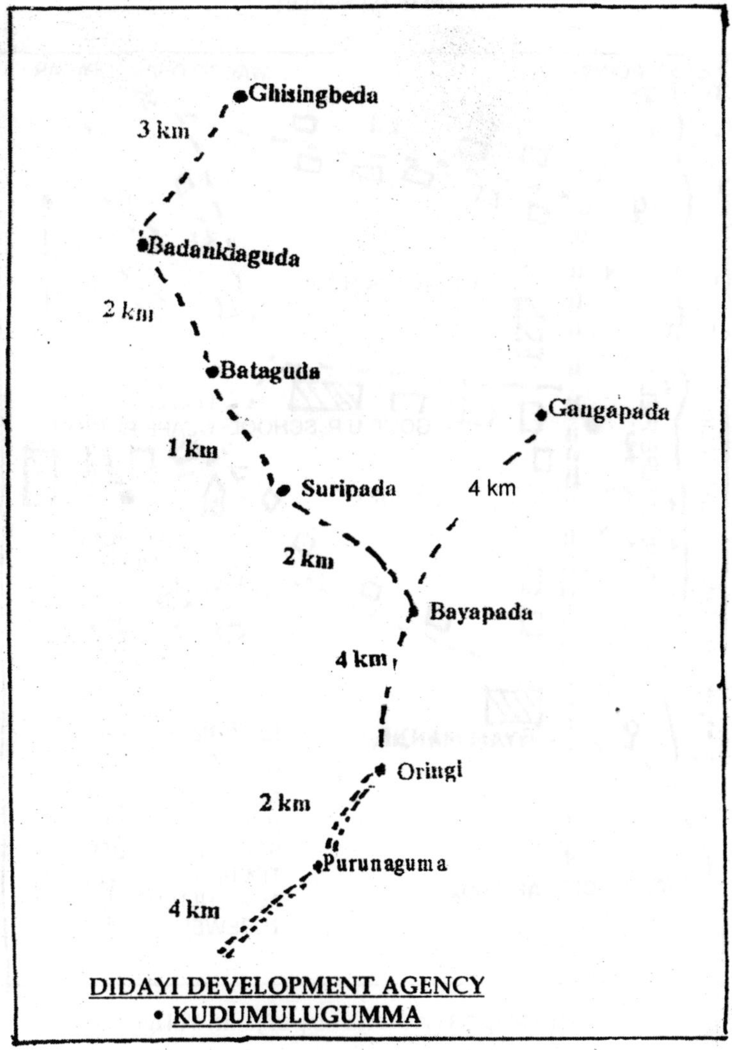

Route Sketch Map 3.1 : Route Sketch of Study Villages in Hilltop Sector

(Orissa State Armed Police Force) of Koraput based battalion is posted here to guard this region to combat the operation of Peoples War Group (PWG). Owing to its large population and multi-ethnic composition reasons, Jantri has been selected as the base village (Sketch Map 3.3). Other four villages are,

(NOT TO SCALE)

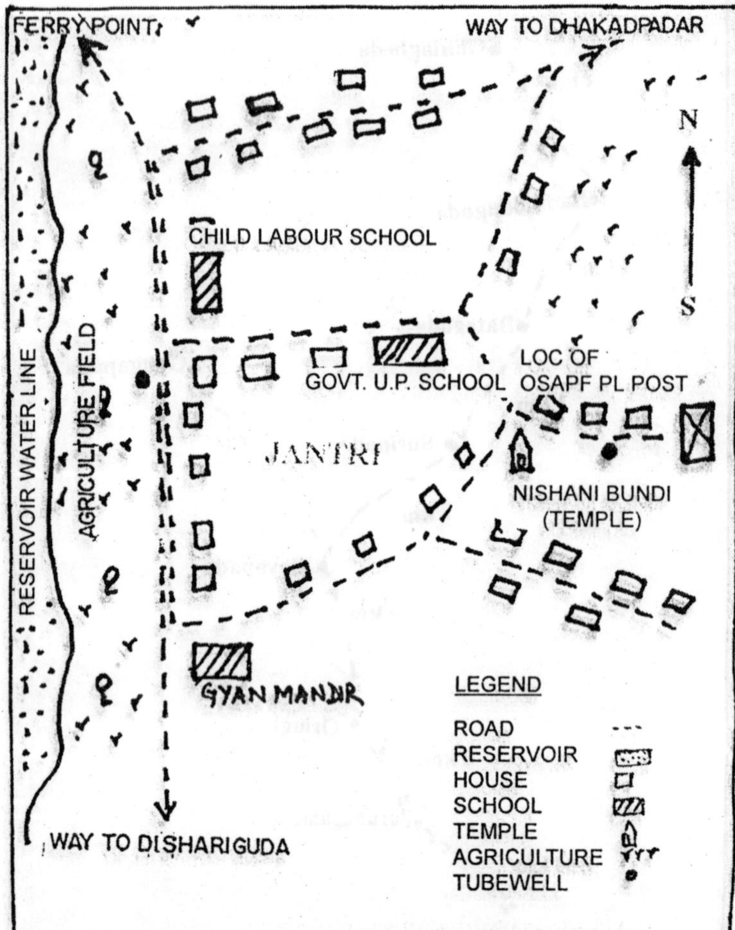

Sketch Map 3.3 : A Sketch Map of Jantri Village

namely Dabuguda, Disariguda, Sanyasiguda and Totaguda. These villages are closer by 3-4 km from Jantri (Sketch 3.2). These villages lie along the Chitrokonda Reservoir (Sketch Map 2.2). Among the five villages, Totaguda is a pure Didayi village except one *Rana* household. The villages : Dabuguda (*Kondh* : 6HH), Disariguda (*Kondh* : 5HH) and Sanyasiguda (*Kondh* : 20HH), are mixed populated villages.

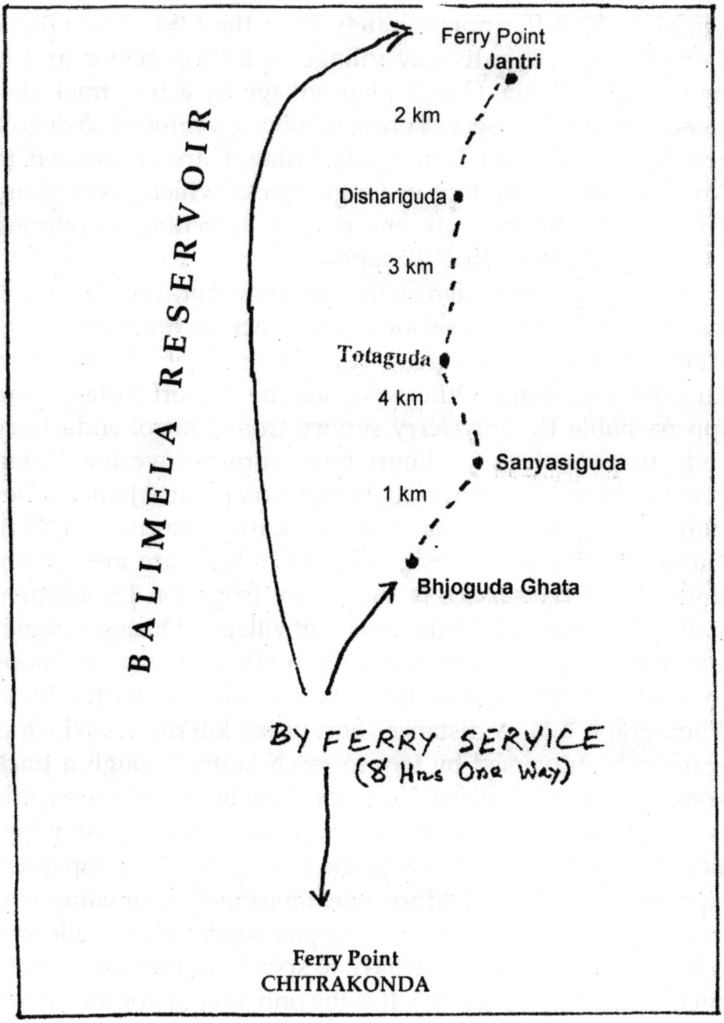

Sketch 3.2 : Route Sketch of Study Villages in Cut off Sector

Location and Communication

The plain villages Oringi and Purunagumma, are approachable by a jeepable road of five km each from the DDA, Kudumulugumma. The hilltop villages are located at the height of 3000 ft. approximately from the MSL. The village Bayapada is the gate-way village of hilltop sector and is connected with the Oringi plain village by a foot-track that passes through a Reserve Forest, involving a climb of 45 degree gradient. The other four study villages are connected to Bayapada either by foot or jungle tracks which takes about three to five hours walk one way to the villages covering 6 to 10 km distance from Bayapada.

If one traverses across the hilltop sector, one can reach the villages of cut off sector crossing across the reservoir of Machkund river covering the distance of 25 km from Kudumulugumma. Otherwise, all the cut off villages are approachable by only ferry service from Chitrokonda ferry point that involves ten hours boat journey covering 30 km through the reservoir to reach the last ferry point at Jantri. Other study villages, viz. Disariguda (2 km), Totaguda (4 km), Dabuguda (5 km) and Sanyasiguda (6 km), are away from Jantri. The ferry service being run by Irrigation Department makes only one trip in a day to cut off villages. During summer season the boat even does not reach village Jantri and stops en-route at Bhojaguda because of shallow water level (Photograph 3.1). A distance short of ten kilometres which is again to be traversed by foot to reach Jantri through a track from Dishariguda village. Very often, the boat man taking this as an excuse, do not go up to village Jantri though on paper they claim to have reached at Jantri. During the study trip much experience was gained. Most of the time the boat remains over-crowded and a number of waiting passengers are not allowed to board en-route and they have to spend another 24 hours to catch the next ferry service. It is the only lifeline for the cut off people who always remain at the mercy of the boat man. Distance and mode of communication to the study villages from the Didayi Development Agency and Community Development Block Office, Kudumulugumma is given (Table 3.2)

Table 3.2 : Distance and Mode of Communication to the Study Villages

Sl. No.	*Name of study villages*	*Distance from Micro Project/Block office, Kudumulugumma (in km)*	*Mode of communication*
Plain sector			
1.	Purunagumma	4	By Road
2.	Oringi	6	-do-
Hilltop sector			
3.	Bayapada	10	By foot.
4.	Suripada	12	-do-
5.	Gangapada	16	-do-
6.	Badankiyaguda	17	-do-
7.	Ghising Beda	20	-do-
Cut-off sector		(35 km by road to ferry point)	
8.	Jantri	30	By ferry
9.	Disariguda	28	-do-
10.	Totaguda	26	-do-
11.	Dabuguda	25	-do-
12.	Sanyasiguda	23	-do-

Village and House Pattern

Plain Villages

The villages are characterized by the nature of housing pattern in the settlement area. The homesteads are fenced with bamboo, twigs and stone enclosures. The kitchen gardens are within the enclosure of the house and settlement pattern is by and large linear.

Oringi is a revenue village and the total area of the village is 633.69 acres. A hill stream flows in east-west direction of the village which serves the purposes of irrigation and potable water sources. It is the foothill village and connects the villages of hilltop sector through the reserve forest. The village Oringi constitutes 122 households with 526 Didayi population. It is the most populous and largest village among the all 37 villages (Table 3.1). The most striking feature is that the dominance of female population over male. Other than Didayi, *Kondha* (11HH), *Paraja* (5HH), *Rana* (7HH), *Gauda* (9HH), *Domb* (10HH) and Christian (1HH) are dwelling. The village is divided into seven zones (*Sahi*), namely *Naik Sahi, Polasi Sahi, Golpeda Sahi, Dolai Sahi, Appukiya Sahi, Ghia Sahi* and *Domb Sahi.* Each zone (*Sahi*) is separated from the other by a narrow village path. *Domb Sahi* constitutes the *Domb* people (Scheduled Caste). The Zones (*Sahi*) have been named after the clan-names. The village has a common place called *'Gulisung'* for ceremonial rituals, village council meeting, folk dances and get-to-gather on various socio-cultural activities.

There are a Primary school (Government), one Upper Primary school (H & Tribal Welfare Department) and one ICDS (Integrated Child Development Scheme) sub-centre. One bio-gas plant and seven tube-wells have been constructed here. Two solar light systems are installed in the central location of the village.

Purunaguma is a compact and big village. The population state of the village is 207, constituting 50 households (December 1998, ICDS survey), out of which the Didayi population is 156 consisting 37 households. Predominance of female over male population is marked as indicated in (Table 3.1). Rest others are *Kondh* (8HH), *Kamara* (3HH) and *Domb* (2HH). The villagers are residing in a row as accordingly their own community and caste. Didayi houses have enclosures of bamboo fencing. There are even 4-5 houses within a single enclosure and a common courtyard.

There is a Government U.P. school, a Girls High school (H&TRW Department), a child labour school and a sub-centre of ICDS located in the village. There are five tube-wells and one solar light system found in the village.

House Pattern

Most of the houses are of tiled roof and rectangular in size. Houses have mud walls with two rooms and a verandah but without windows (Photograph 3.2). The entrance room is used for cooking, living and storage purpose. The inner room is meant for sleeping and worshipping deities. Hearth (*trusu*) is found to be at one corner of the entrance room with an earthen lamp (*batur*). The walls are seen decorated with colourful painting patterns (*jhoti*).

The foodstuffs and grains are stored in large basket wrapped in *siali* leaves and kept on the roof ceiling, approached by bamboo ladder. The pounding hole *(sabo/tanka)*, grinding stone for millet (*feenendir*), pounding wooden log (*pairi*), the baby basket cradle (*ajala*) etc. are found in the verandah.

The doors are made of wood with decorated craft works. The doors possess locking facilities. The pet animals are kept in the animal shed made adjacent to the side of the house. Domestic birds are kept on the hanging bamboo ladder. Also special pots and bamboo baskets are kept for hatching purposes.

Hilltop Villages

Hilltop villages are pure Didayi villages and thickly populated. The villages are characterized by uni-clan settlement pattern. They are usually situated on the higher level of ground. Houses are small and compact with a common approachable road. The distance between the houses is generally close and the houses lie in one side of the village path.

Bayapada village is the gate-way village of hill sector (Photograph 3.3). A stream is flowing, parallel to the village. Both the compact and the scattered houses are found. Houses are having the bamboo fencing (*Turrah*). Mostly, the newly wed couples and the polygynous family stay in the scattered houses.

One non-formal school (*Gyanmandir*) run by DDA and a sub-centre of ICDS are operating. The village has a common place for gathering called '*Gulisung*'. MIP (Minor Irrigation Project) and contour bonding are in operation by DDA.

Among all the study villages of hilltop sector, Gangapada is the largest and the most populous village (Table 3.1). The *Gulisung* (communal gathering place) is used for village meeting, youth dormitory and ceremonial observations.

Badakinyaguda and Ghisingbeda, both of the villages are surrounded by stones and boulders. Due to the lack of place the houses do not have the enclosures. Both the villages have *Gulisung*. The *Gulisung* at Ghisingbeda is used as the youth dormitory for boys and the place to worship. These villages are pure Didayi villages and thickly populated (Table 3.1). Ghisingibeda is an adjacent village of *Bonda hill*. The villagers of Ghisingbeda very often complain against the *Bonda* people who stack their claim on the agricultural produce saying that the land falls under Bonda village jurisdiction. Such dispute at times lead to a serious fights between the two communities and the *Bondas* even snatch away the belongings of Didayis.

House Pattern

Houses are made of mud with thatched roof. Roof is made of a type of grass (*piri*) which is locally available. The houses are rectangular and comparatively smaller than the plain villages. There is no window in the houses. Most of the houses have bamboo mat doors and generally the houses are not locked. Houses of Bayapada, Gangapada and Badiankiyaguda are consisting of a verandah with two rooms. Some houses also consist of one room with a verandah and sometimes without a verandah as in the villages, namely Suripada, Ghisingbeda and Badankiyaguda.

The foodstuffs and the grains are stored in the same way the plain villagers do (Photograph 3.4). All the household assets are kept like the plain villagers. Pet animals are kept in the animal shed made near or side of the house.

Cut off Villages

Cut off villages are larger than the hill villages. Jantri is the largest village among five villages. Except village Totaguda, others are mixed villages. Didayis stay in a separate zone of the village and maintain their distance from the other community. Houses have a bigger enclosure area than the hilltop villages. Generally, the houses are situated at both sides of the village path. The village path is generally wide in most of the villages. In cut off villages the communal gathering, ceremonial rituals and village meetings are held at a place called *'Nisani Hundi'* which is located under a big tree. In these multi-ethnic villages both the dominating communities, namely

Didayi and Kondh have their own *'Nisani Hundi'* located at separate place. There is no *'Gulisung'* (place for communal gathering/youth dormitory) as found in the villages or hilltop and plain sector. It may be due to the impact of multi-ethnic composition of the villages. Totaguda being one of the pure Didayi village has *Gulisung* as a normal practice of the Didayi village.

House Pattern

Houses are rectangular in size having mud walls with tiled roof. Houses are very strong with wooden doors. The doors are beautifully carved and having the locking arrangements. Most of the houses are bigger in height than the hill villages. House generally consists of two rooms and a big verandah. There is no window in the house. Each house has a courtyard and a kitchen garden. Animal shed is found adjacent to the side wall of the house.

The foodgrains are stored in large bamboo baskets wrapped in leaves of *siali* plant. The pounding hole, pounding wooden log, grinding stone, baby basket cradle, etc., are kept in the verandah. Cooking is either done in verandah or in the entrance room. The inner room is used both for sleeping and worshipping deities. They keep money inside a bamboo hole.

Social Structure

Social structure comprises the social institutions that categorically identify the role, relationship as well as occupational position of man and woman with their respective social framework. Social structure of a community whether primitive or modern plays an active role in changing the socio-economic condition.

Eggan has given more emphasis on the relationships between the individuals as well as the groups while describing the social structure. Social organisation as described by Firth is 'The systematic ordering of social relations by act of choice and decision'. Hersksovits, the eminent cultural anthropologist defined social organisation in the terms of kinship and human associations.

To understand the Didayi social structure as well as its role to enhance socio-economic change, it is essential to analyze their family structure, marriage types, political systems and kinship relationships with particular reference to lineage history as well as clan identity.

Family Type

Didayi family, the smallest social unit, is basically organised on patrilocal principle ; as a result it is Patrilocal, Patrilineal, and Patriarchal although certain degree of female dominance is marked in several matters. Both nuclear families and extended families have been found. In an extended family the head of the household looks after his old parents, unmarried brothers, sisters and widowed daughter-in-law (Photograph 3.5). A few single member families are also seen. According to the tradition the married son has to shift into a separate neo-local residence on a plot provided by his father. They are monogamous with certain exception.

It is, however, revealed from Table 3.3 that there are 1.88 per cent families which are single member type, while 54.08 per cent families are nuclear type and 44.82 per cent families are extended type in both the plain villages. In the hilltop sector, the nuclear family type shows a dominant position (79.85%). Few extended families (17.16%) are also found. Whereas 2.61 per cent constitute the single family where the old widow lady or the widower old man stays. One case of polygynous nuclear family is recorded in hilltop sector village Bayapada which is a rare case so far as 12 villages are concerned. Noteworthy feature is that 44.82 per cent extended families of the plain households constitute 20.5 per cent unmarried girls on an average. Whereas, the extended type of families of hilltop villages are having 23.41 per cent unmarried girls on an average (Table 3.4). In the cut off villages 76.82 per cent nuclear families and 18.29 per cent extended types of families are found. These extended families mostly comprise unmarried siblings and old parents.

Table 3.3 : Types of Families in Study Villages

Sl. No.	Name of the Village (HH)	Name of the Sector	Single	Nuclear	Extended	Polygynous nuclear
1.	Oringi (122)	plain	3 (2.45)	64 (52.45)	55 (45.08)	— —
2.	Purunaguma (3 7)	-do-	—	22 (59.45)	15 (40.54)	
	159 HH		3 (1.88)	86 (54.08)	70 (44.02)	
3.	Bayapada (37)	Hill sector	2 (5.40)	24 (65.56)	10 (27.02)	1 (2.7)
4.	Suripada (22)	-do-	1 (4.54)	11 (50)	10 (45.45)	—
5.	Gangapada (86)	-do-	3 (3.48)	65 (75.58)	18 (20.93)	—
6.	Badankiyaguda (64)	-do-	1 (1.56)	57 (89.06)	6 (9.37)	—
7.	Ghisingbeda (59)	-do-	—	57 (96.61)	2 (3.38)	—
	268 HH		7 (2.61)	214 (79.85)	46 (17.16)	
8.	Jantri (17)	Cut off	—	12 (70.58)	5 (29.41)	
9.	Totaguda (16)	-do-	1 (6.25)	13 (81.25)	3 (18.75)	
10.	Dabuguda (30)	-do-	3 (10)	22 (73.33)	5 (16.66)	
11.	Disariguda (13)	-do-	1 (7.69)	10 (76.92)	2 (15.38)	
12.	Sanyasiguda (6)	-do-	—	6 (100)	—	
	Total 82 HH		5 (6.09)	63 (76.82)	15 (18.29)	

Note : Figures in bracket indicate percentage.

Inter-family relationship reveals strong bond of relationship. Head of the household treats individual member of the family in an impartial manner. The old parents are given due respect and looked after. If any family members are found guilty, they are punished by the head of the household. All able body of the family including children above 5 years go to the work field. Inter-family disputes are rare. They are God-fearing people, docile and tolerant.

Didayi family is an economically self-sufficient unit where every individual member performs his/her respective tasks according to their age, sex and the traditional form of division of labour. Giving importance to every individuals ideas, maintenance of harmony, cooperation and mutual understanding, are the most striking characteristic features of the Didayi family. Parents are very broad minded in case of the selection of mates by their daughters as more numbers of unmarried girls are found in plain and hilltop sector.

Marital Status

The socio-economic life of Didayi is mainly reflected through marriage ceremonies. Marriage fulfils their social obligations and customary benefits. It also facilitates their economic status both from the bride price and the compensation. Bride price is to be paid in case of both marriage by arrangement (*toso*) and marriage by capture (*udalia*). If the wife elopes with some other than that person has to pay the compensation (*sagarta*) to the first husband whatever he keeps in demand. In case of cross cousin marriage (*marshaboyi*), the boy has to pay the compensation (*manghar*) to his maternal uncle if he decides not to marry his daughter as this type of marriage is considered to be most ideal type.

They are monogamous. The choices of the boys and girls are considered to be final. As a normal practice, the marriage proposal is required to be initiated by the boy's side known as *'tasawella tashar'*. The girl's family may reject the proposals in case they do not like. A large number of girls between age group of 15 to 35 years from plain and hilltop sector are found unmarried due to lack of suitable proposals pressed from the boys side (Table 3.4). The table reveals that in the plain villages, viz. In Oringi and Purunaguma, there are found 20.5 and 40.5 per cent unmarried girls between the age group of 20-40 respectively. In the hilltop villages, namely Bayapada, Suripada and Gangapada, there are 40.54, 22.72 and 6.97 per cent unmarried girls of the age group 20-40 found respectively. These girls are staying with their parents and giving the economic support to the family by wage earning.

Even though a maximum number of cross-cousin and parallel cousin marriages are held traditionally followed in cut off villages and in some of the hilltop villages, these are not predominantly practised in plain sector villages. At times, the girls even reject the traditional proposals of the Didayi boys of the plain sector who are educated and working. Didayi girls do marry lower Bonda boys who are working. They rigidly follow the principles of village exogamy as well as clan exogamy while establishing marital alliance.

Table 3.4 : Number of Unmarried Girls in the Study Area

Sl. No.	*Name of Village (HH)*	*No. of HH having un-married girls*	*Age*	*Occupation*	*Educational Qualification*
Plain Sector					
1.	Oringi (122)	25 (20.5)	20-30	Daily labour & Tailoring	nil
2.	Purunaguma (37)	15 (40.5)	20-45	-do-	nil
Hill Sector					
4.	Bayapada (37)	15 (40.54)	20-25	Daily labour	nil
5.	Suripada (22)	5 (22.72)	20-27	Daily labour & DWCRA GP	nil
6 .	Gangapada (86)	6 (6.97)	20-40	-do-	nil

Note : Figures in bracket indicate percentage.

Socio-economic Causes for the Growing Number of Unmarried Girls

In addition to the prevailing disparities in the male to female ratio, the socio-economic causes for increased number of unmarried girls mainly from plain and hilltop villages are :

Most of the Didayi boys of plain do somehow hesitate to marry modern village girls for the belief that such girls are not faithful and unable to do hard work in households.

The hilltop, girls having exposed to the plain soft and modern life of the plain area, prefer to get married in plain villages. Even they are not prepared to get married the hilltop employed boys as these girls are aware of the arduous life style of the hill sector.

The plain boys with a little education are seeking alliances with only educated working girls even from other communities. All these girls have become the victims of the attitudinal change of the boys.

Average marriageable age in respect of Didayi girls is about 13 to 15 years and for boys it is 16 to 18 years. In some mountain top villages the boys get married to girls of 3 to 5 years elder to them. This practice is gradually fading away. The months of January and June are considered to be the marriage seasons. Monday and Tuesday are taken as the most auspicious days for the performance of marriage ceremonies.

Various match makings

Though arranged marriage is the common practice among the Didayis, other kinds of marriages also take place. Those are mentioned hereunder :

(a) Cross-cousin marriage

This is also an arranged marriage which is known as *'marshaboyi'* generally practised by hilltop and cut off Didayis. Marriage procedure begins with the proposals from boy's side through a group of village people called *'raiberia'*. The boy's father enters the premises of the girl's house with the group and fixes an arrow on the roof top of the house and declares the proposal. If the girl agrees to the proposal and the bride price, then marriage is fixed. The marriage function is celebrated after two or three years. In the meantime, the boy's father or the *'raiberia'* keep on visiting the girl's house with liquor (*suluppa*) and one kilogram of rice at least once in a month. However, the boy and girl are free to choose their partner and their disagreement for the marriage makes it mandatory for their parents to bear the compensation in lieu of bride-price.

Cut off Didayis prefer cross-cousin marriage because of its economic advantages and fulfilling the social obligation through the marriage of offsprings of brother and sister. During the field study Madhu Pangi, the Sarpanch of Totaguda village has claimed her brother's son to be the son-in-law for her only daughter.

(b) Marriage by Elopement (udeia gube)

If a boy does not marry his maternal uncle's daughter and elopes with some other girl then he can marry her only after he fulfils the compensation demand of his maternal uncle.

(c) Marriage by Capture (gube)

A boy after selecting suitable girl takes her away by force with the help of some of his friends and keeps her hiding in a secret or secluded place. She is entertained with the required food and *salap* wine etc. till the girl's parents come forward to negotiate the marriage after fixing up agreeable bride-price.

(d) Marriage by Service (ghar jamai/ghar jwa)

Didayi boy preferring this kind of marriage puts himself at the service of the would-be father-in-law for at least one to two years before getting married to his daughter without paying any bride-price. Two cases have been recorded, one in Jantri and another in Bayapada (Photograph 6). Both the bride grooms were orphans and married to their maternal uncle's daughters after giving three years service to their respective father-in-law.

(e) Marriage by Negotiation (toshawella marriage)

This is known as arranged marriage and is materialized only through negotiation (*tasher*). The choices of boys and girls are taken into account . The bride-price is fixed before the marriage. As a normal procedure, groom's procession comes to bride's house where marriage is solemnized.

Post-marital love affairs and remarriage

(a) ***Sagarta* (*Post-marital affair*)**: The husband demands the compensation in lieu of bride-price to the eloped lover of his wife. He sends his demand through a group called *'raibedia'*. The group comprises village headman (*Nayak*), messenger (*Chalan*), Priest (*Pujari*) and other elderly persons. A day is fixed for the payment of the compensation (*sagarta*).

(b) ***Widow Marriage***: Widow marriage (*randijhola*), widower marriage (*andirajhola*) and junior levirates are present. The elder brother's widow (*kiming*) sometimes get married to her brother-in-law to avoid property related conflict. In case she gets married to an outsider, the second husband has to bear the compensation (*randijhola*) to her deceased husband's parents. A widower can get married to his deceased wife's younger sister (*embike*).

Divorce

Divorce is an uncommon practice among the Didayis. Except one case of village Oringi, no other case has been found in study villages.

Descent Groups

Didayi family and marriages are based on integrated bond of kin groups which determine a number of cognates and agnates. The Didayis are patrilineal as they trace their descent in the father's line. However, all the genealogical connections seem to end at the grandfather's generation.

Clan and Lineage

The Didayi Clan Organisation seems to be associated with a cluster of totemic groups that symbolize after a totemic animal. Groups of clans under a particular totemic animal follow the clan exogamy. Hence, they are categorized themselves as the brother clan groups.

Totemic objects	Clan surnames
(a) Tiger (*Nkoo*)	*Ghia, Sira, Gudia, Dhangda Manjhi, Mudli, Bagh Palasi, Naga, Khirsani, Golpeda, Raspeda, Palkagiri, Kindge.*
(b) Cobra (*Mala Buoo*)	*Bisoi, Angra, Bhimbhi, Turuk, Ghata, Solpeda, Pujari, Kushaha, Palasi, Chalan, Rimbi, Snobo*
(c) Bear (*Rabeh*)	*Bhoja, Sanyasi, Rajpeda*
(d) Vulture (*Gidha*)	*Pangi*
(e) Honu/Monkey (*Galuri*)	*Sisa, Khillo, Bishoiee*

Earlier study conducted by Shri S.C. Mohanty, Dr. Uma Guha and Dr. Ferriera, have excluded the totemic object 'monkey' (*goluri*) along the clan surnames such as—Sisa, Khillo, Bishoiee and Pangi (Guha *et al.*, 1968 : 56) which have been recorded during the field study in cut off sector. The plain and hilltop Didayis mostly belong to 'Cobra' and 'Tiger' totemic object. The clan surnames like Mudli, Golpada, Naga, Bagha Palasi and Ghia, under tiger totem and Bisoi, Chalan, Angra, Palasi, Pujari and Snobo of cobra group, are extensively found in these two sectors.

Didayis do not worship the totemic objects. Even they do not hesitate to kill the animal that belongs to the totemic group. During Chait festival they can kill any prey including totemic objects. It is learnt from the Didayi elders that each clan (*Gta*) has a mythical origin, associated with the respective totemic symbol and folklore. But in due course of time they have forgotten these folklore as well as the legends. The younger generation of the Didayi community show their ignorance as well as disinterested attitudes to know about their legends. Only a few elder people have knowledge about their myths.

The lineage consists of a groups of patrilineally related families which are either nuclear or of extended type. The families of consanguine parallel cousins of different degree are belonging to a lineage. The importance of the lineage can be marked in socio-economic spheres through the functional roles of eldest living members of the lineage. These eldest members enjoy the special position in the village council. The problem relating to any member of the lineage are referred to these elders before appealing to the village council. During the field study a case of post-martial affair of a woman of Jantri village has been noticed to be solved by the eldest cousins (*dhanang*) of her lineage.

Kinship

Didayi family is based on the integrated bond of kinship and this bond extends in two directions : patri and matrilines. Kinship plays an important role in their socio economic activities. The Didayi society reveals a descriptive-*cum*-classificatory type terminology in which a common term is referred to both the paternal and maternal kin groups. Some of the examples are :

(a) Father's mother and mother's mother—*Injah*
(b) Father's father and mother's father—*Anta*
(c) Father's elder sister and mother's elder sister—*Basa*
(d) Father's sister's daughter and mother's brother's daughter—*Silamboy*

That apart there are specific terms related to specific persons. Some of the kin terms are given to understand the kinship system of Didayi (Table 3.5).

Thus, the kinship terminological tree of Didayi shows the duplication and presence of the dual organization that combines a group of paternal kin and maternal kin to a common kinship term, ignoring the gender status. Avoidance is not strictly followed. However, joking relationship is observed among the friends, elderly person, grandparents and grand-children.

Dormitory Organisation

Most of the PTGs of Orissa have youth dormitory either for boys or girls or for both. The Didayi dormitory is mono-sexual type, meant for only boys. It is known as *'Gulisung'*. It is either centrally located or at the corner end of the village. *Gilisung* is also used as the common place of ceremonial gatherings and

Table 3.5 : Kinship Terminology

Sl. No.	Relationship in different generations	Terms reference in three sectors		
		Plain	Hill	Cut off
A.	**Ego's Grandparents generation**			
1.	Father's	*Anta*	*Dadee*	*Anta*
2.	Father's mother	*Injah*	*Injah*	*Injah*
3.	Mother's father	*Anta*	*Dadee*	*Anta*
4.	Mother's mother	*Injah*	*Baee*	*Injah*
B.	**Ego's parents generation**			
5.	Father	*Umba*	*Aba*	*Aba*
6.	Mother	*Eaang*	*Eaang*	*Eaang*
7.	Father's elder	*Basa*	*Upsa*	*Basa*
8.	Father's elder brother's wife	*Basa*	*Upsa*	*Basa*
9.	Father's younger brother	*Taboh*	*Taboh*	*Taboh*
10.	Father's younger brother's wife	*Umbo*	*Umbo*	*Umbo*
11.	Father's sister (older and younger)	*Aata*	*Ata*	*Ata*
12.	Father's sister's daughter	*Silamboy*	*Silamboy*	*Silamboy*
13.	Mother's elder brother	*Mama*	*Mon*	*Mama*
14.	Mother's younger brother	*Mama*	*Ata*	*Mama*
15.	Mother's brothers	*Ata*	*Ata*	*Ata*
16.	Mother's elder sister	*Basa*	*Upsa*	*Basa*
17.	Mother's elder sister's husband	*Basa*	*Upsa*	*Basa*
18.	Mother's younger sister	*Umbo*	*Umbo*	*Umbo*
19.	Mother's younger sister's husband	*Taboh*	*Taboh*	*Taboh*
20.	Mother's brother's daughter	*Silamboy*	*Silamboy*	*Silamboy*
21.	Mother's brother's son	*Engre*	*Engre*	*Engre*
C.	**Ego's generation**			
22.	Husband	*Gumia*	*Gumia*	*Nehenda*
23.	Wife	*Kanoe*	*Kanoe*	*Neckma*
24.	Elder brother	*Enang/Boan*	*Munang*	*Enang/Boan*
25.	Young brother	*Imb*	*Imb*	*Imb*
26.	Sister	*Baiee*	*Baiee*	*Baiee*
27.	Unmarried girl	*Sela*	*Sela*	*Selamboy*
28.	Unmarried boy	*Ingre*	*Ingree*	*Ingree*

village meetings in many villages. During field study four dormitories have been found in the hilltop sectors. Presence of more number of youth dormitories in the Hill sector states about the attachment to the traditional temperaments as well as the values. Hence, it seems that the socio-economic and cultural importance that the institution enjoyed in the past, is gradually losing its significance.

Photograph 3.1 : Ferry point at Bhojaguda on way to Jantri (Cut off village)

Photograph 3.2 : A house in Purunaguma village (Plain sector)

Photograph 3.3 : A house of Bayapada village (Hilltop sector)

Photograph 3.4 : Storage of foodgrains

Photograph 3.5 : An Extended Family of Oringi village (Plain sector)

Photograph 3.6 : A case of Marriage by Service (Jantri cut off village)

4

Economic Structure

Quest of food has been an age-old practice for the survival of man. Primitive man devised food-gathering technique for his own survival that has been categorized as the primordial economic activity. Man has passed through four stages of livelihood, viz. food-gathering, hunting, pastoral and agriculture to satisfy his hunger. Thus, getting food is a fundamental interest of any community to satisfy its primary need that is hunger.

Karl Marx's 'Economic deterministic theory of social change' states that the socio-economic conditions are the vital factors for changing the social institution and social factors. The history of all existing societies is the history of class struggle being governed by the mode of economic production. Therefore, economic development is always human oriented and sought to be achieved through improving the competitive efficiency of particular community by increasing production.

Kabeer (1994 : 74) states that economic growth is a means rather than an end in itself but tends to agree that achieving economic growth is the first priority. Hence, economic development is not concerned only with economic growth but also with progress in human societies. However, it is very difficult to abstract the economic aspect of primitive societies than the study of industrial societies as the former lacked money and markets in the proper sense of the term. Moreover, while talking about the economic growth of a tribal society such as the Didayi, it is very essential to know its economic structure.

Landholding Status

The Didayi land belonged to the Jeypore Estate and the Maharaja of Jeypore was the landlord. The Estate was abolished in 1952 under the provisions of the Orissa Estate Abolition Act. The Jeypore Estate was divided into two parts for the convenience of administration with headquarters at Rayagada and Jeypore. The Didayi territory came under the former Jeypore subdivision. Each subdivision was further divided into tehsils and each tehsil was placed under an Amin. The Amin was assisted by a revenue sub-inspector. At the village level, the revenue was collected by the village headman or the Mustajar. He was appointed by the Maharaja and the post was hereditary. But the Mustajar did not keep any written records of the landholdings of Didayi. However, the Collector's Land Register documents showed the record of the holdings of each Didayi household.

Senapati (1966 : 286) stated that rent was paid in cash or kind. Where the cash payments were in force, the assessment was usually a certain sum on each plough and hoe used. This varied from Rs. 2 to Rs. 6 on a plough and should now be indicated in paise for hoe. Generally, a farmer (*royat*) was assessed on the assumption that he had one plough and a hoe and was permitted to cultivate as much land as he could.

The land revenue system or the Mustajari system was abolished in July 1955 and the rents were collected directly from the Didayi by the government. The Didayi villages came under Malkangiri tehsil. Out of 401 villages in this tehsil, 286 villages were surveyed in 1963. The remaining 115 villages were not surveyed including 22 Didayi villages. The cash payment was introduced in 1963. A Didayi of the surveyed village had to pay a maximum of Rs. 3.60 as the land revenue per acre of wet land and minimum of Rs. 2.86. But the land revenue per acre dry land varied from 75 paise to Rs. 1.50. In the un-surveyed villages the forest department were collecting Rs. 3 to Rs. 10 per acre forest land (Guha,1968 : 54).

The latest settlement programme covered the entire Malkangiri district excepting about 500 square miles of *Bonda* hill and *Kondakamberu* areas which are the most inaccessible and the least populated and cultivated region in the district. The survey of this area was proposed to be taken up in the year 1969-70 (Senapati, 1966 : 288). The tribal people of the area could not gain much out of this survey as their names were not recorded in the demand register because the Mustajars did not grant any receipt for rents collected from the people.

Subsequently, when the tribal lands were acquired for development project in Koraput district like Mig factory at Sunabeda, Machkund and Balimela Hydro Electric Project, the Revenue officials could not pay desired compensation to them due to lack of any landholding records. Thus, the tribal people who had customarily rights and valid rights on lands have been victimised (Mahapatra, 1999a).

Shroff (1997 : 66) stated that one lakh acres of cultivated lands belonging mostly to tribals and about four lakh acres of forest lands including submersible areas of reservoirs have been utilised for several major development projects in Koraput district. About two lakh acres of forest lands handed over to the Dandakaranya Development Authority, especially in deforestation zone of Umerkote and Malkangiri for resettlement purposes. As a result, nearly one lakh tribal people have been deprived of five lakh acres of private and forest lands on which they depended largely for their livelihood. Since there was no legal rights, the compensation could not be paid to the tribal people. At the same time a very nominal amount was spent towards acquisition of lands. Even, the displaced people have not been properly resettled by providing alternative lands and common amenities because of construction of the Chitrakonda reservoir.

It has been mentioned earlier that a Survey by THRTI was conducted to assess the land position of the people (Adivasi, 1971-72 : 61). It is found in the Report that in 63 villages of wholly submerged, partially submerged and new villages, 62.2 per cent of families were mostly shifting cultivation while 12.5 per cent of families depended on wage earning. It is also ascertained that there has not been any authentic revenue settlement activity conducted in this area.

Therefore, the people used to pay revenue according to the number of possession of the ploughs used for cultivating the lands. It was the norm that a sum of rupees three was to be paid for one plough. Land possession of individuals was demarcated by the trees and the stumps of trees. Even the same procedure was followed at the time of demarcation of land possession of one village from another. The report suggests that actual possession of cultivating land of an individual could be approximately assessed by the amount of seeds the cultivators use.

In view of the above facts the plight of the Didayi can be well understood who have been displaced and badly affected by the reservoir. On verification of the landholding records in the Tehsil Record Office at Chitrakonda, it is found that on an average each Didayi family has only less than half an acre of cultivable land in hilltop and, 1.76 acre in cut off villages, whereas in plain villages the landholding status is 2.095 acre. This indicates that plain villagers are economically better off and the hilltop villagers are found to be extremely marginal. On an average 57.6 per cent households are landless (Table 4.2). Therefore, for their survival they have no choice but to depend on shifting cultivation on the hill slopes and it is difficult for them to eschew the practice of shifting cultivation.

Inheritance and Succession

The inheritance of ancestral property customarily passes in a patrilineal line. Both settled lands and the shifting lands are the major family oriented assets. The right of possession of lands generally goes to the sons after the death of the father only. In case there is no son, the landed property goes to his brother's sons. If none is there to claim the property then that may either be given to the daughter or to the village headman. Usually, principle of succession of fruit bearing trees and *salap* trees are followed in the line of land property. With regard to other household movable goods including implements are generally shared among children or among the secondary kins. Now-a-days, due to more number of unmarried girls in the family, brothers are giving some shares to their sisters at their discretion towards maintenance. Other household assets like utensils, pet animals and house are distributed among the brothers and the unmarried sisters. After the death of the parents, the youngest son normally occupies the house. The ornaments if found with the corpse are burnt during cremation.

Occupation

The Didayi economic structure mainly revolves round the agriculture and forest produce collection. Their primary occupation is the food production by means of settled and shifting cultivation while the secondary occupation involves wage earning, forest produce collection and other casual employment. Hunting and fishing seems to be a tertiary occupation. Generally, these are carried out as a hobby and a part of leisurely activities. They go for communal hunting (*Shikarbenta*) only once in a year during Chait parva which is celebrated between the month of April and May. The details of occupational pattern of the community is to be discussed later because it requires the understanding of division of labour prevalent among Didayis.

Division of Labour

It is found that each member of the family has been engaged in certain economic activities according to age, sex, skill, status and power levels. It is because most families suffer from poverty, so all members contribute to economic support for the maintenance of family. The male members are often accompanied by their wives to the agricultural field and forest or even for wage-earning from early morning. In that case, old people of the family usually look after the infants and children under 7 years while the parents are away in their respective work fields. The children above 7 years are generally engaged in the cattle grazing activities and also assist their parents in forest produce collections. Since there is little diversification of economic activities, the division of labour is mainly based on age and sex.

Primary Occupation

Settled Cultivation

The Didayi of plain and cut off sectors have been practising the settled agriculture due to the availability of the cultivable lands and suitability of the environment. They have adapted themselves to the plough cultivation from an ancient time hoe cultivation. They also use the sloppy up-lands and lands near-by the local streams for cultivation. They utilise indigenous irrigating skill by lifting water manually through a long bamboo from stream water source.

During *khariff* (August-December) season, the villagers produce paddy, millet, red gram, black gram and maize, etc. and in *rabi* season (January-April), they grow crops like oil seed (*alsi*), ground nut and a variety of vegetables. The whole cultivation process involves mainly three stages: sowing, weeding and reaping. Only traditional fertilizer like cow dung and compost manure are being used by them. The whole family works in the field. It is estimated during the field study that the yielding capacity of an acre of plain land is about ten *putties* or 600 kg whereas the yield from shifting cultivation is five *putties* or 300 kg per acre. The agricultural activities are associated with rituals observances like offerings and sacrifices to the Mother earth and other peripheral deities by the head of the household for higher yield of crops and protection of crops from insect infestation and other hazards.

Agricultural Equipment

Almost all households have agricultural implements, even the landless persons. Exchange of agricultural produce and agricultural implement is a common feature in the village, especially during agricultural season. They use the following traditional agricultural equipment :

(a) Plough (*cini*)
(b) The long wooden handle plough (*rirana*)

(c) Spade/Kodala (*korada*)
(d) Ground leveller (*patta*)
(e) Spade with spikes (*insuan*)
(f) Long handle sickle (*hoeas*)
(g) Axe of different sizes (*malle/tange*)
(h) Hoe

These traditional implements are either made by themselves or purchased from local markets to meet the agricultural requirements (Photograph 4.1). Since the Government has schemes to provide agricultural tools, the Didayis now depend more on government subsidy and supply that are made available from DDA, Kudumulugumma.

Due to easy accessibility, the plain villagers are a pivileged group for obtaining the agricultural implements immediately after supply of that by DDA. Moreover, plain villages have the advantage of getting other availing inputs like HYV seeds, pesticides, fertilizers and guidance of the officials for improving their agricultural productivity.

Shifting Cultivation

Shifting cultivation is the main source of the income for the hilltop and cut off villages. For scarcity of the plain and fertile lands, shifting cultivation is to be continued in future although the State Government banned the practice. Hilltop Didayis have their respective terms for each type of shifting cultivable lands which are : (a) The hills used for shifting cultivation is called *guebar; dongar;* (b) The hill slopes or the high lands where water cannot be stored is called *tikra;* (c) The third type of land which is low and where water can be stored is called *jahaloti;* and (d) The fourth type of land is called *beda* which is the recuperated patch of old patch of shifting cultivation.

Types of crops produced in various types of land

(a) *Hills* (*Guebar* or *Dongar*) : Ragi, *Suan* (cereal), black gram, red gram, green gram, gingerly seeds, millet and *Dongar-rani* (cereal);

(b) *High land* (*Tikra*) : *Suan* (cereal), *Alsi* (oil seed), *san dhan* (paddy), ragi, and black gram;

(c) *Foothills* (*Jabaloti*) : Vegetables and *Dongar-rani* (paddy);

(d) *Old Podu patch* (*Badi/Beda*) : Maize, tobacco, vegetables and castor.

The land on the upper ridges and on slopes are used for shifting cultivation. These lands are traditionally owned by families without valid revenue *Pattas*. In hilltop villages all the family members take active part in clearing, maintaining as well as in the whole cultivation process. Whereas in the cut off villages like Totaguda, Dabuguda, and Disariguda cultivation of *podu* land is done by a group of villagers and all of them share the yield. There is no continuity or fixed group affiliation in this practice. Every year the willing families form a group and set out for the shifting cultivation on a pre-determined patch of a hill area which is generally adjacent to their village. Madhu Pangi, the lady Sarpanch of village Totaguda states that they are the displaced villagers. Their low lands for which they possess the *Pattas*, have submerged and they have shifted to adjacent higher foothill area. Depending on the water level in the reservoir, they reclaim their own land and practise settled cultivation. Any loss to their crops due to increase in water level, they demand compensation every year. In order to meet their livelihood all the families of hill top and cut off villagers are doing the shifting cultivation. In this type of cultivation some specific implements are used and these are axe, long handle sickle and hoe. Hence, it requires less implements and is thus involves lesser techno-economic process.

Cultivation Procedure

The process of cultivation is associated with a series of manual activities. In the month of February and March the forest patch measuring approximately one to three acres are cleared by cutting, slashing, and burning the trees and the bushes over the *dongar* land or *podu* land (guenbar/*bri*). However, they do not cut fruit-bearing trees like mango and jackfruit etc. Before first shower of the monsoon in April to May, whole patch is cleared from all unburnt twigs. The second phase follows with the spreading of ass over the patch. Stone boundary and fence are made around the field to protect the crops from the wild animals as well to reduce soil erosion. The third step involves the sowing of mixed seeds of twelve types like millet, paddy, oilseed (*alsi*), maize, cereal (*kangoo*), red gram green gram, black gram, brinjal, tomato, chilly and castor seeds, etc. during month of June and July. The sowing process is followed with certain rituals performed by the head of the household to propitiate the mother earth, trees and spirits. Only coconut and ripe banana are offered to the mother earth without any animal sacrifice as is the practice with many other tribes. Harvesting is gradually done in a phased manner as and when crops are ready for harvest.

A patch so used for shifting cultivation for three to four years consecutively are left unused to rejuvenate the fertility of the soil. This land is known as *beda* land or *bedalio* and reused after a gap of three to four years. In the new patch they selectively go for the crops like millet, paddy (*dongar-rani*), chilly, cereal (*kangoo chaol*), gingelly seeds, black gram and cucumber. Whereas *suan*, a variety of millet and other staple crops are only opted in the next successive years in the old shifting cultivated patch.

Terrace Cultivation

Terrace cultivation has been a traditional and indigenous agricultural practice by the tribes of southern Orissa, especially in Gajapati and Koraput Districts. The Saoras of Gajapati considered to be the pioneer in this field. Perhaps the Didayi because of circumstantial necessity learnt and borrowed the idea of terrace cultivation from Saora and Kondha tribal people.

It has been noticed that the Didayi of hilltop villages have taken into practice of terrace cultivation. In Bayapada village a *podu* patch was seen converted to a terrace land by a four-wheeled wooden leveller. The villagers are also using the water of running stream (*nalla*) for irrigation of terrace land.

Secondary Occupation

Since the primary occupation becomes inadequate to meet the livelihood requirements, secondary occupation is adopted. It usually supports the economic necessities of family and keeps engaged the members to find out alternative income source. In the study villages it is observed that all households have one or more secondary occupation, viz. forest collection and wage earning.

Forest Collection

The Didayi generally derive directly or indirectly a substantial amount of their requirements like edible leaves, fruits, honey, wild game, medicinal plants, etc. from the forest. Besides these, they also collect house building materials from the forest (Photograph 4.2). It is believed that they are one of the creature of nature, hence they grow in the lap of nature and the latter provides all their requirements as is the case with most animals and plants.

Once upon a time, the forest was providing a variety of items to meet their needs almost more than fifty per cent of their requirements. Even, now also they are in habit of collecting various types of forest produce (Table 4.1).

Table 4.1 : Types of Forest Produce

Sl.No.	*Items*	*Purpose*
1.	Varieties of roots and tubes	domestic consumption and sale.
2.	Green leaves	-do-
3.	Mushrooms	-do-
4.	Siali leaves	for storage of food and groceries.
5.	Piri	thatching of house.
6.	Broomstick	self-use and sale.
7.	Mahula flowers	liquor consumption and sale.
8.	Gum	sale.

Out of these items, some are seasonal and some are collected regularly. Most of these items are used for self-consumption and only surplus items are sold in the local weekly market. They get it free of cost and without forest their survival is unthinkable. However, due to substantial decline of forest as a result of shifting cultivation practice, illegal felling of trees by the wood smugglers and failure of afforestation scheme by the Government many of the forest produce have almost disappeared.

Hunting and Fishing

Hunting and fishing are the leisurely activities of the Didayi. The hilltop Didayi are still in the habit of going to the forest in search of prey due to the availability of animals in the surrounding jungles. They are seen carrying their traditional hunting weapons like bow, arrow, traps, etc. while roaming in the forest track. As a normal practice, they carry the weapons any time they go out of the house. On the contrary, the plain and cut off Didayis are relatively less keen in hunting and only participate in communal ritual hunting during Chaiti festival.

The plain and cut off Didayis catch fish once in a while for their own consumption. Rarely, they take fish to the market for sale except the villagers of Taberu and Nandimanjari of cut off sector and Nilapari of hilltop sector. Therefore, no family accrue any income from hunting and fishing.

Exchange

The villagers of plain and cut off sectors prefer monetary transaction to the barter system as they are aware of the disadvantages of the barter system. Due to lack of readily available money, they go for barter and are frequently cheated by the traders. However, the system of exchange of goods for goods still continues within villages as well as in the weekly markets. It is observed that purchasing of certain items like salt, onion, kerosene oil, dry fish, cooking oil, etc. is made not by cash payment but in exchange of some vegetables and pulses like soya bean seeds, black gram, etc. The hilltop dwellers are fully dependent on the barter system. Whatever money they collect by selling their products, they like saving it for posterity than to spend immediately. Except a few items like clothing, kerosene oil, cooking oil, they get all other items on barter.

Weekly Market

The weekly market is known as *'hatt'*, a common place for get-together of all the kith and kin groups as well as the friends of Didayis. It has a great socio-cultural and economic impact on Didayis. This is a place for coming in contact with the Didayi youths as well as elders of different villages. It is the only place from where they get their cloth, ornaments, cosmetic items and a lover gives a gift to his beloved and moves freely along with other friends. It actually breaks the monotony of life. Hence, in a way market is viewed as a place of entertainment. They eagerly wait for the market day and unless they are sick, they do not miss it.

It is the centre of economic activity as well as social interaction. Here they come in contact with the other tribal brethren, outsiders and the traders. At the end of the day, both males and females consume country liquor sitting in one corner of the market place. It starts around 8 a.m. and continues till 4 p.m. Besides marketing, they also collect the rations of PDS from the Micro Project Office.

The weekly markets located are as under :

(a)	Monday	Naringijhola	Hilltop sector
(b)	Wednesday	Janbai	Cut off sector
		Ankadali	Cut off sector
(c)	Thursday	Kudumulugumma	Plain sector

Herewith, the market of Kudumulugumma is discussed with the details of activities. Other markets are similar in pattern but smaller in size. Traders from nearby areas like Mathili, Malkangiri, Jeypore, Gobindpalli and Motu, come to this weekly *hatt*. Generally, they occupy their own shade for specific items and have to pay the tax to the Panchayat of Kudumulugumma. It is noticed that each of them keep the specific item such as cloth, utensils, grocery, vegetables, sweets and fancy items. Moreover, other trades men like blacksmith, goldsmith, potter, barber, liquor, cattle seller and ice-cream vendor are also seen. However, they are not the tax-payee as they don't occupy a shade.

Mostly, the people of nearby villages of Kudumulugumma and Khairiput G.P. depend on this weekly market. The *hatt* is very crowded with a gathering of more than 300 people. All types of people, viz. general, Scheduled Castes, Scheduled Tribes and other backward communities come to *hatt*. However, the traders behave in a different manner with different customers. During the visit it is seen that the Bonda women are treated with utmost caution because of mere apprehension. On further inquiry, it is told that the Bonda women even sometimes snatch away the items if they are not treated carefully. At times, the Bonda males also attack the traders. However, the traders are found to be very friendly with other tribal people including Didayis.

Income and Expenditure

In order to get a comprehensive idea about the socio-economic condition of the Didayi, an attempt has been made to assess their income and expenditure per annum. Agriculture is the primary source of income. In addition to agriculture, they generate income from wage-earning, animal husbandry, liquor selling, and selling surplus forest produce. For meeting the requirements the cultivable land is inadequate, therefore, they resort to other economic activities to supplement the family income (Table 4.2).

The landholding status among the Didayi have been calculated on the basis of their revenue records as well as from personal interviews. It is evident from Table 4.2 that 42.39 per cent constitute the landholders and 57.6 per cent of landless. The plain Didayis on an average possess two acres of cultivable lands whereas the villagers of other two sectors have less than two acres of cultivable *podu* land. Again it is a matter of agony that they do not have any land rights over these *podu* lands.

Most of the time, the forest officials threaten them and collect bribes while using the forest *podu* land.

Table 4.2 : Landholding Status of Didayis

Sl. No.	*Village*	*No. of HH*	*Average area (acre) Cultivated per HH*	*Land-holders*	*Landless HH*
Plain Sector					
1.	Oringi	122	2.43	51(41.8)	71(58.2)
2.	P.gumrna	37	1.76	23(62.16)	14(37.84)
			2.095		
Hilltop Sector					
3.	Bayapada	37	1.72	27(72.97)	10(27.03)
4.	Suripada	22	0.14	14(63.63)	8(36.36)
5.	Gangapada	86	0.012	19(22.09)	67(77.91)
6.	B.guda	64	0.026	16(25)	48(75)
			0.475		
Cut off Sector					
7.	Jantri	17	1.83	12(70.58)	5(29.41)
8.	T.guda	16	1.69	8(50.8)	8(50)
			1.76		
	Total	401		170(42.39)	231(57.6)

Note : Figures in bracket indicate percentage.
Source : Tehsil Records Room, Chitrokonda.

Production

The primary source of income is from agriculture which accounts for 85.91 per cent of their annual income (Table 4.8). It is found that 509 households of the three sectors primarily enjoy the agricultural production. The major crops they produce are paddy, suan, millet, pulses, oil seeds and vegetables. The maximum production is the paddy which is 15.7 qtls. of the total produce followed by millet (5.24 qtls.) and pulses (3.15 qtls.) as depicted in (Tables 4.3, 4.4 and 4. 5). However, the plain dwellers do not cultivate suan. The agricultural produce the Didayi households procure hardly meets their requirements for 5-6 months. In spite of low production, they at times sell off or barter a portion of the crop to meet other requirements. Generally, they sell off all the oil seeds in addition to certain forest produce. A hilltop household on an average gets a total amount of 9.39 qtls. yearly agricultural produce which accounts Rs. 5,180 according to the local market value. Whereas, a cut off Didayi procures 12.33 qtls. agricultural produce of Rs. 7,424 based on the local market value. On the other hand, a plain Didayi gets 12.56 qtls. agricultural produce of Rs. 8,479 which is according to the market value of that locality (Tables 4.3, 4.4 and 4.5).

Table 4.3 : Crop-wise Production and the Value of Produce (Hilltop Sector)

Sl. No.	*No.of HH*	*Name of Crop*	*Quantity produced (in. Qt. HH)*	*Value (per Qt.)*	*Value of produce (in Rs.)*
1.	268	Paddy	4.12	334.95	1380.00
2.		*Suan*	1.58	518.98	820.00
3.		Millet	1.76	500.00	880.00
4.		Pulses	0.45	2044.00	920.00
5.		Oilseeds	0.62	1209.00	750.00
6.		Vegetables	0.86	500.00	430.00
		Total	9.39	5107.00	5,180.00

Note : In terms of market values in the locality.

Table 4.4 : Crop-wise Production and the Value of Produce (Cut off Sector)

Sl. No.	*No.of HH*	*Name of Crop*	*Quantity produced (in. Qt. HH)*	*Value (per Qt.)*	*Value of produce (in Rs.)*
1.	82	Paddy	5.24	334.95	1755.00
2.		*Suan*	1.35	518.98	700.00
3.		Millet	1.73	500.00	865.00
4.		Pulses	0.86	2044.00	1757.00
5.		Oilseeds	1.25	1209.00	1394.00
6.		Vegetables	1.9	500.00	953.00
	-	Total	2.33	5107.00	7424.00

Note : In terms of market values in the locality.

Table 4.5 : Crop-wise Production and the Value of Produce (Plain Sector)

Sl. No.	No.of HH	Name of Crop	Quantity produced (in. Qt.HH)	Value (per Qt.)	Value of produce (in Rs.)*
1.	159	Paddy	6.34	334.95	2132.00
2.		Millet	1.75	500.00	875.00
3.		Pulses	1.84	2044.00	3747.00
4.		Oilseeds	0.53	1209.00	641.00
5.		Vegetables	2.10	500.00	1084.00
		Total	12.56	5107.00	8479.00

Note : In terms of market values in the locality.

Average annual income

Average annual income is a standard criterion for assessing the economic status of a person, group or community. In order to find out the average income, from all sources, production and their income of the whole year, have been taken into account. The annual income of 509 households have been recorded through personal interview. After careful analysis, it is found that their major income is from agriculture which is 85.93 per cent (Table 4.8). The table also depicts that the second source of income is from wage earning which accounts for 7.17 per cent of their income. The income both from livestock and forest produce is very meagre which accounts 4.19 per cent and 1.91 per cent respectively. On the whole, average annual income of plains per household is Rs. 9,723 whereas in hilltop as Rs. 6,347 and in cut off, it is Rs. 8,464 (Table 4.8).

The 'poverty line' has been defined in terms of annual income of a family consisting of five members on an average. The poverty line has been changing from plan to plan. It was Rs. 3,500 per family in the Sixth Plan which increased to Rs. 6,400 during Seventh Plan and further to Rs. 11,000 in the Eighth Plan. However, the income level of Rs. 8,500 in Eighth Plan, is taken as the cut off point for assessing the economic status of the Didayi households. According to the norms of Government of India, the types of poor are categorized against the annual income as depicted in Table 4.6. Therefore, the annual household income of a plain Didayi comes under the category of Poor. Whereas, the annual household income of a hilltop Didayi falls in the category of V.V. Poor and of a cut off household in the V. Poor category. Therefore, they all come undcr the BPL category.

Moreover, the economic status of the people has also been assessed on the basis of their agricultural production. For this, the average agricultural production of the individual household has been taken into account and the findings have been given in Table 4.7. It is seen that only the plain sector constitutes a few (3.7%) households of A.P.L. category. On the other hand, the hilltop and cut off sectors have more (98.1% and 71.9%) number of destitute households respectively. However, from the overall point of view it can be stated that a maximum number of households (70.1%) are belonging to the destitute groups based on their agricultural production.

Table 4.6 : Categorisation of Poor by GoI (VIII Plan)

Sl.No.	*Range of Annual Income*	*Per Capita Income*	*Types of Poor*
1.	8500-11000	961-1280	Poor
2.	6400-8500	701-961	Very poor
3.	3500-6400	454-700	Very very poor
4.	Up to-3500	453	Destitute

Table 4.7 : Economic Status of Didayis on the Basis of Agricultural Production

Economic Status	*Plain HH* (%)	*Hilltop HH* (%)	*Cut off HH* (%)	*Total* (%)
A.P.L.	6 (3.7)	—	—	6 (1.2)
Poor	19 (11.9)	—	5 (6.09)	24 (4.8)
Very poor	42 (26.4)	—	6 (7.3)	48 (9.4)
V.V.Poor	57 (35.8)	5 (1.8)	12 (14.6)	74 (14.5)
Destitute	35 (22.2)	263 (98.1)	59 (71.9)	357 (70.1)
Total	159 (100)	268 (100)	82(100)	509(100)

Note : Figures in bracket indicate percentage.

Table 4.8 : Average Annual Income from Various Sources

Sl. No.	Sector	No. of HH	Agri-culture	Wage	Live-stock	MFP	Misc.	Total (in Rs.)
1.	Plain	159	8479 (87.20)	680 (6.99)	358 (3.68)	150 (1.54)	56 (0.57)	9723 (100)
2.	Hilltop	268	5180 (81.61)	560 (8.82)	357 (5.62)	178 (2.8)	72 (1.13)	6347 (100)
3.	Cut off	82	7424 (87.71)	520 (6.14)	315 (3.72)	142 (1.67)	63 (0.74)	8464 (100)
Overall Average per		HH	21083 (85.93)	1760 (7.17)	1030 (4.19)	470 (1.91)	191 (0.77)	24534 (100)

Note : Figures in bracket indicate percentage.

Average Expenditure

On an average, a plain Didayi household spends an amount of Rs. 9,748 per year (Table 4.9). The table also indicates that a hilltop and a cut off household spends Rs. 6,354 and Rs. 8,504 respectively. Of this, consumption expenditure accounts for 92.96 per cent and rest only 8.04 per cent is utilized for income generation activities like agricultural production and acquiring of domestic animals.

Expenditure on food items of three sectors, alone accounts for 69.8 per cent of the total expenditure. Cloth, liquor and tobacco constitute next major expenditure of plain and cut off Didayi. However, the hilltop Didayi hardly spends on liquor and tobacco (2.18%) as they grow tobacco and share liquor freely among themselves (Photograph 4.3). Expenditure on other heads are minimal. Except the hilltop Didayi, the villagers of other two sectors are found to spend a very negligible amount (0.25 %) on education of the children.

Savings/Indebtedness

It is seen from the income-expenditure pattern that the Didayi families of the 12 study villages somehow manages to run in a balanced budget with a meagre difference of Rs. 25, 7 and 40 respectively (Table 4.10 & Graph 4.1). They do not have any

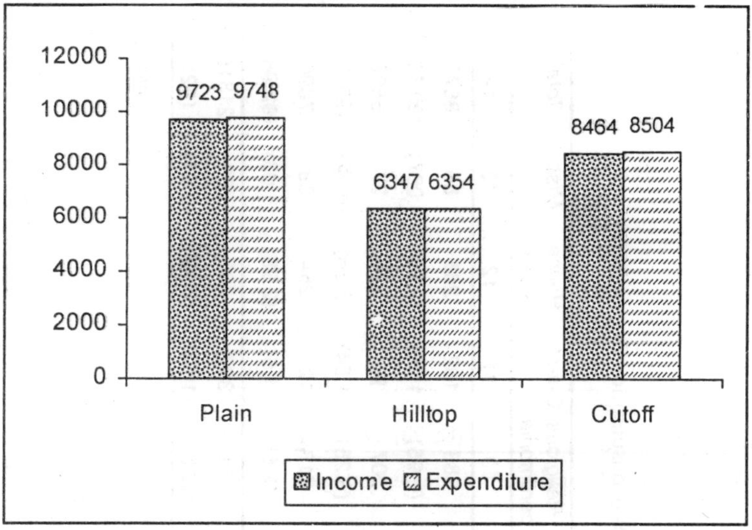

Graph 4.1 : Annual Average Income and Expenditure State of a Didayi Household

savings in the bank as recorded during the field study. However, it has been noticed that they are in habit of saving the money inside a bamboo hollow. Those who can afford to save, they save the currency notes inside the bamboo and hide it in their houses for safe custody which they rarely take out.

They do not prefer to owe or lend monetary help from any other outsiders except their own kith and kin. They apprehend to borrow money from outsiders as some of them who have availed the TRYSEM loan have been experienced cheating by the VLW who had demanded Rs. 150 from their loan amount. At times, the outsiders like forest officials and the police persons charge allegation and demand money from them. Within the village though they help each other in socio-cultural functions but cannot get the economic assistance as all of them are in the same economic bracket (BPL). It is revealed from the opinion survey that except the Micro Project they do not ask monetary help from others as they are aware of the fact that the DDA is only functioning for their beneficial sake. The on-going schemes like DWCRA under CD programme and income generating schemes by DDA, have been providing

Table 4.9 : Average Expenditure incurred on Different Items (Consumption Expenditure)

S. No.	Sector	No. of HH	Food	Cloth	Liquor & Tobacco	Kero-sene	Medi-cine	Edn.	Religious ceremonial	Guests	House repair	Misc.	Total
1	2	3	4	5	6	7	8	9	10	11	12	13	14
1.	Plain	159	6551	703	505	156	52	37	288	162	288	85	8827
			(67.2)	(7.21)	(5.18)	(1.6)	(0.53)	(0.37)	(2.95)	(1.66)	(2.95)	(.087)	(90.55)
2.	Hilltop	268	4668	391	139	87	49	—	207	98	226	27	5892
			(73.4)	(6.15)	(2.18)	(1.36)	(0.77)		(3.25)	(1.54)	(3.55)	(0.42)	(92.7)
3.	Cut off	82	5951	632	484	98	34	25	213	127	254	88	7096
			(69.9)	(7.43)	(5.69)	(1.15)	(0.39)	(0.29)	(2.5)	(1.5)	(2.98)	(1.03)	(92.96)
Total			17170	1726	1128	341	135	62	708	387	768	200	21815
			(69.8)	(7.01)	(4.6)	(1.4)	(0.54)	(0.25)	(2.9)	(1.57)	(3.12)	(0.81)	(92)

(contd.)

Note : Figures in bracket indicate percentage.

Table 4.9 (Contd.) : Average Expenditure incurred on Different Items (Consumption Expenditure)

Sl. No.	*Animal/Husbandry*	*Agriculture*	*Grand Total*
	15	*16*	*17*
1.	35	886	9748
	(0.36)	(9.09)	(100)
2.	27	435	6354
	(0.42)	(6.88)	(100)
3.	30	568	(8504)
	(0.35)	(6.68)	(100)
Total	92	1889	24606
	(0.37)	(7.67)	(100)

Table 4.10 : A Comparative Statement of Annual Income and Expenditure

Sl. No.	*Sectors*	*Households*	*Total income (in Rs.)*	*Total expenditure (in Rs.)*	*Balance budget*
1.	Plain	159	9723	9748	25
2.	Hilltop	268	6347	6354	7
3.	Cut off	82	8464	8504	40

economic assistance to the people. Moreover, the study on beneficiary HH reveals that the developmental programmes, namely DWCRA (20.63%), horticulture scheme (12%) and agriculture scheme (44%), have economically benefited the households respectively (Tables 7.1, 9.3 and 9.5). These income oriented schemes have helped the people to bridge the household budgetary gaps to some extent. Even though, they are in below poverty line still they do not prefer to be indebted as no such case has been recorded.

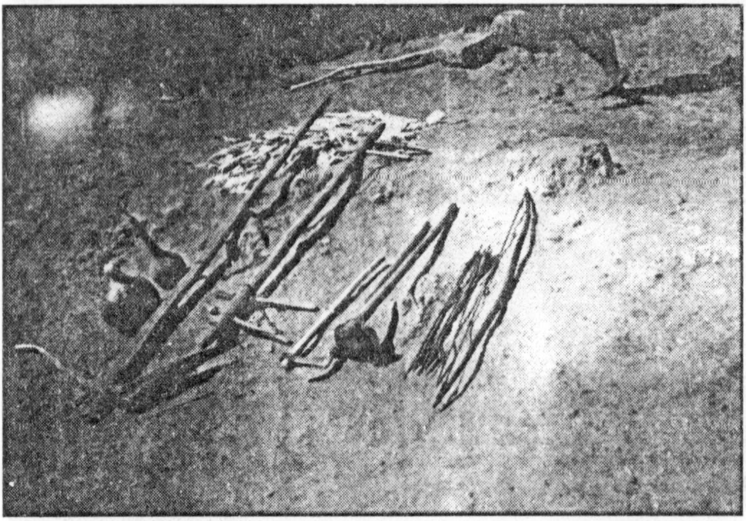

Photograph 4.1 : Agricultural Implements

Photograph 4.2 : A Didayi utilising his skills on bamboo for making household articles (Bayapada Hilltop village)

Photograph 4.3 : Unique way of storing pumpkins, tobacco and sweet gourds (Hilltop village)

5

Political Organisation

Political participation is closely associated with the political awareness of any community because it largely influences the socio-economic development process. Political awareness has a strong correlation with the participatory orientation, cynicism and political efficiency of voters of any community. The Didayi community of at present shows interest towards the modern electoral system as well as the existing traditional village political structure at the same time. The people have exercised their franchise during the current Parliamentary Election, held in July 1999 and information from primary sources reveal that about 55 per cent voters had cast their votes in respective booths including the aged women.

The women are equally aware of the political affairs of the state and the nation. They understand the functioning of the *'Panchayati Raj'* system. Even there are ladies who have actively participated in political processes at grassroots level and got elected as Sarpanch, Naib Sarpanch and ward members. The women participants in the system get a support from not only the family members, but also of the community as a whole. To focus on the present issue, there is a need to discuss the importance of traditional political organization of the community.

Traditional Political Organization (Village Council)

The village council is headed by the *Naik* (village headman) to whom the other members like *Golpeda* (next to *Naik*), *Chalan* (village messenger), *Pujari* or *Palasi* (village Priest) and *Dishari* (village medicine man) do assist him in solving the inter- and intra-village disputes, socio-religious conflicts and even economic issues.

Every village meeting is conducted in presence of the members of both the traditional village council and the modern panchayati system in which the Naik and the Sarpanch take the leading roles. Both of them are respected equally by the villagers. It is seen in village Totaguda that woman Sarpanch usually seek the assistance of traditional village heads in order to arrive at a decision. The status and the role of the village council members are briefly discussed below :

Naik **:** The post of *Naik* is hereditary. He presides over all the village meetings and in his absence the *Golpeda* conducts the meeting but keeps the decision pending for necessary approval of the *Naik.* He negotiates the fixation of bride-price as well as compensation for extra martial affairs (*sagarta*). He decides the nature of punishment and quantity of penalty for the wrong doers considering the econornic condition of the latter.

Golpeda **:** His post is also hereditary and in some villages he is called as *Muduli.* He enjoys the power next to *Naik.* The position of *Golpeda* is not so mandatory as in many villages nobody is elected or nominated for the position. So far, the position have been occupied by male Didayis only. A female cannot be a contestant for the post as the job is unsuitable to accomplish by a woman.

Chalan **:** The *Chalan* plays the role of a messenger and his post is not hereditary. The selection takes place on Wednesday only during Nandi Parva (February to March) or Push Parva (December to January). Incidents like child birth, date of funeral ceremony of the kith and kin, probable dates for meeting including the important days of community festivals are conveyed to him for dissemination in the village. If he becomes sick, he deputes a member of his family to accomplish the work.

Pujari/Palasi **:** He is the village priest and he is nominated by the villagers. In the hilltop and plain villages there are usually two *Pujaris* in each village; one is known as *Handi Pujari* or *Bada Pujari* and the other is *Thata-kulla Pujari* or *Sana Pujari.*

The post of *bada Pujari* is hereditary and *sana Pujari* is generally selected by the villagers during February-March in order to assist the *bada Pujari* for carrying winnowing fan during Chaitra festival. He is selected only for the purpose. The *bada Pujari* worships the *Nishani Hundi* (Shrine) near *Gulisung* (a public place for conducting community socio-religious activities). Both the *Pujaris* decide the duration, venue and time of each festival to be observed in the village.

Dishari : He is the village medicine man. The post of *Dishari* is neither selective nor hereditary because it depends on the quality of knowledge one acquires in the field of traditional medicine and healing practices. He takes active part in funeral purification ceremonies and also performs the magical art like chanting hymns including sacrifice of animals with a belief that it would keep away the evil spirits from the patients and thus heals the patients affected by the spirits, ghosts and other supernatural beings.

Community Meeting

A suitable place which is a centrally located area in the village, is used as the meeting place of the village committee. It is usually held at *Gulisung*. Normally, eight important people take active part in the meeting and they are the *Naik, Pujari, Dishari* and five other elderly persons of the village. While dispensing the disputed cases, the juries demand some liquor from each party involved in the case.

Sani Angra, aged 50 years of Oringi village, the head of the Didayi community, attends various meetings held in the DDA office and Block ofice. He also represents in various seminars conducted at District and state levels on Tribal and Welfare Schemes. In 1990, he also met the then Chief Minister, Mr. J.B. Pattanaik on the matters of local development schemes and programmes and urged him to allocate substantial amount of money to DDA for rapid development of the Didayi community.

An important decision has been noticed at Oringi, a plain village where a Didayi man and his family members were excommunicated owing to conversion to Christianity. It provides enough evidence that the decisions of traditional political organization is often more powerful than even the modern political system.

Political Awareness of Didayis

Democracy survives on people's active and effective participation in the decision-making process. Active political participation is essential because it determines the magnitude of socio-economic development of the community. In other words, political participation enhances political awareness. The objectives of the section is to analyze the level of political awareness, hence certain views and opinions are required to assess the awareness.

In order to find out the political awareness regarding electing their representatives, knowledge about the number of political parties and opinion survey has been conducted in 12 study villages of three sectors. In each village, opinion of 10 males and 10 females are recorded, making a total of 120 respondents. The responses collected through personal interviews have been analyzed. It is revealed that 59.1 per cent males and 54.1 per cent females are aware of the location and functioning of the GP (Table 5.1). The table also depicts that the knowledge about the local member of Assembly (MLA) and Member of Parliament (MP) has been found to be quite limited because only 9.1 per cent males and 5.8 per cent females have responded correctly. Furthermore, it can be stated that a few men and women personally know them (MP & MLA) but many do not as these members belong to different villages and have not visited their villages during election. Although, 37.5 (male) and 29.1 (female) per cent know about the Chief Minister, none of them are aware of Governor of Orissa and President of India. Only the people's representatives like Sarpanchs and Ward members (16.6 per cent) of the villages know the name of the present PM, Mr. Atal Behari Vajpayee. However, more people (M : 70.8%, F : 40.8%) are aware about late Smt. Indira Gandhi and still believe that she is alive. More than 76 per cent males are aware of two political parties, i.e. Congress and BJP. Only 30.8 per cent are in knowledge of third party namely BJD. The females are relatively less aware about political parties than the males. Their knowledge about father of the nation is also limited to 15.8 and 9.1 per cent amongst males and females respectively.

Table 5.1 : Level of Political Awareness of Didayis

Sl. No.	*Questions*	*Responded correctly* (M : 120)	*Per cent*	*(F : 120)*	*Per cent*
1.	Name of GP.	71	59.1	65	54.1
2.	Name of MLA	11	9.1	7	5.8
3.	Name of MP	11	9.1	5	4.1
4.	CM of Orissa	45	37.5	35	29.1
5.	PM of India	22	18.1	11	9.1
6.	Governor of Orissa	—	—	—	—
7.	President of India	—	—	—	—
8.	Late Smt. Indira Gandhi	85	70.8	25	20.8
9.	Mahatma Gandhi	19	15.8	11	9.1
10.	Name of Political Parties:				
	(a) Any Two	92	76.6	63	52.5
	(b) Any Three	37	30.8	13	10.8
	(c) More	—	—	—	—

Note : Relating to current situation, 1999.

6

Religious Life

Religion is an important integral part of the life. Every activity in the society is guided and regulated by the religious deities, festivals and values in the Didayi society. The Didayi consider the Mother Goddess (*Adi Mata*) as the supreme being. Next to it, is the God of Nature (*Biru*).

On various occasions, they also worship different Hindu deities like Lord Shiva, Sri Ganesh, Lord Krishna, Brahma, Rama and Sita and Goddess Laxmi. Apart from worshipping these deities, ancestral worship is prevalent in all households. In Chait festival ancestral worship is commonly held at Nishani Hundi (cut off villages) and at *Gulisung* (Photograph 6.1). The plain Didayi are more influenced towards Hindu religion and celebrate almost all Hindu festivals. *Pujari* of the area follow both the traditional as well as Hindu ritual procedure while worshipping. For example, observance of *'Trinath mela'* is conducted on 21st day of new-born baby and on the name-giving ceremony. But it is important to state that they have not yet given up beef eating, which contradicts the Hindu ideology. The Didayi of cut off sector are more influenced by the Bengali refugees of Dandakaranya area and outsider Hindus. However, the hilltop Didayis have retained their traditional religious identity and ritualistic procedure, not adopting much of Hindu style of worshipping.

In every festival and socio-religious events, their forefathers are worshipped with a belief that their happiness would provide life long security and prosperity to the individual and to the Didayi community as a whole. The *Pujari* or *Palasi* performs rituals in all the ceremonies and festivals like *Landi Parva, Chaiti Parva, Pusa Pandu.* The annual cycle of festivals celebrated by the Didayi are given in Table 6.1.

Table 6.1 : Annual Festival Calendar of Didayi Community

Festival	*Month*	*Duration of Observance*	*Purpose*	*Offerings*	*Deities*
Pushkar Pandu	Dec.-Jan.	3 days	Worship cattle, Selection of *Pujari*, Marriage negotiation	Sacrifice of Goat, Chicken	*Go-mata*
Jhati Parva	-do-	8 days	-do-	-do-	*Adimata*
Nandi Parva or *Lindi Pande*	Feb.-Mar.	3 days	For better crop	Coconut, Banana No sacrifice	*Adimata*
Dosra Hia	March-April	1 day	Chait-Festival	White chicken, white goat	*Bhairo*
Chaiti Parva	April-May	7-8 days	Communal hunt, Eating	Sacrifice of pig, hen	*Biru, Adimata*
Osarke Pande	Jun.-Jul.	2 days	Sowing ceremony	Sacrifice of brown chicken, egg, milk, rice, etc.	*Adimata*
Asha Parva	Aug.-Sep.	8 days	Eating of new vegetables, crops	Sacrifice of pig, chicken, coconut	*Biru/* Mango Kernel
Diali Arbe or *Hini Hundi*	Oct.-Nov.	1 day (First Monday)	Village deity Puja	-do-	*Biru*

The village priest fixes the exact date and duration for celebration of each festival for his respective village. All these festivals are celebrated in all the sectors. 'Chait Parva' is the most important festival (Photograph 6.2). This is a festival in which the Didayi men demonstrate their hunting skill and the females show their capability in safeguarding the houses from the wild animals. The Didayi women decorate their houses to welcome the male folks when they return from the ceremonial hunting. The males are only allowed and welcome to the village if they return with the game. The ladies wash the feet and put a vermilion mark (*tika*) on the foreheads of the Didayi men. In return, the male members give 25-50 paise to the Didayi ladies. The prey is chopped and distributed among the villagers according to traditional rules. The person whose arrow first hits the animal, gets a thigh of the killed animal and a red *saree* from the village *Naik* as a token of prize in lieu of the bravery deeds. The second hitter gets the neck portion and rest are distributed among the villagers. The festival is celebrated with folk dance, special foods and country liquor (Photograph 6.3).

Conversion

The Didayis are not in favour of conversion, although a number of households belonging to Bondo tribe of the adjacent area have embraced Christianity. Only one family of Oringi plain village, Sama Pujari got converted to Christianity. Though his son Dabi Pujari is earning approximately Rs. 2000 per month from Missionary Organization, he is not acting as a role model for others as stated by Sani Angra of Oringi village who is the headman. Because of conversion, this family has been excommunicated from the village. Sani Angra states that they

Photograph 6.1 : Nishani Hundi of Jantri village (Cut off sector)

would not embrace other religion than Hinduism since they are getting various benefits from the government. It is again a strong belief they have that their God (*Biru-vairabi*) would cast curse.

Photograph 6.2 : Didayi on Hunting Spree (Chait Festival, Hilltop sector)

Photograph 6.3 : Musical Instruments being played during Chait Festival (Hilltop village)

7

Policy and Practice for the Didayi Development

Introduction

An important aspect of administrative evolution in India since Independence and from thereafter, the advent of development planning, has been a tremendous increase in the point of contact between the functionaries connected with tribal development administration on the one hand and tribal people on the other. It must be emphasized on the quality of relationship between the administrative system and the tribal groups at large is basic not only for the successful implementation of development programmes but also for the operations of a democratic system of the type in India.

Every society goes through a developmental phase which is called autonomous development. But, sometimes this autonomous development may not be sufficient to attain a socially desirable living standard of a particular community within a society. So in this case, some sort of government intervention is needed to initiate and foster a higher rate of development, i.e. Planned development. However, the planning should not be forcefully implemented which may result into negative growth. It should ensure peoples active participation in such a way, the objectives should be achieved within the targeted period. The programmes in tribal development field has to be properly designed taking into consideration of the present needs, environmental conditions and cultural factors. Under the programme, the specific plan oriented actions are framed, called a scheme. The schemes are the stepping stones of any development programme, thus are the effective tools of the planned development.

Before Independence

The policy of isolation by the British government resulted in poor administration in tribal areas, as a result they remained cut off from the rest of the population. They were ignorant and helpless to know and understand the happening around them. This isolation led to exploitation by non-tribal money-lenders, contractors, Zamindar and middlemen. A few roads were constructed to enable contractors to exploit the forest produce and the communication with the other people was discouraged. Consequently, a sense of separatism had developed in them.

During the British period Didayi country land was under the Jeypore Zamindar under Madras Presidency as already has been discussed earlier. However, a new chapter in the history of the Jeypore began with the formation of Koraput district. Jeypore estate was abolished with effect from 29 December, 1952 in Government notification No. 8231-R, under the provision of Orissa Estate Abolition Act, 1951.

In 1936, when the Indian Legislative Assembly criticised the British Government policy of partial exclusion, the political leaders condemned the exclusion and also blamed several anthropologists who had advocated for the isolation. Varrier Elwin said, "Otherwise intelligent persons declared that the excluded areas were a trick of the Anthropological preserve the Aboriginal as museum specimens for the exercise of their blessed science" (Elwin, 1950 : 107). Elwin (1939 : 511-519) also advocatsd for establishment of a sort of National Park of the tribal people and advised that their contact with outside world should be reduced to the minimum and supported the idea of isolationism.

The policy of isolation and drift meant nothing more than a maintenance of *status quo.* It resulted in reducing the tribal people to a state of penury in most parts of India. They were at the lowest level of development in every field. Their land was heavily accumbered and a good portion had already passed into the hands of non-tribal people. Their rights in forest were definitely encroached upon. Outside elements introduced for the purpose of government and forest work continued to exploit them. On many an occasion, the tribal people rose in the revolt with their demands. Even the reformative steps were taken into action but all these proved futile (Prasad, 1988 : 85).

The Didayi likewise have remained isolated and cut off from the mainstream till independence without any arm of administration reaching them. The contact with the administration was limited to only deposition of rent or tax through the headman of the community.

Post-Independence Era

The Constituent Assembly of free India accepted the tribal problem as an integral part of the development of the Indian people as a whole. The Article 46 lays down the safeguards for the Scheduled Castes and Scheduled Tribes to protect from the social injustice and all forms of exploitation. Socio-economic development has been undertaken as a part of national development planning.

Planned Development Efforts

Rural development in the post-independence era became the major thrust of planned effort in the country since 80 per cent of the population used to live in rural areas in disadvantaged conditions. The government initiated systematic plans and strategies to help the rural communities to move faster along the path of development towards the realization of national goals through the Community Development Programmes (CDP) from 1952. During the same time, i.e. from 2-10-1952, National Extension Service Programmes (N.E.S. Blocks) were launched in areas of tribal concentration with a view to ameliorate the socio-economic conditions of the tribal people (Srichandan, 1993 : VI).

A more intensive approach was adopted for tribal welfare with the launching of special projects called multi-purpose tribal blocks in 1956 by the Ministry of Home Affairs in co-operation with the Ministry of Community Development and Cooperation (*ibid.* : 165).

Out of 43 Special Multi-purpose Tribal Blocks (SMPT Blocks), only four such blocks in Keonjhar, Koraput and Mayurbhanj districts of Orissa started as pilot projects during Second Five Year Plan. This was further extended to 480 blocks in the Third Five Year Plan and 504 tribal development blocks were established in the Fourth Five Year Plan. A special programme for the selected tribal area was initiated during the Fourth Five Year Plan in Bihar, Orissa, Andhra Pradesh and Madhya Pradesh. One such special programme known as Tribal Development Agencies were started in Orissa. Over a period of 10 years, in two stages of 5 years each, the T.D. Blocks received additional money grants of Rs. 10 lakh (stage I) and Rs. 5 lakh (stage II) over and above the normal investment under the C.D. Block Programme. Thereafter, during the Fourth Plan period an additional investment of Rs.10 lakh (stage III) was made for the consolidation of T.D. Blocks (Mohanty, *et al.*, 1996 : 55-56).

On the eve of Fifth Five Year Plan, the Planning Commission appointed the Shilu Ao Committee in 1972 to look into the problems of tribal development. The Committee pleaded for the policy of integrated development of tribal areas and recommended three types of areas, viz. macro, meso, and micro in order to make it administratively viable. The sub-plan concept was introduced during the Fifth Plan Period (1974-1979) and it included setting up Integrated Tribal Development Project (I.T.D.P.) in the area with more than 50 per cent concentration of tribal population and the total sub-plan areas for the country was 179. By and large, the major development programmes, namely : IADP, SFDA, MFAL, CSRE, MNP, WEP, NREP, RLEGP etc. were launched in the state through the C.D. Blocks. However, these could not substantially benefit the tribal people nor could the programmes gain any kind of popularity among the tribes. During the Seventh Plan Period, the tribal sub-plan approach gave major thrust on the development of Primitive Tribal Groups (PTGs).

In Orissa, the tribal sub-plan area covers 118 development blocks spread over 12 districts, viz. Mayurbhanj, Sundergarh, Keonjhar, Balasore, Phulbani, Deogarh, Malkangiri, Nowrangpur, Koraput, Rayagada, Gajapati and Kalahandi. The entire sub-plan area is divided into 21 Integrated Tribal Development Agencies (ITDAs) for operational purpose. In these areas concentration of tribal population is 50 per cent or more. In these projects family oriented development programmes are implemented with 25 to 30 per cent subsidy.

The working group during VII Plan made several recommendations for the development of the PTGs. These include family-wise economic development, coverage of ICDS, ban on sale and purchase of tribal land by the outsiders, peoples participation in all stages of programme implementations, incentives for the staff working in primitive tribal areas, involvement of NGOs and additional special central assistance. Furthermore, the Ninth Plan acknowledges the need for a National Tribal Policy about which has already been discussed.

Community Development Programmes (CDPs) for the Didayi

DRDA is the nodal organization at the district level to carry out all developmental activities. The District Rural Development Agency (DRDA), Malkangiri has been implementing its various schemes, namely DWCRA (Developnient of Women and Children in Rural Areas), Industrial Development Projects, Employment Assurance Scheme (EAS), Kutirajyoti Yojana and schemes in Non-Conventional and Renewable Energy System executed through OREDA. All these schemes are also operating through the Didayi Development Agency for the development of Didayi tribe.

Since the inception of the Micro Project from 1986 to 1994, the ITDA, Malkangiri has been releasing the monetary assistance of about Rs. 5,38,215. The Didayi Development Agency has kept its record as accordingly the scheme-wise utilization of the funds in various heads. The utilization of funds and physical targets made during the stipulated period, viz. 1992-93 and 1993-94, have been produced in Annual Action Plan (Action Plan, 1994-97 : 24). The Micro Project has spent this fund in many fields like Agriculture programme, Horticulture programme, Human Resource Development, Infrastructure development, Natural Resource development and animal husbandry scheme. An amount of Rs. 2,00,000 has been received from DRDA by the Micro Project to take up construction of Non-Formal schools (*Gyanmandir*) at Taberu (cut off sector) and Bodankiyaguda (hilltop sector) under EAS (Action Plan, 1999-2000 : 4). DRDA has provided assistance for execution of l4 km road work in the Hill section (Government Report, 1998-99 : 3).

Execution of Schemes

DWCRA

Development of women and children, a sub-scheme of IRDP was started in 1982-83. It aims at a collective endeavours of women groups which are known to work better than individual manuals. It also emphasizes on making them more self-reliant by providing additional opportunities for self-employment. Under this scheme Didayi women are organized in groups of 10-15 for taking of economic activities like broom binding, spice and turmeric powder making and tailoring. There are 11 DWCRA groups in operation in different income generating activities like broom binding, spice grinding and tailoring in the Didayi villages (Table 7.1). The table reveals that seven DWCRA groups of 105 women (20.63%), are in operation in two plain, three hilltop and two cut off villages. It also depicts that DWCRA is successfully functioning in the beneficiaries of three sectors. The scheme has been imparting various training with an aim of persuading their sustainable earning capacity while simultaneously learning the art of running their own small scale industry, viz. broom binding, spice powder/ turmeric powder grinding and tailoring. The 18.86 per cent ladies of plain, 16.79 per cent women of hilltop and 36.58 per cent ladies of cut off sector, have been benefited. Since the programme is found to be more potential, therefore, more importance should be given to it in terms of organizing the women group.

TRYSEM

Training of Rural Youths for Self-Employment scheme aims to impart technical skill to the tribal and rural youths from the families below powerty line and to enable them take up self-employment activities. The upper age limit of 35 is relaxable up to 40 years in the case of widows, freed bonded labour persons displaced due to large development projects and cured leprosy patients. But it has been found that only 16.98 per cent plain, 7.08 per cent hilltop and 14.63 per cent cut off villagers have received the loan respectively (Table 7.1) and simultaneously paid back to the State Bank of India, Orkal Branch of Balimela as has been recorded in their passbooks. Hence, TRYSEM training modules are to be restructured to include more number of the Didayi youths.

NOAPS

The National Old Age Pension Scheme (NOAPS) is a component of National Assistance Programme, which came to effect from 15 August, 1995. Under the NOAPS, the men as well as women above 65 years can get benefit of old age pension of Rs. 75 per month, provided they have little or no regular sources of financial support.

The Didayis are availing the NOAPS. However, the coverage under the scheme is found to be very limited as 14 per cent HH (plain), 2.61 per cent HH (hilltop) and 4.87 per cent (cut off), have availed the scheme (Table 7.1). On the whole, only 6.67 per cent people have been benefited.

Besides the NOAPS, Didayis are also obtaining widow pension. But the number of beneficiaries are very limited as only 4.4 per cent (plain), 0.74 per cent (hilltop) and 1.21 per cent (cut off) households have been recorded.

Table 7.1 : Community Development Programme for the Didayis

Sl. No.	Schemes	No. of Ben.HHs Sector			Total
		Plain 159 (100%)	Hilltop 268 (100%)	Cut off 82 (100%)	No. of HH 509 (100%)
1.	ITDA & OREDA				
	Solar PV lights	3 (1.88)	—	2 (2.43)	5 (0.98)
	Solar Cooker	5 (3.14)	—	—	5 (0.98)
	Bio-gas plant	1 (0.62)	—	—	1 (0.19)
2.	ITDA-TRYSEM				
	Agriculture loan	27 (16.98)	19 (7.08)	12 (14.63)	58 (11.39)
3.	RWSO				
	Tube-wells	11 (6.91)	6 (2.23)	7 (8.53)	24 (4.71)
4.	DWCRA	30 (18.86)	45 (16.79)	30 (36.58)	105 (20.68)
5.	Roof Tiles	136 (85.5)	—	8 (9.75)	144 (28.29)
6.	Old age pension	23 (14)	7 (2.61)	4 (4.87)	34 (6.67)
	Widow pension	7 (4.4)	2 (0.74)	1 (1.21)	10 (1.96)
7.	ICDS-Centres	3 (1.88)	1 (0.37)	2 (2.43)	6 (1.17)
8.	PDS-BPL cards	151 (94.9)	268 (100)	73 (89.02)	492 (96.66)

Note : Figures in brackets indicate percentage.

OREDA and RWSO

Orissa Renewable Energy Development Agency has provided improved five solar cookers and one bio-gas plant to the villagers of Oringi of plain sector. But the villages of other two sectors are yet to be accessible to the scheme.

Under the RWSO (Rural Water Supply Organization), tube-wells have been dug out in the villages of three sectors. During field study, 24 tube-wells have been recorded in the 12 study villages. However, the tube-wells in the plain villages are only found to be in working condition as the villagers have been using the water.

In addition to these schemes, DRDA has also provided tiles. However, the plain villagers are only benefited out of the scheme as 85.5 per cent households have been recorded to access to the scheme and 15 per cent are yet to get the benefit (Table 7.1). It is also learnt that these people have made their tiled roof on their own expenses and will be getting the tiles subsequently. On the other hand, the hilltop households are deprived of the tiles. There are only 9.75 per cent cut off households who have received the tiles (Table 7.1). It is learnt from the cut off villagers that they are not interested for these supplied tiles as they have to bear the transportation charge of the tiles.

In addition to the above CD programmes, the people are also being benefited through BPL Scheme. Almost 97 per cent households possess the BPL Card (Table 7.1). However, during the field study, it has been found that the ration items which are already mentioned in the card, are not yet provided to the card holders. Even, in some cards, both the ration items and the date of disposal are mentioned in advance of the month. Hence, in reality the people are deprived of the ration items both qualitatively and quantitatively.

Integrated Child Development Service (ICDS), Kudumulugumma has only six sub-centres in 12 study villages which are found to be inadequate as 98 per cent children and women are noticed in malnourished state.

Integrated Tribal Development Agency, Malkangiri has been providing monetary assistance to DDA. Under ITDA, solar PV system are installed in both the plain villages (Oringi & Purunaguma) and cut off villages (Jantri and Totaguda). Whereas, the hilltop beneficiaries are deprived of this PV light system. Furthermore, it is found during field study that not a single system is in operative state. The principal reasons for the poor reliability and performances are :

(a) Lack of involvement of the beneficiaries in decision relating to the installation of PV and its use;

(b) non-availability of spares;
(c) non-availability of training on system maintenance;
(d) sub-standard quality of the component parts and poor system design; and
(e) poor awareness levels about the PV system.

Therefore, in order to overcome the poor field performance, PV system requires regular maintenance and periodic checks by trained technicians.

Didayi Development Agency

In the process of functioning of Bondo Development Agency, the Government authorities took the notice of the pitiable plight of the Didayi who are inhabitants of the adjacent locality. On the recommendation and efforts of the Scheduled Castes and Scheduled Tribes Research and Training Institute (SC & STRTI), then known as Tribal Harijan Research and Training Institute (THRTI), a Micro Project for the Didayi named as Didayi Development Agency (DDA) was established at Kudumulugumma of Malkangiri district in the year 1986, *vide* Government Resolution No. 23449/TW, under the Society Registration Act, 1860. As per the decision of the Union Ministry of Home Affairs, a location specific project report covering family oriented benefit schemes is prepared for Micro project. An officer specializing in the field of agriculture, soil conservation, horticulture, etc. is appointed as the Project Officer. He with his staff are in-charge of all developmental schemes. The Micro project functions as an autonomous body with the District Collector as the chairman and subordinate sub-divisional/block officials, local MLA, MP, and tribal leader as members of the governing body of the agency. The special officer of the Micro project acts as the member-secretary of the Governing Body of the Agency. In the yearly meeting, the action plan of the previous year is reviewed and a fresh annual action plan of the current year constituting the outlay of the developmental action oriented proposals are discussed and finalised. The details of the various ongoing programmes and schemes have been discussed subsequently in Chapter 8.

Role of NGOs

The question of cooperation and coordination between the government and the voluntary agencies is really a matter of fact for any developmental planning. The two can cooperate and coordinate with each other without jeopardizing their interest and the areas where there could be possibility of clash of interest.

Addressing the role of voluntary organization, Roy (1987 : 454-464) has brought out a ten-fold character :

(a) To supplement government efforts and not to complete.
(b) To be eyes and ears of the people at the village level.
(c) To set an example.
(d) To activate the systems and make it responsive.
(e) To disseminate information.
(f) To illustrate how local village and indigenous resources would be used for their own development.
(g) To make communities as self-reliant as possible.
(h) To train a cadre of grassroots workers who believe in professionalizing voluntarism.
(i) To mobilize financial resource from within the community.
(j) To mobilize and organize the poor demand quality service and to improve a community system of accountability on the performance of grassroots government functionaries.

However, in the process of participated development, emphasized in the Ninth Five Year Plan, the role of voluntary organizations is found very important. Some voluntary organizations (NGOs) have put their effort to organize the tribal villagers especially of the more primitive groups against exploitation, dis-empowerment and for securing the rights and privilege and developmental inputs, being earmarked for the ignorant tribal people.

Mahapatra (1994 : 30) stated that the Sarvodaya Movement in various states, the Navjivan Mandal of Orissa and other non-governmental organizations have ultimately run foul of the government and bureaucracy apart from running counter to the vested interests of the exploiters, money-lenders and land grabbers in tribal area.

However, the role of NGOs is found to be very negligible in Didayi areas. Except the cut off sector, no such organization has come into notice during the field study. In the cut off villages, namely Totaguda, Jantri, Disariguda, Dabuguda and Sanyasiguda, a NGO, named 'REACH' with its Headquarters at Bhubaneswar, has set up a branch in Jantri village. This organization is basically providing additional knowledge about various schemes and programmes being undertaken by the government. Its worker, a lady who is popularly know as 'REACH didi' among the villagers, has taken up many steps for betterment of the villagers. The lady Sarpanch, Laxmi Pangi of Totaguda village stated that under the guidance of the REACH supervisor (*didi*), they have been saving one rupee per day. In addition to that, whatever may be the production of the cash-crops like, *alsi*, chilly, etc. they have been trying to deposit at least Rs. 30 in the mini bank out of sale proceeding, of these crops. About 50 per cent to 60 per cent villagers are found to be motivated towards this saving scheme. It has been realised that the people's participation as well as cooperation with 'REACH' NGO, is further making this programme a successful achievement.

8

Didayi Development Agency (Micro Project)

The Micro project in the name of Didayi Development Agency (DDA) was constituted in August 1986, *vide* Government Resolution No. 23449/TW, dated 5 August, 1986. In the same year DDA started functioning at Kudumulugumma, a Block headquarters under Chitrakonda Tehsil with a view to undertake overall developmental programmes exclusively for the Didayi. The agency covers a total of 37 villages of Khariput and Kudumulugumma blocks. Micro project has also proposed to include four secluded Didayi villages, namely Dabuguda, Sariguda, Samakunda and Phulpadar R.C. Colony-1 which are shown in Map 8.1. The total geographical area of the DDA is 140 sq. km. The agency has since been registered under the Societies Registration Act, 1960, on 7 October, 1986.

Objectives

The objectives of the project are as under :

(a) Family-oriented income generating economic activity schemes for Didayis.
(b) Fulfilment of the basic needs of PTGs through some of the schemes.
(c) Imparting skill building training for familiarizing with modern income generating activity schemes.
(d) Infrastructure development and social service support.
(e) Providing irrigation facilities to enhance agricultural production in the limited area and homestead lands.

(Not to Scale)

Map 8.1 : Map of Didayi Development Agency

Structure of the Governing Body of the Micro Project

The district collector is the chairman of the Governing Body. The subdivisional officers, block level officers and non-officials including chairman of the Panchayat Samiti, local MLA, MP and a tribal leader act as its members and the special officer of the Micro Project as the Member-Secretary of the Governing Body of the Agency.

Governing Body of the Micro Project

↓

Chairman (District Collector)

↓

Micro Project Special Officer (Member-Secretary)

↓

Members

Official	Non-Official
District/ Sub-Divisional Officers	Member of Parliament (MP)
Block Level Officers	Member of Legislative Assembly (MLA)
	Chairman of Panchayat Samiti
	Didayi Leader

Function of the Governing Body

It is observed that the Governing Body (GB) convened meetings once in a year, particularly in the month of March and April (Table 8.1). In the meeting, the GB reviews the last meeting proceedings after circulating it among its members. In case, there is no objection to the proceedings, the same is passed and confirmed. The GB also reviews the progress of various schemes, programmes and any special activities for the current

Table 8.1 : Year-wise Dates of G.B. Meeting held (1987-1999)

Sl. No.	*Dates of Meeting*	*Remarks*
1.	03-03-87	1st GB Meeting to discuss the Action Plan
2.	12-05-98	12th GB Meeting
3.	07-05-99	13th GB Meeting

Source : Action Plan, 1994-97, 1999-2000, DDA.

year. Suggested Action Plan for the next year is vividly discussed. The suggestions of members, if any, is incorporated into the Action Plan. Broad allocation of funds for the year on various heads is also finalized in the GB meetings.

Financial Outlay

The Didayi Development Agency has been getting financial assistance from Tribal Welfare Department on special Central grant, ITDA, DRDA for carrying out various schemes of the DDA. The details of the allotment received and the expenditure covering the period from 1986 to 1999 is shown in Annexure-I. It is found that the DDA has been able to spend less than one-fourth of the allotted amount in the initial stage. Subsequently, from 1989 to 1996, it has been able to spend about 75 to 80 per cent of the annual allotted amount and balance is carried forward to the next year. However, by the year 1999 the DDA has been able to utilise 93 per cent of the total allotted fund. The expenditure on establishment has been 24.54 per cent amounting to Rs. 35,35,096 and the expenditure on various developmental schemes accounts for Rs. 1,08,69,681 which is 75.45 per cent of the total utilised amount (Table 9.7). So far, Rs. 1,44,04,777 has been spent out of the total allotted fund from 1986-99 (Fig. 9.3). Furthermore, considering the number of households being 1285 covered by DDA, expenditure on developmental schemes per household comes to Rs. 8451.11 since its inception till 1999. Therefore, DDA has spent less than one-fourth of the allotted amount.

Programmes and Schemes

The DDA has undertaken a number of schemes and programmes with a view to provide assistance for integrated socio-economic development of the Didayi tribe on sustainable basis under the broad framework of the objectives. The project has adopted the following major developmental schemes :

(a) Natural Resource Development (NRD) and Family Oriented Income Generating Scheme (IGS).

(b) Human Resource Development (HRD).
(c) Infrastructure Development.
(d) Establishment and Administrative facilities.

The developmental schemes being carried out by DDA is illustrated in a diagram form (Fig. 8.1).

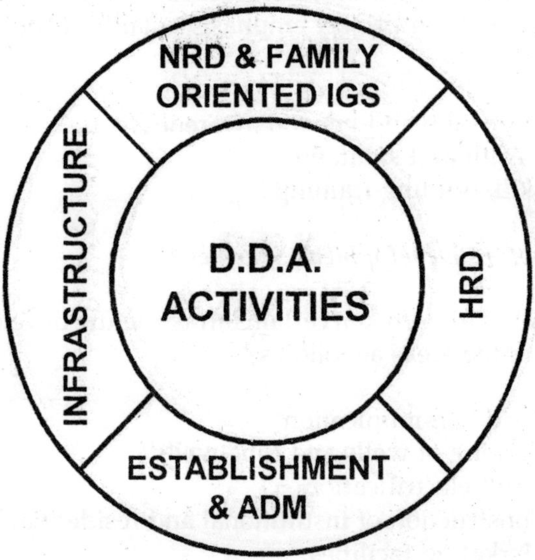

Fig. 8.1 : Sustainable Developmental Activities by DDA

Natural Resource Development (NRD) and Family Oriented Income Generating Schemes

As the name suggests, the Micro project has devised a numher of schemes to develop and exploit the available local natural resources of the area for the benefit of the tribal population and to provide avenue for them to enhance their income. The schemes undertaken by NRD are :

(a) Horticulture
(b) Agriculture
(c) Land development and Agro-forestry

(d) Irrigation
(e) Animal Husbandry and Fishery
(f) DWCRA and TRYSEM progammes

Human Resource Development Schemes

In order to develop the human resource of the tribal population of the area special project emphasis is laid on the following schemes :

(a) Education and general awareness
(b) Health and sanitation
(c) Skill building training.

Infrastructure Development Schemes

The DDA has undertaken certain infrastructure developmental schemes in the areas as follows :

(a) Road communication
(b) Digging of wells and tube-wells
(c) Rural electrification
(d) Construction of institutional and residential buildings
(e) Marketing facilities.

Establishment and Administration

This part deals with the organizational aspect of the DDA. In order to make it an effective body, so that it can meet the requirements and aspiration of the Didayi towards its sustainable development.

Details of Schemes and Programmes implemented

NRD and Family Oriented Income Generation Scheme

Horticulture

The micro project has given assistance to promote horticulture in the area in order to provide perennial source of income on sustainable basis to the beneficiaries. The details of various types of saplings provided over the period are as under :

(a) Perennial Crops Plantation: Saplings of mango, guava, pine apple, coconut, lemon, banana, custard apple and jackfruit have been given to the beneficiary households for plantation at the backyard. Cashew and tamarind saplings are being supplied for plantation on hill slopes. It is learnt that a nursery was started to grow saplings for further distribution in different phases. The saplings were not supplied every year to the beneficiaries, only in 1994, DDA for the first time initiated the activity. About 6212 beneficiaries benefited from the programme (Table 8.2). Since, no concrete figure on expenditure on sapling plantation was available in the office, it is ascertained that approximately Rs. 2 lakh have been spent on the programme.

(b) Vegetable Crops : Vegetable minikits have been distributed among the beneficiaries under *Khariff* and *Rabi* programmes, viz. potato, ginger, turmeric, tomato, cabbage, radish, cucumber, bitter gourd, pumpkin, lady's finger and water melon, etc.

Table 8.2 : Expenditure on Horticulture by DDA

Sl. No.	*Year*	*Expenditure (In Rs.)*	*No. of Beneficiaries (Families)*
1.	1986-87	25,000	30
2.	1987-88	35,114	375
3.	1988-89	6,076	700
4.	1989-90	9,366	709
5.	1990-91	64,660	1138
6.	1991-92	17,095	586
7.	1992-93	55,920	493
8.	1993-94	1,21,094	259
9.	1994-95	1,11,368	371
10.	1995-96	1,93,758	668
11.	1996-97	1,49,853	477
12.	1997-98	1,430	6
13.	1998-99	71,600	400
	Total	8,62,334	6212

Source : Annual Action Plan, DDA, Kudumulugumma.

The year-wise expenditure on horticulture scheme indicates that the horticulture programme has been meticulously implemented by the Micro project from the beginning. It has spent more than eight lakh rupees covering 6212 families (Table 8.2). However, the beneficiaries covered are mostly from villages, namely Oringi, Muduliguda, and Purunaguma of plain sector and hill villages like Bayapada and Suripada. Other villages have not been given due priority in this regard.

(c) Nursery-*cum*-Demonstration Farm : A horticulture nursery-*cum*-demonstration farm has been developed in Purunaguma village of plain sector to raise nursery of perennial saplings, vegetables and demonstration of different agricultural practices needed for crop harvesting. According to the Action Plan 1999-2000, it has been proposed to cover 2000 beneficiaries but actually 1000 people were benefited, although Rs. 42,180 is spent over a period of 12 years (Table 8.3). Table states that the total expenditure on the nursery maintenance is Rs. 42,180 over the period of past ten years. In order to give necessary exposure and training to the hill sector people, the DDA had proposed to make a green house at village Bayapada at a cost of Rs. 50,000 in addition to the expenditure incurred in the nursery at Purunaguma for the year 1995-96. However, there has been no emphasis given to establish such nursery and training facilities to the people of cut off area.

Table 8.3 : Maintenance of Nursery-*cum*-Demonstration Farm

Sl. No.	*Year*	*Expenditure (In Rs.)*
1.	1987-88	5,840.00
2.	1988-89	1,565.00
3.	1989-90	1,123.00
4.	1990-91	nil
5.	1991-92	nil
6.	1992-93	7,038.00
7.	1993-94	8,804.00
8.	1994-95	3,300.00
9.	1995-96	14,510.00
10.	1996-97	NA
11.	1997-98	nil
12.	1998-99	nil
	Total	42,180.00

Source : Action Plan. 1994-98, DDA. Kudumulugumma.

Agriculture

Agriculture is the main occupation of the Didayis. They consider it more stable, independent and regular than all other income generating activities. Their agricultural productivity has been limited due to non-availability of high yielding variety of seeds, non-utilization of fertilizers and pesticides, age-old practice of cropping without use of modern implements and limited irrigation facilities. The DDA has taken appropriate measures through this scheme to alleviate the above deficiencies.

Under Agriculture scheme following incentives have been given :

(a) Supply of inputs like High Yielding Varieties of seeds, fertilizers and pesticides.
(b) Supply of improved agricultural implements such as crow bar, pick axe, spade and plough. (Annual Action Plan, 1994-97 : 26)
(c) Providing irrigation facilities to take up second/third crops even during drought situation.

It is evident from the expenditure pattern that focus on agriculture schemes has been given by the DDA since very beginning (Table 8.4). Every year, they have identified the suitable beneficiaries and provided them with required quantity of good variety of seeds. However, it is only after 1995-96 onwards, fertilizers and pesticides have been provided. The table also depicts that total money spent so far on agricultural schemes, amounts Rs. 12,46,107 covering 8,502 beneficiaries. The details of beneficiaries and their villages could not be ascertained from the DDA records. Moreover, it has been mentioned that only three plain villages, namely Oringi, Purunaguma and Muduligudda have been benefited out of the supply of HYV seeds, fertilisers and pesticides during both *Rabi* and *Khariff* crops. However, the Micro project has proposed to supply the HYV seeds to the hilltop and cut off Didayis as these villages have not been supplied yet. (Annual Action Plan, 1999-2000 : 3-4).

Table 8.4 : Expenditure on Agriculture by DDA

Sl. No.	*Year*	*Expenditure in Rs.*	*No. of Beneficiaries*	*Name of the items*
1.	1986-87	57,000	50	Plough
2.	1987-88	71,323	117	-do-
3.	1988-89	67,145	1207	-do-
4.	1989-90	67,823	531	-do-
5.	1990-91	2,49,061	1017	-do-
6.	1991-92	2,03,524	1017	Crow bar, spade
7.	1992-93	76,800	322	-do-
8.	1993-94	1,52,944	1152	(Paddy, ragi, niger, maize, arhar, black gram)—*Khariff* crops. (Wheat and mustard)—*Rabi* crops
9.	1994-95	1,03,536	1120	(Paddy, arhar, ragi, ground nut, maize)—*Khariff* crops (Wheat, green gram and ground nut)—*Rabi* crops
10.	1995-96	62,117	617	Seeds as above, fertiliser, and pesticides
11.	1996-97	1,00,221	1052	-do-
12.	1997-98	5,605	200	-do-
13.	1998-99	29,008	340	-do-
	Total	12,46,107	8502	

Source : Annual Action Plan, 1994-95, DDA, Kudumulugumma.

Supply of improved agricultural implements

The DDA has supplied a number of improved varieties of agricultural implements to the beneficiary households of hill-top sector. It seems that agricultural implements have been provided to 267 beneficiaries of the hilltop villages in 1994-95 (Table 8.5). Villages of other sectors have not yet been supplied with the implements. The details of other beneficiaries, covering during the year of 1995-96 and 1996-97, has not been mentioned in the records of DDA, produced for this study. This indicates that there is a disproportional distribution of benefits. Hence, it has partially fulfilled requirements of the people.

Table 8.5 : Expenditure on Implements

Sl. No.	*Year*	*Expenditure (In Rs.)*	*No. of Beneficiaries*	*Name of Implements*	*Sector/ Village*	*Remarks*
1.	1994-95	29,140	267	Crow bar, spade and pick axe	Hill top	Rs.300 per set
2.	1995-96	21,420	255	pick axe		
3.	1996-97	45,155	200	crow bar, axe		
	Total	95,715	722			

Source : Annual Report, 1994-97, DDA, Kudumulugumma.

Land Development

In the Didayi area, there are a number of streams and *nallas.* Particularly in the region all these streams overflow and destroy the crops and cause soil erosion. It has been a perennial problem. In order to solve these problems, the Micro project has undertaken land development works with a view to ensure the following purposes :

(a) To stop soil erosion and conservation of soil.
(b) To harvest the rain water and thus raise the productivity.
(c) To encourage the traditional shifting cultivators *(Podu* farmers) and landless families to adopt settled agriculture by reclaiming, developing, and levelling the foothills.

After identification of the problems and the affected sites, the DDA has taken up following measures :

(a) Vegetative Bunding : In order to check soil erosion of the nearby hills, DDA decided to have planting of vetivera grasses in hilltop villages. It is a deep rooted grass which can grow in dry and waste land. The grass has the capability to multiply by slips due to its deep roots thus would help to check the soil erosion. Furthermore, it would also fulfil the requirement of the people since it is helpful for thatching.

However, not a single patch of vetivera plantation was noticed in the hilltop sector during the field study.

(b) Stone Bunding : This programme has been taken up to improve the land by bunding with stones. A contour stone wall of 2.25 ft to 3 ft wide (at cross-section) and of 2-3 ft height is made on the slope by collecting stones from the same field. This helps in both conserving the soil and moisture as well as increasing the productivity of the field by enlarging the effective area for cultivation. The work on contour and stonewall bunding has been noticed in the Bayapada and Suripada villages of hilltop sector during the field study. The villagers of these villages are seen working as the daily labourer. Each of the labourer has been getting Rs. 30 per day according to the prevailing wage rate of the State Government.

(c) Land Levelling/Terracing : Land levelling and terracing is being done near the newly constructed water harvesting structures, diversion weirs, cross bunds, dug-wells and the backyard kitchen garden of the Didayi households.

(d) Development of Drainage System : Existence of a number of perennial streams in the project area cause problem when overflow during rainy season. It washes away the loose soils from the fields, damaging the bunds. Many a times, these damage the standing crops. Therefore, the drainage system has been developed to allow the free flow of rain water.

(e) Construction of Gully Control Structure : In the foot-hills of *Kondakamberu* mountain ranges, many ridges and gullies have been formed due to un-bunded and sloppy terrain. Hence, different measures have been taken to control the gullies by constructing dry stone structures, plantation of vegetative grass like vetivera grass root systems.

(f) Stream Bank Erosion Control Measure : The Micro project has taken up plantation of *neem* tree, *chakunda* tree and *siali* creeper along the stream banks to check the soil erosion. However, no such trees have been noticed during the study.

(g) Avenue Plantation : An effort has been made to plant trees like *neem,* black berry, *chakunda,* etc. along the sides of the project roads connecting different Didayi villages under the scheme of avenue plantation. However, the scheme is only implemented in the plain village roads.

(h) Sisal Patch Plantation : In order to check the soil erosion of the deforested and degraded hills, Micro project has gone for Sisal plantation on those areas. Again in side of the patch plantation of sisal, various types of fruit bearing trees namely, jackfruit, mango, timber, etc. have also been planted. Noteworthy feature is that no such plantation area has been recorded during the field study.

The details of the expenditure on land development programme reveals that land development programme has been covering mostly the hilltop villages, namely Bayapada and Suripada. During the field-study in the hilltop sector, the work on contour bunding and stonewall bunding was found to be in progress at Suripada village and most of the labourers were from the nearby villages. In the last six years, the DDA has spent an amount of Rs. 1,92,560 on land development work, covering about 1537 acres of land belonging to 71 Didayi families of hilltop sector (Table 8.6 and Annual Reports). Furthermore, the villagers have understood the importance and benefit of the scheme. A hill villager of Bayapada named Dama Mudli of 35 years old was seen levelling his *beda* land (old *podu* patch) for terrace cultivation. It is learnt from the informants that the villagers follow the technique of terrace making to collect a good deal of water both from the perennial source (stream) and the rain water. However, the villages of other two sectors are yet to be benefited out of the scheme.

Table 8.6 : Land Development Expenditure

Sl. No.	Year	Expenditure in Rs.	Beneficiaries
1.	1992-93	1,29,754.00	53
2.	1993-94	13,147.00	6
3.	1998-99	49,659.00	12
	Total	1,92,560.00	71*

Note : (*) indicates the LD works in the fields.
Source : Annual Report, DDA, 1994-95, Kudumulugumma.

Agro-Forestry

Ago-forestry encompasses some components of agriculture, horticulture, soil conservation and forestry. It aims at maintaining the ecological balance while providing food security to the tribal population who have been practising shifting (*Podu*) cultivation on the hill slopes. The Agro-forestry has been found very effective to prevent *Podu* cultivation and ensures food supply, while conserving the water and soil. This is a sort of composite farming which involves simultaneous planting of annual and perennial crops, including fuel, fruit, fodder, oil, timber and house building materials to meet the basic requirements of the tribal population. However, compatibility of various plants identified to be grown in a particular region is to be carefully seen because these must match with the existing flora of the area both ecologically and culturally.

The DDA has not so far given adequate emphasis to this aspect, though they have proposed and approved expenditure outlay on Agro-forestry scheme based on SALT (Sloping Agricultural Land Technology). This has been tried out at Kasipur under the OTDP (Orissa Tribal Development Project). Under this project, Government of Orissa has issued *Pattas* rights to the beneficiaries so that participant households could claim their proportionate sharing benefit. Agro-forestry scheme based on SALT has also been strongly recommended for implementation in the adjoining area of *Bondo* Development Agency of Malkangiri district (Mahanty, 1996 : 52).

The proposed financial outlay for Agro-forestry made by DDA indicates an estimation of expenditure of Rs. 26,31,860 for the Agro-forestry scheme for the year 1995-96 and 1996-97 (Table 8.7). Furthermore, the expenditure sheet of DDA for the above period does not specify any such programme implementation in the area. However, the schemes like cashew plantation, sisal plantation, vegetative bunding, fencing and stone wall bunding, etc. have been carried out at different places under the other schemes like agriculture, horticulture and land development works. So far, the concept of 'composite farming' of Agro-forestry has not yet been implemented in the Didayi project area.

Table 8.7 : Outlay for Agro-Forestry on Different Components

Sl. No.	*Schemes*	*Cost in Rs. Per Unit*	*1995-96*		*1996-97*		*Total (in Rs.)*
			Physical (km)	*Finan-cial*	*Physical (km)*	*Finan-cial*	
1.	Misc tree plantation	7,746	20	1,54,920	40	3,09,840	4,64,760
2.	Cashew plantation	2,900	30	87,000	60	1,74,000	2,61,000
3.	Fruit tree plantation	5,574	10	55,740	20	1,11,440	1,67,180
4.	Annual cropping	500	40	20,000	80	40,000	60,000
5.	Sisal fencing	9,214	10	92,140	20	1,84,280	2,76,420
6.	Vetivera bunding	750	20	15,000	40	30,000	45,000
7.	Stone wall/ bunding	22,550	10	2,55,500	20	5,11,000	7,66,500
8.	Discontinuous trench	1,850	20	37,000	40	74,000	1,11,000
9.	Compost pits	100	100	10,000	200	20,000	30,000
10.	Stone wall fencing			1,50,000		3,00,000	4,50,000
	Total	51,184	260	877300 (33.33)	520	1754560 (66.66)	26,31,860 (100.00)

Note : Figures in bracket indicate percentage.
Source : Action Plan, 1994-99, DDA.

Irrigation

In order to improve irrigation facilities in the area, the DDA has taken steps by execution of Diversion weirs through RCC channels and constructing check dams at suitable locations. The Micro project has spent more than Rs. 34 lakh till 1997 on irrigation projects covering one hilltop village and two plain villages (Table 8.8). However, during field study, it has been observed that many of the check dams and WHS are in dilapidated condition and serves no purpose. It may be due to poor quality of construction and lack of periodic maintenance.

In spite of spending Rs. 14,11,908, the purpose has not been met. Even weirs diversion at many places are found to be damaged. During the field study in hilltop sector, a check dam has been noticed in Bayapada village. The check dam seems to have been constructed at a wrong site as the flow of the stream has taken a wrong diversion.

Table 8.8 : Details of Irrigation Projects

Sl. No.	Irrigation schemes	Year	Village	Beneficiaries	Expenditure in Rs.
1.	NK	1991-92	—	251	4,54,334
2.		1992-93	—	251	3,06,897
3.	Construction of Diversion Weirs	1993-94	—	251	3,91,371
4.	WHS	1996-97	Naring Jhola	251	1,98,853
5.	—	1997-98	—	—	—
6.	WHS	1998-99	Oringi & Muduliguda	—	60,453
	Total				Rs. 14,11,908

Source : Annual Action Plan, 1994-95, DDA, Kudumulugumma.

Animal Husbandry Schemes

The Didayis domesticate cattle, goat, sheep, pigs, poultry, dogs, cats etc. Even some of the wild animals and birds like mongoose, jungle fouls, parrot, etc. are also kept for consumption. Milking is not in the practice but beef is the most priority non-vegetarian food item. Cows are offered as bride price and also given to the married daughter in case of a marriage by service (*ghar jammai*). During the ceremonial rituals the cattle, pig, goat, sheep and poultry birds are offered for sacrificial purpose.

In a non-mechanized agrarian economy of the Didayi, livestock is the chief source of farming power. The bullocks and buffaloes are used for multi-purpose activities. Apart from economic benefits, those help to earn social rights and obligations which are involved in the agro-economy. The cattle are used for cultivation of lands, carriage of loads and harvesting of crops.

The goats, pigs, sheep and poultry birds are easy to maintain since they involve not much cost and serve as an important source of income. These also meet their food requirements. Pigs do the job of scavengers in the Didayi villages. All domesticated animals are kept with a view to obtain more economic benefits with less inputs and minimal maintenance cost as the environment provides them most of the requirements like fodder namely grass, straw, leaves, and left over cooked/uncooked foods.

Livestock Population

Livestock population has been collected from 12 study villages of three sectors of DDA (Table 8.9). It is evident from the table that a Didayi household possesses cattle 3.05 number on an average. This shows that the cattle are the economic backbone of the tribe in addition to the poultry which is 6.76 per household. In addition to cattle and poultry, goat and sheep

Table 8.9 : Livestock Population

Sl. No.	*Village*	*No. of HH*	*Cattle*	*Sheep*	*Goat*	*Pig*	*Poultry*
Plain sector							
1.	Oringi	122	324	78	97	108	615
2.	Purunagumma	37	136	32	45	72	325
Hill sector							
3.	Bayapada	37	117	12	38	60	295
4.	Suripada	22	97	07	28	43	268
5.	Gangapada	86	236	45	76	89	362
6.	Badakinyaguda	64	196	33	68	60	332
7.	Ghising *Beda*	59	173	28	56	74	317
Cut off Sector							
8.	Jantri	17	56	08	19	25	186
9.	Totaguda	16	71	13	21	—	178
10.	Disariguda	13	48	12	16	30	234
11.	Dabuguda	30	87	19	25	66	273
12.	Sanyasiguda	6	14	5	9	18	56
	Total	509	1555	292	498	645	3441
		(100)	(305.5)	(57.36)	(97.83)	(126.71)	(676.03)
	Average no. per HH		(3.05)	(0.57)	(0.97)	(1.26)	(6.76)

Note : Figures in bracket indicate percentage.

are kept by less number of families. Although, the number of pig per household is 1.26 but it is observed that 90 per cent Didayis keep pigs. Dogs are most commonly kept in all villages for hunting and safeguarding purpose.

Implementation of A.H. Scheme

Under this scheme, following programmes have been launched since 1990 for additional income generation of the Didayis :

(a) Supply of bullocks and plough.
(b) Rabbit rearing scheme and supply of ducks.
(c) Goatary.

(a) Plough and Bullock : Plough and bullocks are supplied to the villagers to assist in the cultivation practice so that it would enable them to enhance their agricultural production. The beneficiaries of the scheme stated that although they were very much anxious to avail the benefit of the scheme but in turn the scheme failed to fulfil their hopes and aspirations. They felt utter dissatisfaction owing to the fact that they had been supplied with diseased and substandard ones. Although, the scheme seems to be very promising one still could not be successful because of the environmental and the socio-cultural constraints as discussed subsequently (Chapter 9).

(b) Rabbit Rearing and Supply of Ducks : DDA had started Rabbit rearing programme in 1990-91 and Duck farming in 1994-95. The Micro project had spent Rs. 10,348 on the Rabbit rearing scheme benefiting only four beneficiaries (Table 8.10). The table also states that Ducks were supplied to 20 beneficiaries of cut off sector on 50 per cent subsidy and DDA has spent Rs. 26,000 on the Duck farm programme. However, these schemes have been discontinued owing to the poor response from the people.

(c) Goatary : The scheme has been implemented in 1998-99 in which there are 25 beneficiary families belonging to only two plain villages, viz. Purunaguma and Tikarpada. It is learnt that the people are not satisfied with the quality of supplied goats as these animals hardly survive. So, they kill these supplied goats for consumption rather than to generate further income. Hence, the scheme is found to be not encouraging one.

Animal husbandry scheme has been implemented since 1990 and the DDA has spent an amount of Rs. 4,86,296 on the scheme (Table 8.10). Furthermore, it is revealed from the table that most of the schemes like supply of plough and bullocks, rabbit rearing and the goatary are only limited to the three villages of plain sector, namely Oringi, Purunaguma and Muduliguda. Rest of the two villages, viz. Tikarpada and Chilipadar are found to be less benefited. Likewise, only in four out of 18 villages of hilltop sector and three out of 14 cut off villages, where the A.H. scheme operates. The scheme has benefited only 343 beneficiaries (26.69%) out of 1285 households. On an average, each beneficiary household has availed the benefit of Rs. 1418. However, the A.H. scheme did not give much gain to the people as discussed later (Chapter 9).

Table 8.10 : A.H. Scheme showing Expenditure Pattern (1990-1999)

Sl. No.	*Year*		*Expenditure in Rs.*	*Benefi-ciaries*	*Village*
1.	1990-91	Bullocks and Plough	89,838	104	Muduliguda, Oringi & Purunaguma
		Rabbit Breeding	10,348	04	-do-
2.	1991-92	Bullocks and Plough	1,13,105	60	-do-
3.	1992-93	-do-	4,000	20	-do-
4.	1993-94	-do-	50,000	20	-do-
5.	1994-95	-do-	50,000	20	Totaguda and Dabuguda (On 50% subsidy)
		Supply of Ducks	26,000	20	—
		Medicines and Vaccine	4,000	20	—
6.	1995-96	Bullocks and Plough	80,650	30	Bayapada, Suripada, Gangapada, Bataguda
		Supply of Medicine	15,000		
7.	1996-97	Bullocks and Plough	6,455	20	—
		Medicine	12,000	—	—
8.	1998-99	Goatary	25,000	25	Purunaguma, Tikarpada
	Total		4,86,396	343	

Source : Annual Action Plan, DDA, Kudumulugumma.

In the project area, there is only one Livestock Aid Centre (LAC) functioning at Jantri village and a Veterinary Dispensary at Kudumulgumma. These facilities are not adequate to meet the requirements of the Didayis of the hilltop and cut off area. The Livestock centre actually does not serve the purpose of the villagers since all the employees are highly irregular in their duties. During the field study not a single employee of LAC was noticed in Jantri village of cut off sector.

Fisheries

The Didayis of cut off sector are staying closer to the water line of the Machkund river, DDA has provided boats and fishing nets to them to increase their income sources. This programme has been taken by the Micro project as per the scheme approved by the Assistant Director of Fisheries, Malkangiri. Each unit of equipment (one boat and one fishing net) has been given to the persons from two households for joint fishing operation. During the field-study in the cut off villages, the boats are found to be in broken state. Even, the wooden planks of boats are being re-modified to the sleeping cots as recorded in Jantri and Totaguda village.

After observing the wreckage of boats, it was imperative to know the reasons thereof. From the opinion gathered, these are the following reasons for which the Boat scheme failed :

(a) It was expected that fishing activities would be made jointly, but in practice it was done individually.
(b) There is no repair facility available in the area and the people lack technical knowledge to repair the boat.
(c) It has also been noticed that due to conflict between two households, at times the boats get damaged as these lay un-attended at the water line.
(d) Sometimes, the submerged tree stumps in the reservoir water cause damage to the boats.

The scheme has been operating since 1991, benefiting 336 HH of cut off sector with an expenditure of Rs. 6,03,010 (Table 8.11). Noteworthy feature is that the total number of beneficiary households (336) exceeds the total number of households (302) of the cut off sector.

Furthermore, it has been noticed that the Didayis of the study villages mostly prefer the communal fishing. Individual members of the family also do fishing by their hand woven nets. They catch fish for domestic use. The area is inaccessible and they do not have any access to the market places except one ferry service that takes 10 hours to reach at Balimela ferry point. Now-a-days, the Bengali Refugees from Dandakaranya settlement colonies are rather seen deriving maximum benefits from the reservoir with their inherent fishing skill. Even, the Didayis are seen buying fish from them.

However, Didayis of Taberu, Nandimanjari and Maribeda villages which are located in the southern part (Map 8.1) of the cut off sector, are seen selling fish along with Bondas in the Onkadally weekly market which is about four to five hours walking distance from their villages. While exchanging views regarding fishing activity, it has been noticed that they seem to be more enthusiastic about the fishery programme of the DDA as it may help them in enhancing their income. But the DDA is yet to cover these villages.

Table 8.11 : Expenditure on Fisheries

Sl. No.	*Year*	*No. of boat and net (in Units)*	*Expen-diture (in Rs.)*	*Benefi-ciaries (in No.)*	*Village*
1.	1991-92	—	81,670	80	Sanyasiguda, Dabuguda
2.	1992-93	30	1,47,582	116	-do-
3.	1993-94	NA	92,148	60	-do-
4.	1994-95	10	67,700	20	Totaguda, Dabuguda
5.	1995-96	10	67,950	20	
6.	1996-97	10	nil		
7.	1997-98	NA	66,580	20	—
8.	1998-99	NA	79,380	20	Naringijhola, Ambli *beda*, Khajuriguda, Tikarpada and Orapader
	Total		6,03,010	336	

Note : NA means not available.
Source : Annual Action Plan, 1994-95, DDA.

Human Resource Development Scheme

A lot of work has been undertaken by DDA in order to improve human resource of the Didayi community. Under this scheme, emphasis has been given on their spread of education, imparting skill building training, health, hygiene and sanitation, etc.

Education

Education is a powerful means of removing disparities, discrimination and disabilities in society. It plays a vital role in the socio-economic profile of any group or community. A literate person is able to read, write, react and understand on his own and helps himself to enhance his economic status. Education is at the same time a potential instrument of individual development as well as social upliftment. In spite of various provisions and educational efforts made by the government so far, tribal population in general and Didayis in particular are far away from desired standards. 'Right to education' or 'Education for all' is still a distance vision which is yet to be achieved. As we are aware, a nation is judged not only by its economic, industrial or military power but by the well-being of their people in terms of their health, nutrition, education and living standard in addition to the factors like their opportunity to earn a fair reward for their labour, their ability to participate in the decision-making process that affects their lives.

Education plays a vital role in the socio-economic profile of any tribal group through learning only the tribal communities can maintain their ethnic identity, while avoiding social disintegration and becoming an active participant in the wider national life.

Successful implementation of the development programmes in the tribal areas can only be carried out through active involvement, understanding of the purpose as well as the appreciation of the details of the ongoing development schemes by the concerned tribal communities. It is only possible through the development of mass literacy of the tribal people.

The International Consultation Liaison Committee for Literacy has explained it as "Literacy is not the simple reading of a word or a set of associated symbols and sounds, but an act of critical understanding of men's situation in the world" (UNESCO, 1972). Accordingly, the literacy concept for the people has been categorized as under :

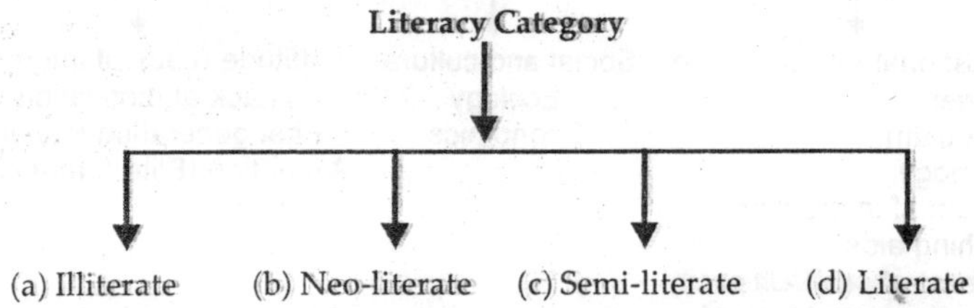

(a) Illiterate : A person who is unable to read and write. So to say, if he is ignorant and unlearned.

(b) Neo-literate : A person who can only do the signature and understand the verbal meaning of the words. He can also write the alphabets or few words.

(c) Semi-literate : He is the person who knows to read, write and understand the things in a rude manner. He is in the half-way of his learning achievement.

(d) Literate : A person is a literate if he is able to react, write and understand on his own.

Tribal Literacy Status

Scheduled Tribes in India constitute 9.5 per cent of the total population of the country (1991 census). There are more than 573 tribal groups with a varying range in their socio-cultural, economic and educational status. Literacy rate of STs since the year 1971 is steadily increasing from 11.3 per cent to 16.35 (1981) and 29.6 per cent (1991). In spite of various measures being adopted by the Central and State Governments, still their progress is in the rudimentary stage of development. Various research findings conclude that there are three sets of constraints, i.e. Internal, External, and Psychological factors affecting the educational participation, achievements and progress which is described in Fig. 8.2.

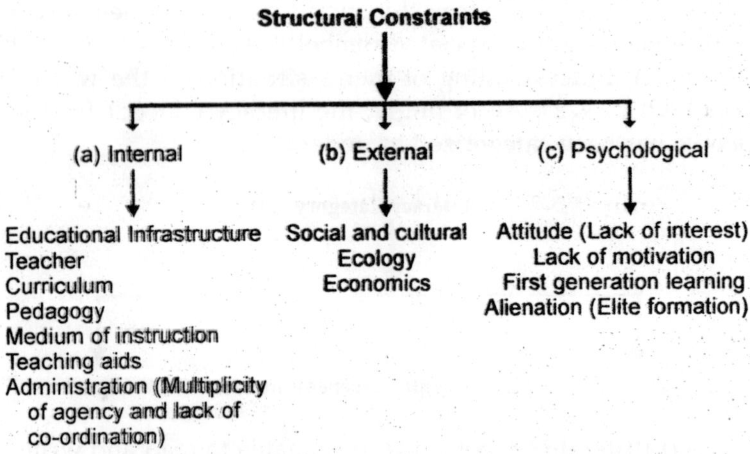

Fig. 8.2 : Structural Constraints in Tribal Education

Literacy Position : The total literacy rate in Orissa according to 1991 census is 49.09 per cent with a male literacy rate of 63.09 per cent and female literacy of 34.68 per cent. As against this the percentage of literacy in Malkangiri district is only 20.04 per cent out of which male and female percentages are 28.22 per cent and 11.69 per cent respectively. Whereas, the Scheduled Caste literacy rate constitutes 33.76 per cent out of which 46.09 per cent and 21.15 per cent are male and female respectively which shows that tribal population lack behind SCs in terms of literacy rate. Literacy rate of STs of Malkanigiri district is 6.77 per cent out of which male : 11.21 per cent and female : 2.32 per cent (Statistical Out-line, 1997 : 23-27). To have a comparative view on the literacy rate of General, STs and Didayi population, the percentage of literacy among General, STs, and Didayi population of Orissa, the data are shown Table 8.12.

The literacy rate has gone up to 30 per cent from 4 per cent by the end of 1998-99 since 1981 census (DDA Governor's Report, 1998-99 : 3). However, the field study conducted in 12 sample villages in 1999 indicates that the average literacy state in plain is 34.13 per cent, in hilltop 5.26 per cent and in cut off 14.28 per cent, thus average literacy state is found to be 15.93 per cent, accounting both the Neo-literate and the literate (Table 8.13) for the Didayi. It is evident from the table that in spite of all the disadvantages and constraints in the area, the Didayis have shown certain positive signs towards the efforts put in by DDA to spread literacy among them. The 'Neo-literate' who can put their signature is 9.49 per cent out of 15.93 per cent of total literate 334 Didayis (literate and neo-literate). However, at present 'Post Literacy Continuing Education' (PLCE) and 'Continuing of Education Programme' (CEP) are not in operation for Didayis. Although, the Micro Project claims that 2000 male and 1685 female Didayis have been benefited from the adult education programme and become literate even though the adult education scheme have been discontinued.

Table 8.12 : Literacy Rate among General, STs and Didayi Population (1971, 1981 and 1991)

Sl. No.	*Year*	*General (%)*	*Scheduled Tribes (%)*	*Didayi (%)*
1.	1971	29.45	11.30	0.8
2.	1981	36.23	16.35	3.2
3.	1991	49.09	22.31	30*

* DDA Governor's Report, 1998-99.

Source : Annual Report, 1995-96, Govt. of India, Ministry of Welfare, New Delhi, and Census of India, 1971-1981.

Table 8.13 : Average Literacy Status of Didayis (1998-99)

Sl. No.	*Sector*	*House-holds*	*Popu-lation*	*Neo-Literate*	*Literate*	*Illiterate*
1.	Plain	159	682	149 (21.9%)	84 (12.23%)	477 (65.6%)
2.	Hill	268	1120	26 (2.32%)	33 (2.94%)	1061 (94.7%)
3.	Cut off	82	291	24 (8.16%)	18 (6.12%)	252 (85.7%)
	Total	509	2096	199 (9.49 %)	135 (6.44%)	1790 (85.4%)

Note : Figures in bracket indicate percentage.

During the field-study in hill sector villages, many neo-literates have expressed their inclination for availing a chance to become literate. It has been noted that many neo-literates have put their signature in the medicine issue register, maintained by the *Gyanmandir* (a non-formal school being run by the micro project) teacher in Bayapada village for hilltop villages. Nearly, 50 people's signature has been collected (Annexture-II).

The spread of literacy can be attributed to the following efforts made by the Micro Project, since its inception :

(a) Adult Education Programme.
(b) Pre-School Education.
(c) Non-formal school.
(d) School run by Education Department.
(e) Special schools run by H & T Welfare Department.
(f) Child labour schools.

Pre-school Education

Formal education could not make much appreciable achievement both in the tribal and general areas due to the nature of rigid and form system. Therefore, it has been felt to provide pre-school education, based on the play-way method to create interest among tribal children about learning process in their own language. The need is being fulfilled by ICDS (Integrated Child Development Services) and Non-Formal schools, namely *Gyanmandir* by DDA.

ICDS is running eight Anganwadi centres which are located at Purunaguma, Oringi, Muduliguda, Bayapada, Khejuriguda, Totaguda, Orapadar, and Jantri. These centres are irregular in their functioning and operating with a lot of constraints. Their contribution towards pre-school teaching is found to be inadequate.

Non-Formal school (*Gyanmandir*) : DDA is running 10 *Gyanmandirs*, non-formal schools in the interior pockets of the hill and the cut off sectors. There is no *Gyanmandir* in plain villages since adequate number of formal schools run by Education Department are there. There are six *Gyanmandirs* in hilltop and four *Gyanmandirs* in cut off sector. During the field study four *Gyanmandirs* have been noticed, two in hilltop and two in cut off sectors respectively. On an average, 75.82 per cent children are getting benefited every year, according to the attendance registers, maintained at each *Gyanmandir* (Table 8.14). The table reveals that the girl children (36.81%) have also got equal opportunity to be enrolled in the non-formal school as of boys (39.01%). However, the maximum number of female children (44.15%) are from Bayapada of hilltop sector. Furthermore, it has been recorded that three girls from the same village are studying in Upper Primary classes in Sindhiguda Shevashram School.

The non-formal schools are established with a purpose to impart pre-school teaching to Didayi children who are the first generation learners before getting them enrolled in the formal schools of education, namely Sevashrams (residential school, Classes I - V). In *Gyanmandirs,* the children are acquainted with Oriya alphabets in addition to their mother tongue. The children are conditioned to a school environment where some interests for learning process is inculcated within them by providing an exposure to the outside world.

The *Gyanmandir* teachers are appointed by the DDA under the Multi Purpose Education Workers Scheme (MPEWS). Presently there are 10 MPEWSs, all of them are working with a salary of Rs. 750 per month. Most of them are under-matriculates and belonging to Didayi community. In addition to teaching in *Gyanmandirs,* MPEWSs also perform following duties in the respective areas:

(a) Act as interpreter.
(b) Assist in providing PDS.
(c) Assist in Postal distribution (since no post office operates in the sector).
(d) Pulse Polio programme.
(e) Assist in all government sponsored activities like election operation, Census survey, Health camp, etc.
(f) Assist in identifying beneficiaries and distribution of Micro project aids.
(g) Assist in identification of BPL & APL beneficiaries.
(h) As a representative from DDA and link between the villager and DDA.

The MPEWs are not able to devote adequate time for educational purpose and found to be dissatisfied for the unusual work-load with meagre salary.

Table 8.14 : State of Children in Gyanmandirs (1998-99)

Sl. No.	Village/ Sector	No.of children (In total)	No. of children enrolled (Age groups) (3-5)			Total No. of children (in enrolment) (5-8)			G. Total
			M	F	M	F	M	F	
Hill top									
1.	Bayapada	77	7	15	17	19	24	34	58
		(100)	(9.09)	(19.48)	(22.07)	(24.67)	(31.16)	(44.15)	(75.31)
2.	B. guda	73	22	18	11	05	33	23	56
		(100)	(30.13)	(24.65)	(15.06)	(6.84)	(45.19)	(31.49)	(76.68)
Cutoff									
3.	Jantri	15	01	02	05	03	06	05	11
		(100)	(6.66)	(13.33)	(33.33)	(20)	(40)	(33.33)	(73.33)
4.	Totaguda	17	03	01	05	04	08	05	13
		(100)	(17.64)	(5.88)	(29.41)	(23.52)	(47.05)	(29.4)	(76.47)
Total		182	33	36	38	31	71	67	138
		(100)	(18.13)	(19.78)	(20.87)	(17.03)	(39.01)	(36.81)	(75.82)

Note : Figures in bracket indicate percentage.

Primary Education

On completion of pre-school learning, the children are usually enrolled to the various Sevashrams with the consent of the parents. The Sevashrams accepting children from the hilltop and cut off sectors are as under :

Hilltop Children	Cut off Children
(a) Sindhiguda Sevashram	Andrapalli Sevashram
(b) Ras*Beda* Sevashram	Ras*Beda* Sevashram
(c) Kadamguda Sevashram	Panasput Sevashram
(d) Khairiput Sevashram	Khairiput Sevashram
(e) Residential school Kudumulugumma	Residential school Kudumulugumma

The number of children from *Gyanmandirs* joining Sevashrams from Hilltop sector is given in Table 8.15. The table states that out of 18 hill villages, 46 children of six *Gyanmandirs* have been enrolled in three Sevashrams since 1994. Furthermore, it indicates that dropout rate varies from 40 to 100 per cent in Sevashram schools among the newly admitted Didayi children, barring some years (1996 & 1999).

The number of enrollment in Sevashram school for Didayi children is gradually falling which shows a negative trend of educational achievement of *Gyanmandir* run by the DDA.

Table 8.15 : Year-wise Enrolment/Dropout of Hilltop Children in Sevashrams (1994-1999)

Name of Village	*Year*	*No. of Enrolment*	*Name of Sevashrarn*	*Dropout (in No.)*	*Retained (in No.)*
Bayapada	1994	5	Sindhiguda	2 (40)	3
	1995	5	Khairiput	5(100)	nil
	1996	2	Kadamguda	nil (0)	2
	1997	7	Sindhiguda	5 (71.43)	2
	1998	6	Kadamguda	5 (83.33)	1
	1999	5	Sindhiguda	nil (0)	5
Suripada	1995	1	Khairiput	1(100.0)	nil
	1996	2	Kadamguda	nil (0)	2
	1997	—	—	—	—
	1998	4	-do-	4 (100.00)	nil
	1999	4	Sindhiguda	nil (0)	4
Tlkarpada	1994	1	-do-	nil (0)	1
	1995-98	—	—	—	—
	1999	1	-do-	nil (0)	1
Ghising*Beda*	1996	2	Kadamguda	2 (100)	nil
	1997-98	—	—	—	—
	1999	1	-do-	nil (0)	1
	Total	46		24	22

Source : Records of Gyanmandir and Sevashrams.

The reasons of dropout gathered from the dropouts and their parents in the respective villages to know the nature of difficulties towards continuation of education are as follows :

(a) The children are hesitant to go to the residential schools located in the plain areas as they found themselves to adopt to the new environment. Hence, they expect a Sevashram in their locality.

(b) The restricted as well as confined environment of the residential schools do not make them feel like at home.

(c) The children feel uncomfortable while donning the school uniforms as they remain bare or put on scanty cloths in the villages. Uniforms may be supplied at *Gyanmandir* stage.

(d) They become home sick. They miss the parents as well as their staple food (gruel) and kins.

(e) As the children are also assisting their economic system, the parents need them in economic pursuit while continuing their education in the nearby school.

(f) *Gyanmandirs* are located at some selective villages, thus making it difficult for the children of other far off villages which are approximately 6-7 km away to attend the school.

(g) Mid-day meal system should be introduced in *Gyanmandirs* to attract the children.

(h) More educational kits and training aids should be supplied to inculcate interest within the children.

Upper Primary Education

There are 11 Upper Primary Schools of Education Department and one Kanyashram that is run by H & T Welfare Department for only girls, are located in the Project area. The details of the schools are given in Table 8.16.

Performance of these schools are found to be less than satisfactory, as most of them are functioning in very irregular manner. The reasons found during opinion survey are discussed as under :

(a) Most of the schools are functioning with only one teacher who has to collect the mid-day ration, transport it through hilly terrain and jungle trails and arrange for its cooking besides teaching. Hence, he remains

Table 8.16 : Details of Schools in the Project Area

Sl. No.	*Sector*	*Village*	*Type of school*
1.	Plain	Purunaguma	Girls High School (H & TRW DEPT)
2.		Muduliguda	U.P. School (Education Department)
3.		Chilipader	-do-
4.	Hilltop	Nilapari	-do-
5.		Damder*Beda*	-do-
6.		Muduliguda (B)	-do-
7.		Naringijhola	-do-
8.	Cutoff	Jantri	-do-
9.		Dabuguda	-do-
10.		Kodigandhi	-do-
11.		Orapader	-do-

mostly busy in mid-day meal activities than teaching. The teacher remains absent from school for about six to seven days to get the ration from the block office.

(b) Besides, he also remains absent for getting his salary and for complying various queries in connection with school education as well as administration.

(c) Almost all teachers keep their families away from the place of work. For any trouble in the family, they have to go home at a stretch 7 to 10 days.

(d) Sickness of their health are found to be major cause of most teachers. They remain absent on account of medical grounds also.

(e) Additional duties assigned to them like Election duty, census duty, survey duty, etc. also eats up about 15 to 20 days every year.

(f) The existence of the non-formal school, the child labour schools and other educational institutions in the same village, are creating confusion among the villagers to choose the particular educational institution for their children.

H & TRW Girls High School

The school was established in 1997 and situated at Purunaguma village about 2 km. distance from DDA office. The school has

160 boarders from different tribal groups like *Gadaba, Paraja,* Bhumia, *Rana,* Bonda, and Didayi. There are six Didayi girls from plain villages and hilltop villages studying in Vth and VIIth standard. Among them one girl of VIIth standard has been doing well and securing 3rd position in the class. The school Head Master is quite satisfied with the performance of the Didayi students.

This school is now running in a new building constructed for DDA office and their staff. The project Administrator, ITDA, has been asked by the Chairman, Collector of Malkangiri District to refund Rs. 4,00,000 to the special Officer DDA Kudumulugumma on this account so that they can construct their own building subsequently at a suitable location (Annual Report, DDA, 1998-99). The Kanyashram is the only Girls High School catering to the educational needs of Khairiput and Kudumulugumma Block area.

Child Labour School

Regarding importance of providing education to the child labour, the former Prime Minister, Mr. P.V. Narashimha Rao stated, "Child labour is a sad reality of our world. Wherever it is practised, it has to be eliminated introducing children to education, is clearly the means to achieve this objective" (*The Indian Express,* July 23, 1995 : 3).

Besides, non-formal schools and the education department schools, there are also child labour schools in the project area, providing education up to Vth standard in non-formal teaching method. They are situated in Purunaguma and Jantri of Plain and cut off sectors respectively. However, there are no child labour school functioning in the hilltop villages but steps are being taken to have one such school in the next session.

Purunaguma Child Labour School : Located in Kudumulugumma GP and Block at a distance of 2.3 km. from the DDA office. Total strength of the school is about 50. Staff position of the school is three in total. It has its own building with teaching aids. Out of 50 students, there are 12 girls. Most of the students are engaged in cattle grazing, collecting forest produce and also assisting their parents in various agricultural activities.

Jantri Child Labour School : The school is located at extreme far end of the cut off sector in Andrapalli GP of Kudumulugumma block. It consists of 52 students from nearby six villages out of which number of Didayi children are 12. There are one teacher and one helper managing the activities of the school. The school is functioning in a temporary *kuccha* home with thatched roof. There is neither adequate teaching staff nor a black-board available in the school.

Functioning of the Child Labour School

This school gives stipend of Rs. 100 to each student per month which is deposited in the pass book issued by the nearest post office. On completion of non-formal studies, the money is given to the child either to pursue higher studies or for self-employment purposes. Besides, they also get mid-day meal and educational kits. Therefore, more number of children are preferring to enroll in this school instead of other formal schools. Thus, the child labour schools have been a threat to Education Department schools as the parents are more interested in getting their children enrolled in child labour schools. Hence, the schools of Education Department of the area are facing acute shortage of students.

It is interesting to find that the children enrolled in child labour schools were neither daily labourers nor the bonded labourers but are mostly dropouts. It seems that during enrolment neither the child's occupational status nor the parent's status have been properly verified by the concerned staffs. The teacher on the other hand is facing threats from the villagers to give admission to children and for immediate release of the stipend money instead of depositing in pass books. The child labour schools have been blocking the further educational attainment of the children because they do not have necessary examinations for admission of their students in the formal High Schools and Colleges.

For secondary and college education the Didayi students are generally taking admission in the following educational institutions of the area :

(a)	H & TRW High school,	Mudulipada	Khairiput Block.
(b)	-do-	Govindpalli	Govindpalli Block
(c)	Government College,	Malkangiri	Malkangiri Block
(d)	Private college,	Kudumulugumma	Kudumulugumma Block

Generally, the Didayi boys from Plain sector villages like Mudulipada, Oringi and Purunaguma are only pursuing their studies in the above institutions as these are approachable and there is parental support. Didayi students of other two sectors, i.e. Hilltop and Cut off sectors are not pursuing their studies beyond Upper primary standard as the institutions, are quite far off (one to two days transit time each way) and lack of motivation for study.

Educational Status : Educational status indicates the achievements of the Micro Project as well as the educational achievement of Didayi students. Taking the levels of educational standards during the operation of educational schemes of DDA, the assessments would partially justify the educational fulfilment of the area. It is observed that during the decade 260 children have completed Upper Primary level, 65 students cleared Middle School level and 22 students are still in High School level. So far, only six students have been admitted in colleges and they are in +2 level. Not a single student has been a graduate yet not acquired any technical education.

In brief, the detailed achievement by DDA with regard to educational success is given in Table 8.17.

Table 8.17 : The Educational Status Achieved by Didayi Children

Sl.No.	*Educational Level*	*No. of students*
1.	Upper Primary level	260 children
2.	Middle Education	65
3.	High School	22
4.	College level	6

Source : Annual Action Plan, 1998, DDA.

It appears from Table 8.17 that DDA should take further steps to improve the educational status of the Didayi people particularly in cut off and hilltop sectors. This objective could be achieved if a non-formal school up to High school be instituted in this area.

Apart from school education, the DDA has opened opportunities for imparting job-oriented training programmes which would be discussed henceforth.

Job-oriented Skill-building Training Programmes

The Micro project has undertaken initiatives in providing skill-building training to Didayi youths for enhancement of their employment opportunity since 1995. The training in the following disciplinaries has been outlined :

(a) Tailoring
(b) Typing
(c) Driving
(d) Technical training.

(a) Tailoring : Generally, the boys and girls are now using stitched clothing, hence they have to depend on tailors staying outside the village. DDA observed that the Didayi people could save a substantial amount of money, if they are trained on tailoring. Keeping the idea in mind, they started conducting tailoring training programme at Kudumulugumma, DDA office premises by procuring six number of sewing machines and some pieces of cloth. DDA has also appointed one Master tailor belonging to General Caste.

In the first batch of the training programme six unmarried girls of Oringi and Purunaguma (Plain sector) got trained for a period of three months in 1998. Two of them have started their own tailoring shop in their respective houses. They are regularly receiving tailoring assignments for both boys and girls of Sevashrams and Kanyashrams.

In the second batch another six unmarried girls have been trained on tailoring to generate income as well as employment.

(b) Typing : The three Didayi youths of Oringi and Purunaguma (Plain sector) who have not passed the Graduation examination have been undertaken typing training with the assistance of DDA since 1997. Out of them two are working as clerks in District Collectorate (Table 8.18).

(c) Driving : Generally, the Didayi youths who have not got through the Matriculation examination, are undergoing the driving training at Similiguda of Koraput district. A total number of 10 Didayi youths have been trained in driving since 1998 (Table 8.18). All of them are employed as drivers in various private organizations.

(d) Technical Training : A 20 number of Under-matriculate Didayi boys have been ITI trained (Table 8.18). Among them six are working as Draughtsmen and Mechanics in various motor garages and private organizations.

Table 8.18 : The Skill Building Training for the Didayi Youths

Sl. No.	*No. of Youths*	*Qualifications*	*Training*	*Employment*
1.	10	Under-matric	Driving at Similiguda	Drivers
2.	20	-do-	ITI training	Draughtsman and Mechanics
3.	8	-do-	Training by DDA	MPEWs in DDA
4.	3	Under-graduate	Typing	Clerks in District Collectorate
Total	41			

Source : Action Plan, 1998, DDA.

The details of the expenditure incurred by the Micro project relating to educational facilities and skill building training to the Didayi children and youths, depict that an amount of Rs. 7,86,230 is spent (Table 8.19). It is evident from the table that the expenditure accounts for the cost of dress materials/uniforms, cost of supply of reading and writing materials to the students and the training costs. This also includes the cost of conducting the state and district level exhibition publicity such as : *Parav* 1997-98 (Koraput). AIR (Jeypore) and Adivasi Mela (Bhubaneswar) etc.

In an effort to bring them into mainstream, the DDA usually encourages them to participate in State and district level Tribal exhibitions or festivals. In the year 1998, DDA sponsored a troupe of members for participation in Tribal Exhibition, held at Bhubaneswar in the month of April. They exhibited dance programme in their specific costume and also brought carpets made by them for sale in the exhibition. In the exhibition, tribal groups of northern and southern Orissa also participated. It had the scope to meet and exchange views among different tribal members. This exposure had a great impact on the Didayi participants.

Table 8.19 : Expenditure on Education and Training

Sl. No.	*Year*	*Items*	*Amounts in Rs.*	*No. of Beneficiaries*
1.	1986-87	Education pgme	10,848	125 students
2.	1987-88	-do-	10,808	121
3.	1988-89	-do-	8,927	166
4.	1989-90	-do-	40,388	515
5.	1990-91	-do-	68,024	317
6.	1991-92	-do-	51,038	230
7.	1992-93	-do-	41,034	981
8.	1993-94	-do-	89,616	981
		and Driving	33,071	10
9.	1994-95	Education pgme	51,339	270
10.	1995-96	-do-	21,976	217
11.	1996-97	-do-	98,964	505
12.	1997-98	-do-	97,299	270
13.	1998-99	-do-	1,62,898	289
Total			7,86,230	4997 students including drop-outs at stages

Source : Annual Action Plan, DDA, 1994-98, Kudumulugumma.

However, the remuneration paid to 10 *Gyanmandir* teachers (MPEWs) at the rate of Rs. 750 per month amounting to Rs. 90,000 depending on the number of MPEWs employed in that year, is not included in the above expenditure. The said amount has been spent on educational programme over the last 13 years, providing facilities to 4,997 students since 1986.

Moreover, considering the number of students attaining various educational standards, the expenditure made by DDA seems to be not satisfactory. Out of 4,997 student beneficiaries, 260 have reached only Upper primary, 65 to M.E, 22 to High school and only 6 have gone to college. Rest all are dropouts or repeaters at different levels. Most of the promising students belong to plain sector villages only.

A resume of the annual educational action plan for the year 1999-2000 approved by governing body of DDA meeting held on 7 May, 1999 is placed as under :

(a)	Remuneration to 10 MPEWs (Rs. 900 PM x 12)	Rs.	1,29,600
(b)	Supply of dress, reading and writing materials for 400 pupils	Rs.	40,000
(c)	Exhibition and publicity State/district level exhibition, tribal dance/cultural programme	Rs.	10,000
	Total	Rs.	1,79,600

There is a proposal to increase the remuneration amount of teachers of *Gyanmandirs* (MPEWs) from Rs. 750 to Rs. 900PM, which is again inadequate considering their job assignments. Organizing the Didayi folk-dance at the District/State level exhibition, DDA has taken initiatives to bring the Didayi to the mainstream. Such exposure, helps to remove certain apprehensions in the minds of the tribal people which restrict them to mix with the mainstream population. They always suspect outsiders those who venture into their area or visit them. The suspicion created in their minds are basically due to lack of communication, i.e. language barrier, their way of life, carefree nature and lack of exposure to world. It has been found that 95 per cent villagers do not even possess a radio set. Wherever, a radio set is available, they use it indiscriminately without understanding the language of broadcast of any programme except some tribal programmes by the AIR Jeypore.

Health, Hygiene and Nutrition

Health and hygiene are the main components of the socio-economic profile of any community. One of the major challenges in the new millennium is to enhance the outlay for health, ensure its equitable distribution status, narrow the rural-urban gap and remove the shortcomings in delivering the health-care services at the community level both in rural, tribal and in urban areas where a sizeable population is living below the poverty line.

The PHC constitutes the backbone of the present rural health-care services in the country. The health-care services as has been envisaged in order to reach every nook and corner of the country are : (a) a health sub-centre for population of 5,000-8,000; (b) a primary health centre for 20,000 to 30,000; and (c) a community health centre for every four PHCs.

However, there is no health sub-centre located in the Didayi inhabited 37 villages under the Micro Project. There are PHCs located at Kudumulugumma and one at Khairiput which are looking after the medical needs of Didayis. The Didayis of plain sector avail the facility of PHC of Kudumulugumma and Khairiput. While the people of hilltop and cut off sector mostly depend on the local medicine men as most of the time additional PHCs located at Jodamba and Jantri of cut off sector remain closed. The medical facilities are grossly inadequate.

Medical Assistance by DDA

DDA has been providing immediate first-aid and certain essential medicines through the *Gyanmandir* teachers. During the field study it is found that a medicine issue-register being maintained by the *Gyanmandir* teacher (Annexure-II) and he also gives medicine whenever any Didayi patient approaches him. The medicines for the diseases like diarrhoea, malaria, headache, stomach pain, acne, skin diseases and first-aid for wounds, etc. are available for the villagers. It seems that they are developing faith towards the modern allopathic service. However, due to non-availability of the medical service within their reach, the Didayis still depend on their traditional magico-religious practitioners like village medicine man (*Dishari*) for day-to-day immediate requirements. Only on deterioration of the patient's condition, they rush to DDA who in turn take them to PHC, District Hospital and Medical College Hospitals, Berhampur if so required. The Micro project bears all the cost. The DDA has proposed to organize first-aid training for the *Disharis* and village midwives; so that, their services can be utilized in the villages of the hilltop and the cut off sectors.

During the field-study, a case has been recorded in Bayapada hill sector village. In an inter-family dispute, Sukri Muduli made a fatal attack on her brother-in-law with an arrow at 3 PM to save her husband while having a brawl between them over a land dispute. This attack with an arrow caused severe damage to the abdomen with 3-4 inch cuts. Even, the intestine of the individual was out when he was brought to DDA office for immediate medical treatment. Under the guidance of the project officer, the patient was shifted to District hospital, Koraput after first-aid at the Kudumulugumma PHC. Some of the villagers donated blood. His life was saved due to timely action and efforts taken by the villagers and the DDA.

General Health Status

A sample study has been conducted in 12 study villages of three sectors to find out the general health status of the Didayis. It has been found that out of total population of 2096, there are 987 males and 1109 females (Table 3.1). It indicates that for 1000 males, the female population is 1123, which is higher than national level Sex ratio (927).

Analyzing entries made in the Medicine Issue Register, it is found that 221 Malaria, 152 fever, 123 skin disease, 326 diarrhoea and 11 injury cases have been recorded during 1993-95. However, the Register is found to be not maintained in the successive years as shown in the (Annexure-II). Thus, out of the common diseases prevalent in the area, malaria is the most common fever which the Didayi frequently suffer from (Table 8.20). Since there is no mention of sex of the patients, it was not possible to analyze the data on sex line.

They are not aware of the preventive measures to be taken against it. Both the hilltop and cut off areas are hyper endemic for malaria. The environment itself has an effect on the vector borne parasitic disease called Malaria. A study undertaken by the Vector Control Research Centre, Jeypore run by IGMR, has indicated that the major breeding habitats of the vectors are slow streams, rivulets and paddy growing areas by terracing technique. The Didayi land conforms to the above terrain and a suitable parasitic breeding site. Besides, Didayis also suffer from snake bites and injury caused by wild animal attacks.

Table 8.20 : Common Diseases of Didayis (Number of cases reported)

Sl. No.	*Year*	*Malaria*	*Other fever*	*Diarrhoea*	*Skin diseases*	*Injury*
1.	1992-93	72	50	55	11	4
2.	1993-94	65	46	37	12	5
3.	1994-95	84	56	31	9	2
	Total	221	152	123	32	11

Source : Medicine issue registers, *Gyanmandirs*, DDA.

Health Programme

Under the health programme, the Micro project has been spending money on organizing the health camps, transport cost of the patients, expenses of attendants of the patients, medicines and on the dietary charges. Immunization programme on pulse polio has been carried out by the teachers of *Gyanmandirs* along with health department staffs. But the effectiveness of the programme is doubtful as the vaccine is required to be kept at a temperature between 2-8 degree centigrade to maintain its quality (*The Hindu*, 12 December, 1999). The polio vaccine vials are carried in person from the PHCs to the villages that involves 6 to 10 hours walk thus exposing the vaccine to higher temperature and ultimately making the Immunization programme to a failure one. The year-wise expenditure on health programme states about the total number of beneficiaries (6179) but at the same time has been found to be silent about the villages of the respective sector (Table 8.21).

Table 8.21 : Expenditure on Health Programme

Sl. No.	*Year*	*Expenditure (in Rs.)*	*No. of Beneficiaries*
1.	1988-89	513	404
2.	1989-90	10,098	250
3.	1990-91	24,474	850
4.	1991-92	22,760	768
5.	1992-93	25,932	220
6.	1993-94	31,339	1,185
7.	1994-95	20,817	835
8.	1995-96	38,582	405
9.	1996-97	32,744	504
10.	1997-98	703	7
11.	1998-99	64,013	751
	Total	2,74,975	6,179

Source : Annual Action Plan, 1998-99, DDA, Kudumulugumma.

The Health Department of Malkangiri district had carried out a survey on the general health status of all the PTGs of Malkangiri district in the year December 1999. On the basis of the survey being conducted in Didayi villages on 20th December, 1999, it has recorded a number of diseases and the cases, commonly prevalent in the areas. These are enlisted as follows :

(a) Malaria fever 677 cases
(b) Cough 358 -do-
(c) Diarrhoea 87 -do-
(d) Skin diseases 1487 -do-
(e) Tuberculosis 557 -do-
(f) Acute Respiratory Infection (AIR) 272 -do-
(g) Leprosy 33 -do-
(h) Eye diseases 37 -do-

From the above data, it is clear that maximum Didayis are suffering from skin diseases which is due to the poor sanitation conditions and residing nearer the Reservoir (cut off people). Next to it, more number of people are also suffering from Malaria fever and T.B. The cause of malaria is already discussed. It has been observed that the rising cases of T.B. is due to the chronic habit of smoking and liquor consumption.

Furthermore, the acute cases like Leprosy, ARI and Eye diseases are occurring owing to the poor nutritional and hygienic condition of the people. However, all these cases can be prevented with proper initiative steps taken by DDA and the Health Department. Further, a few suggestions have been discussed in Impact analysis (Chapter 9).

Nutrition of the Didayis

Nutrition is considered as one of the important measure of health. In fact, health and nutrition are the two sides of the same coin. For maintaining good health, necessary nutrition is required. The staple food is the *gruel*, prepared out of millet and rice. It is consumed along with *suan* rice, vegetables, leaves, soya beans and pulses. They rarely use oil and spices. Mostly, boiled and roasted items are consumed with little salt and chilli. They relish non-vegetarian food, as and when it is available. The food taken by Didayis are found to be rich in carbohydrates and proteins. A rough estimation by the researcher reveals that an ordinary meal provides 1700 calories of energy to an individual and about another 200-400 calories is available from fruits and liquors. But all of them do not get sufficient quantity of food even up to 2400 calories per day. They lack in fatty acids and the vitamins required for a healthy living. In all the 12 study villages, it has been noticed that 60-70 per cent of children are suffering from malnutrition which has caused enlarged spleen and bloating eyes (Photograph 8.1). The ICDS centres located in the hilltop and cut off sectors, are found to be non-functional. The DDA has proposed to open another 7 ICDS centres in these interior villages of the project area. Hence, the desired benefits targeted towards the weaker section of women and children by the ICDS, are not found to be availed of by 90 per cent of Didayis.

Hygiene and Sanitation

As far as personal hygiene is concerned, Didayis lack it too much. They neither brush their teeth nor take bath regularly.

They do not care to wash their hands before eating or after defecation. Occasionally, they use soap and oil, etc. But they do comb their hair. They do not cut nails. The day starts with country liquor, food and a *bidi* smoke. Therefore, they suffer from skin diseases like scabies, acne etc.

The Didayi houses do not have windows. So, there is no ventilation and adequate light inside the house. Normally, a house consists of two rooms and a veranda. Both the rooms are used for multi-purpose activities including cooking. The adjacent side area of the house is converted as animal sheds, with a kitchen garden at the backyard. In the side of the veranda, wooden hangings and earthen pots are kept for poultry birds for hatching purpose. Dogs, pigs and poultry birds are allowed freely in and around the house. They do not have any toilet and bathroom. The children defecate in the courtyards of the house which is cleaned by pigs and the dogs. Generally, the women clean the utensils and the clothes near the stream site. They also take bath there. However, they collect the drinking water from a different point (*chua*) of the stream.

Drinking Water

They generally prefer water from nearby running streams. They dig out a sandy patch near the water line of the running streams called a *Chua*, where the water gets accumulated after filtration through the sand and is used for drinking purpose. However, the bathing place and water collecting point for cooking and drinking purpose, are located separately.

In order to provide pure drinking water, Rural Water Supply Organisation (RWSO) has dug out tube-wells in all the three sectors. During the field study 24 tube-wells are recorded in the 12 study villages. It has been found that out of 24 tube-wells, nine are found to be out of order. Moreover, the people are found to be less bothered about the repair work of the tube-wells as they prefer *Chua* water and also the repair facility is not available. The DDA has made 16 cisterns at hilltop villages i.e. Bayapada, Suripada, Damdorbeda, Burlabandh, Bamiring and Karkaguda (Annual Action Plan, 1999-2000 : 3). Further, the details of the drinking water facilities are discussed in succeeding paragraphs.

Infrastructure Development

Under infrastructure development programme, DDA has carried out developmental schemes like providing drinking water, road construction and construction of non-formal school buildings (*Gyanmandirs*) in the project areas. These are described in subsequent manner.

Drinking Water Facility : DDA has spent Rs. 4,51,575, within a period of seven years for providing drinking water facilities in 2 plain and 12 hilltop villages (Table 8.22). It is also evident from the table that DDA has constructed 31 numbers of works that include open wells (6), cisterns (16) and open wells and tube-wells platforms (9) in plain and hilltop villages. The cut off villages are yet to be benefited of the drinking water programme of the Micro project. Furthermore, it can be stated that the open wells and the cisterns are found to be in disused state as has been noticed during the field study in Bayapada village of hilltop sector. Therefore, the people depend on the *chua* water which is not always found to be safe. Considering these factors, a few plausible suggestions are discussed in Impact analysis (Chapter 9).

Table 8.22 : Expenditure on Drinking Water Scheme (1992-1999)

Sl. No.	*Year*	*Amount Spent*	*Name of Items*	*No. of Works*	*Sectors*
1.	1992-93	96,661	Open wells	5	—
2.	1993-94	29,716	Platforms of Tube-well and openwell	4 & 1	—
3.	1994-95	49,731	Open well and Cisterns	1 & 2	Plain
4.	1995-96	1,22,327	Open wells and Platforms	4	—
5.	1996-97	1,39,004	Cisterns	6	Hilltop
6.	1997-98	nil	—	—	—
7.	1998-99	14,136	Cisterns	8	Bayapada and Suripada
Total		Rs. 4,51,575		31	

Road Communication

The communication is the vital factor for the socio-economic development of an area. The lack of the communication facilities in the project area has almost segregated the Didayis from the mainstream. This also acts as a major hindrance for implementation of the developmental activities.

In the project area, the plain sector 5 villages are connected with jeepable *katchha* roads from Kudumulugumma. Whereas, all the villages in the hilltop sectors are linked by foot tracks and jungle tracks through a reserve forest over the hills with 60 degree gradient. The villages of cut off sector are only connected with a motor boat-ferry service which takes about 6-10 hours one way from Chitrokonda Reservoir Ferry point. The Reservoir is about 30 km away from the DDA office Kudumulugumma. One can walk through the hilltop villages and go down the hill range to reach the cut off villages within two days.

There are many villages in the hill and cut off sector, seem to be untouched by the government officials other than some of the DDA staff. The researcher learnt that before her coming, no outsiders visited the villages like Badankiaguda and Ghisingbeda of hilltop sector. There has been a pre conceived idea that people of these villages are still dwelling in the rock caves but it is not true.

The Micro project has constructed a few link roads and developed the foot tracks to improve inter-connectivity between the hilltop villages. Some of link roads constructed by DDA are given below :

(a)	Oringi to base of the hill on way to Bayapada		3.5 Km	motorable road
(b)	Bayapada	Damdor*Beda*	5 km	Track
(c)	Bayapada	Naringijhola	6 km	-do-
(d)	Bataguda	Badankiaguda	4 km	-do-
(e)	Badankiaguda	Ghisingbeda	6 km	-do-
(f)	Suripada	Bataguda	3.5 km	-do-
(g)	Oringi	Pujariguda, Jantri	5 km	motorable road

The details of expenditure made by DDA on construction of roads/tracks and their maintenance in the area states that an amount of Rs. 37,29,184 has been spent for construction and maintenance of 8.5 km of *kachcha* motorable road in plain sector and 22.5 km of foot tracks in hilltop sector (Table 8.23). Furthermore, out of 14 cut off villages, construction of road has been undertaken only in Jantri village.

Table 8.23 : Expenditure on Road/Track Development by DDA

Sl. No.	*Year*	*Amount (in Rs.)*	*No. of Works*	*Type of Works*	*Length*
1.	1988-89	3,40,000	1	Constr. of roads	6 km
2.	1989-90	20,00,000	1	Constr. of roads	6 km
3.	1990-91	23,427	1	Constr. of road	1 km
4.	1991-92	78,025	1	-do-	2 km
5.	1992-93	nil	nil	nil	nil
6.	1993-94	3,94,262	2	-do-	3 km at two places
7.	1994-95	6,16,451	2	-do-	6 km Origni-Bayapada Bayapada-N. Jhola Bayapada-Damdor*Beda* *Pujari*guda-Oringi
8	1995-96	1,10,783	1	-do-	1 km Oringi-Bayapada
9.	1996-97	1,03,635	2	-do-	3 km at two places
10.	1997-98	nil	—	—	—
11.	1998-99	62,601	1	-do-	5 km Oringi-Purunaguma
	Total	37,29,184	12		33 km of roads/ tracks.

Source : (1) Governor's Report on Annual Administration of Scheduled areas in Orissa for 1998-99 for DDA.
(2) Annual Action Plan, 1994-98, DDA, Kudumulugumma.

In the year 1998-99, a survey has been carried out by State Government to construct a village road which would connect Oringi village of plain sector with Bayapada village of hilltop sector, situated at a height of 3500 ft. from the MSL. The proposed road has to pass through a patch of Reserved forest. According to the project officer of the DDA, the proposal has been fowarded to the concerned authority for obtaining necessary permission from the Forest department. Until and unless, necessary sanction comes through from the State/

Central Government, the road connecting a plain village to a hilltop village cannot be constructed. Till then, all the 18 villages of the hilltop sector will remain segregated and isolated from the mainstream. Once such road comes up, the villages of the cut off sector would be easily accessible in few hours.

Gyanmandir Construction

In the interior villages *Gyanmandirs* have been constructed for imparting non-formal education amongst the Didayis. The construction of *Gyanmandir* was in phased manner by the DDA. Initially, temporary structure was erected using materials like stone, mud and thatch and subsequently in 1999, the *Gyanmandirs* were made by bricks and cements due to allocation of funds by DDA. During the field study, two permanent cement constructed *Gyanamandir* buildings are found in two villages of Bayapada and Jantri. Expenditure on construction of *Gyanmandirs* depicts that an amount of Rs. 4,45,670 has been spent on construction of 10 *Gyanmandirs* since 1987 (Table 8.24). The table also reveals that about Rs. 44,500 have been utilized for each *Gyanmandir* building construction. However, the details of location and type of works against the expenditure done, are not mentioned in the reports.

Table 8.24 : Expenditure on Construction of Gyanmandir

Sl. No.	Year	Amount in Rs.	Physical No. of Construction
1.	1987-88	3,893	—
2.	1988-89	1,000	1
3.	1989-90	8,927	3
4.	1990-91	9,531	2
5.	1991-92	24,613	2
6.	1992-93	nil	—
7.	1993-94	18,862	1
8.	1994-95	57,132	7
9.	1995-96	2,94,346	6
10.	1996-97	nil	—
11.	1997-98	nil	—
12.	1998-99	27,366	2
	Total	Rs. 4,45,670	

Source : Annual Action Plan, DDA, 1994-99, Kudumulugumma.

Housing Scheme

In order to provide fireproof house to Didayis, DDA has purchased Corrugated Galvanized Sheets (CGS) and supplied to the needy villagers under the Housing scheme. For the purchase CGSs, the DRDA, Malkangiri provided the financial assistance. The scheme was implemented since 1994-95 for the needy families. During 1995-96, Rs. 4 lakhs had been proposed to be placed at the disposal of the Special officer to purchase and supply GCI sheets and GCI ridges etc. for 80 Didayi Households. Under the scheme, the beneficiaries are to collect the items and to contribute free labour for construction as per the house plan. It is proposed to cover 80 households in 1995-96 and 100 households in 1996-97. However, during the field study not a single CGI sheet roofed house has been noticed except the office building and the resting place for Didayis within the premises of DDA (Photograph 8.2). In stead, some villagers have been supplied with fire resistance tiles as has been learnt. According to the DDA expenditure sheet, only Rs. 5096 have been spent for purchase of CGI sheets in the year 1998-99. The details of the beneficiaries could not be ascertained.

The DDA has the purpose to electrify all the 37 villages under Rural Electrification Scheme as a measure to improve the quality of life of the Didayis. The necessity of electricity has also been felt by the villagers since they are deprived of viewing Television. However, the scheme is still in pipeline. Its implementation requires coordination between the State Electricity Board and the DDA.

Administration and Establishment

The Didayi Development Agency for the Didayi (Photograph 8.3), has a sanctioned staff strength of one special officer who is the executive head of the project, one welfare officer, one field attendant, one ameen, one chainman, one clerk-*cum*-accountant, two peons, and a driver (Photograph 8.4). The orgaized structure is depicted below :

Organisation of DDA

↓

Special Officer (Project Officer)

Office staff	Field staff
Clerk-*cum*-Accountant (1)	Welfare Officer (1)
Peons (2)	Field Attendant (1)
Driver (1)	Ameen (1)
Chainman (1)	

Special Officer is the head of the office and belongs to a senior Class I Cadre of Orissa Administrative Service. The Post of Welfare Officer and Clerk-*cum*-Accountant are lying vacant for more than one year. With the present staff position, it is difficult to look after the entire project area. Therefore, the Micro project has suggested for appointment of more number of field staff. The details of the new organization is discussed in impact analysis (Chapter 9).

In an interview the Special Officer expressed that the staff should be provided with basic amenities as they have to serve in such remote area where they are devoid of facilities. Adequate incentives must be given to them. Otherwise, no officer and other staff will be willing to serve in these areas. As a result, the vacancies will remain unfulfilled for a long time. At present, the DDA Project Officer is also having the additional charge of Bonda Development Agency which is an adjacent Micro Project where the Project Officer post is lying vacant for quite some time. Thus, the functioning of the project is being adversely affected.

The DDA is located approximately 100 km away from the district collectorate, Malkangiri. The Special Officer is required to visit the district collectorate at least twice a month. The vehicle is used for transportation of serious patients to District Hospital, Koraput which is around 120 km. away from Kudumulugumma. This explains the heavy amount of expenditure on the petrol and the vehicle repair head (Table 8.25). On the whole, the expenditure on establishment has been only 24.54 per cent of the total budget of DDA. It is more than the expenditure amount on Income Generation Scheme that accounts for 23.15 per cent (Figure 9.3 & Table 9.7).

Table 8.25 : Yearly Expenditure on Office Establishment by DDA

Sl. No.	*Year*	*Pay and Allowance*	*Office Contingency*	*Vehicle-repair & Petrol*	*Total (in Rs.)*
1.	1986-87	—	2,158	1,25,756	1,27,914
2.	1987-88	1,49,571	54,252	14,794	2,18,617
3.	1988-89	1,39,709	2,796	19,343	1,71,848
4.	1989-90	1,63,491	17,007	16,146	1,96,644
5.	1990-91	2,18,566	21,639	34,040	2,74,245
6.	1991-92	2,72,743	7,323	33,459	3,13,525
7.	1992-93	2,73,822	8,817	38,245	3,20,884
8.	1993-94	2,93,426	7,868	57,989	3,59,283
9.	1994-95	3,76,027	11,767	37,540	4,25,334
10.	1995-96	4,26,047	30,469	55,462	5,11,978
11.	1996-97	—	—	—	—
12.	1997-98	1,80,111	1,060	13,957	1,95,128
13.	1998-99	3,76,069	32,538*	21,089#	4,29,696
	Total	28,69,582	1,97,694	4,67,820	35,35,096

- • Rs. 3,00,000 have been paid towards ITDA loan obtained for Office establishment earlier in addition.

\# Hiring charge of a jeep as the office jeep is out of order.

Source : Annual Action Plan, DDA, Kudumulugumma.

Photograph 8.1 : Malnourished children of Gangapada Hilltop village

Photograph 8.2 : Resting place of Didayis at DDA Office

Photograph 8.3 : DDA Office at Kudumulugumma

Photograph 8.4 : Researcher with the Project Officer (DDA Office)

9

Impact Analysis of DDA

An assessment of impact of any programme has to be taken into account to the extent of success and failures achieved by various inputs of development invested in different sectors. The right approach to development requires to re-examine the ends and means of developments. An attempt has been made to assess the nature and efficacy of inputs and to find out the extent of success made by each and every programme and their limitations. It has also been examined how far a particular programme or scheme has been able to bring about sustainable, development in harmony with the Didayi society and culture.

Bhowmik (1994 : 17) illustrates a twin approach for tribal development which are : (1) Respect for cultural values of the tribals, and (2) Raising their level of living through the instrumentality of developmental measures in plans and projects or programmes initiated by the government and implemented by the organizations, as also getting actual response through realization of self-sufficiency will prove the extent of success.

A development programme generally consists of a number of time-bound and result oriented schemes. The tribal community is not to be treated as only grant-receiving beneficiaries but also co-partner in the development process. Human efforts and necessary material inputs together constitute the building block of development, hence these are to be utilized to achieve self-reliance after a few years of operation, so that they can develop on their own without any external help. Simultaneously favourable factors required for sustainable development are to be created during the development period.

In reference to Bhowmik (1994 : 17) and Gaikwad (1991 : 10-11) comprehensive guidelines have been drawn before analyzing the success of the impact study. The success of the development programmes mostly depends on the following seven factors :

(a) The plans and schemes being formulated should have clear and unbiased idea about the culture of the people as well as their history and tradition.
(b) Understanding the people with their cultural ethnicity, image profile, mental make-up and attitude to development. It needs to be people-oriented.
(c) The people's active participation in planning, execution and following up schemes.
(d) The ecological setting and environmental conditions of the area need be considered.
(e) Sustainable exploitation of local resources for maximizing advantage.
(f) Provision for changing the plan or welfare programme when becomes unsuitable or retards development.
(g) Seeking constructive suggestions from experts and the people in order to improve the implementation of plans and programmes.

Gaikwad states, "Today, a number of organisations both government and non-government are facing resistance from tribal beneficiaries as far as developmental schemes and programmes are concerned. Some of the reasons for this is the lack of understanding of people's cultural tradition, lack of good rapport with beneficiaries, inability to involve people in planning, implementation and following up schemes, lack of understanding their problems as perceived by them" (Gaikwad, 1991 : 10-11).

Having such criteria/parameter for assessment, there is a need to focus on the activities and temperaments of DDA officials. The success of developmental agency in fact depends upon the officials who operate them and the method of functioning of these agencies. Hence, information on these aspects is very essential for judging the effectiveness of the developmental agencies. Accordingly, the opinion of the respondents on their active involvement and implementation of the schemes has been taken into account.

The Didayi Development Agency (DDA) has been operating since 1986 and has taken up various schemes for development of the Didayi, one of the PTGs of Orissa. Over decade, it has been implementing a series of developmental programmes under three major heads as under :

I. Natural Resources Development and Family-Oriented Income Generation Scheme.
II. Human Resource Development Scheme.
III. Infrastructure Development Scheme.

Before we carry out an assessment on overall impact of various programmes relating to enhancement of the socio-economic status of the Didayi community, it will be prudent to analyze effectiveness of each and every scheme adopted by DDA over the period. The scheme-wise analysis in respect of their success or failure and the reasons thereof are vividly discussed and analyzed to arrive at both qualitative and quantitative assessment of each scheme, on the basis of developmental factors as has been enumerated earlier.

Impact of Development Programmes

One way of assessing the impacts of the developmental programmes is to compare the socio-economic status of the beneficiary households before and after the implementation of the programme in order to assess their income potentiality. For this purpose, scheme-wise evaluation has been carried out per beneficiary household (HH) and also an effort has been made to assess the overall impact on the community.

For the sake of convenience, the benefits out of the programme have been analyzed in terms of average annual income of each individual beneficiary household over the period of participation in the programme. The beneficiary HH have been categorized on the basis of the poverty line as per the norm of VIII Plan; Government of India (Table 4.5). Accordingly, beneficiaries in the income brackets of up to Rs. 3500 are designated Destitute, Rs. 3501-6400 as very very Poor, Rs. 6401-8500 as very Poor and Rs. 8501-11000 are Poor, which constitute the BPL category and above Rs. 11000 as APL category have been taken into account for scheme-wise analysis. During the field-study as many as 50 number of beneficiary households were recorded. Hence, these beneficiary households from the study villages have been surveyed on random basis to calculate the level of pre- and post-programme income. Based on the survey findings, the scheme-wise economic impact has been analyzed. Besides, to get a qualitative assessment of the schemes, an opinion survey has also been conducted covering all HH of the study area, so that the parameters for assessing the impacts can be analyzed in a better manner (Table 9.1). The findings of the opinion survey have been discussed along with analysis of various schemes implemented by DDA subsequently.

Natural Resources Development and Family Oriented Income Generating Schemes

Horticulture

DDA has spent an amount of Rs. 8,62,334 on horticulture scheme, providing vegetable mini kits, saplings of fruit trees, seeds and pesticides to 6212 beneficiaries during 1987-99. Out of which, 80 per cent of the beneficiaries belong to the plain villages, namely Oringi, Muduliguda, and Purunaguma, whereas other two plain villages such as Chilipadar and Tikarpada have not been benefited. In the hilltop sector, only Bayapada and Suripada have got their share (12%) out of 18 villages. In the cut off sector, Jantri and Totaguda only have been benefited (8%) and the rest 12 villages have not been benefited at all (Annual Action Plan 1994-97, p. 27). Thus, it is seen that equal attention by DDA has not been given while identifying the beneficiaries belonging to three sectors. Hence, there has been a growing dissatisfaction, bitter attitudes against the DDA as found in the opinion survey (Table 9.1). The survey

Table 9.1 : Opinion of Didayi Regarding Benefits from Income-Generating Scheme

Sl. No.	Sector	No.of HH	Awareness (%)	No. of Ben.HH	Opinion on Scheme: V. Good	Good	Satisfactory	Bad	Scheme to Continue: Yes	No
Horticulture										
1.	Plain	159	156 (98)	82 (100)	08 (9.76)	39 (47.56)	22 (26.83)	13 (15.85)	69 (84.1)	13 (15.9)
2.	Hilltop	266	32 (12)	12 (100)	—	—	4 (33.3)	8 (66.6)	4 (33.3)	8 (66.6)
3.	Cut off	82	7 (9)	9 (100)	—	1 (11.1)	3 (33.33)	5 (55.5)	4 (44.5)	5 (55.5)
Agriculture										
1.	Plain	159	154 (97)	88 (100)	12 (13.6)	18 (20.4)	27 (30.6)	31 (35.3)	57 (64.7)	31 (35.6)
2.	Hilltop	268	35 (13)	15 (100)	—	2 (13.3)	3 (20)	10 (66.7)	5 (33.3)	10 (66.6)
3.	Cut off	82	7 (8)	8 (100)	—	1 (12.5)	2 (25)	5 (62.5)	3 (37.5)	5 (62.5)
Animal Husbandry										
1.	Plain	159	156 (98)	89 (100)	6 (6.7)	13 (14.6)	3 (3.3)	66 (74.1)	22 (24.7)	67 (76.3)
2.	Hilltop	268	21 (8)	8 (100)	—	—	2 (25)	6 (75)	2 (25)	6 (75)
3.	Cut off	82	4 (5)	4 (100)	—	—	1 (5)	3 (75)	1 (1)	3 (75)
Fishery										
1.	Cut off	82	6 (7)	11 (100)	—	—	1 (9.1)	10 (90.9)	1 (9.1)	10 (90.9)

Note : Figures in bracket indicate percentage.

depicts that 98 per cent HH of plain, 12 per cent hilltop and only 09 per cent HH of cut off sector are aware of the scheme. Again out of 82 plain beneficiary HH, 69 (84.1%) have expressed their positive attitude towards the scheme whereas 13 (15.9%) have shown their dissatisfaction. The number of beneficiaries are found to be very insignificant in other two sectors (hilltop : 12% and cut off : 9%). Out of these beneficiaries, 23.4 per cent of hilltop and 44.5 per cent of cut off are found satisfied with the scheme. Whereas, 66.6 per cent hilltop and 55.5 per cent of cut off sectors are found to be not happy.

However, for the sake of convenience, the benefits out of the programme here have been analyzed in terms of average annual income of each individual beneficiary household over the periods participating in the programme. Table 9.2 indicates that the selection of beneficiaries constitutes 50 per cent destitute and 28 per cent very very poor category. Whereas, 16 per cent beneficiaries HH are from very poor and 4 per cent from poor category. Only 2 per cent of beneficiaries belong to APL category. However, it is evident from Table 9.2 that maximum number of beneficiaries (64%) are from plain sector, whereas 16 per cent HH from hilltop and 20 per cent are from cut off sector. It is observed that the respondent beneficiary had the annual income between Rs. 2000-8000 prior to their participation in the Horticulture scheme. The financial status of the beneficiary HH have been calculated and categorized as viz. (1) Up to Rs. 3500 (25% HH), (2) Rs. 3501-6400 (28% HH), (3) Rs. 6401-8500 (16% HH), (4) Rs. 8501-11000 (4% HH); and (5) above Rs. 11000 (2% HH).

On comparing with the pre and post-programme income state of the beneficiaries HH (Table 9.3), it is revealed that only 12 per cent of destitute group could enhance their income and enter into the very very poor group but the rest 88 per cent HH could not gain much out of the scheme and still remain in the destitute line. In the very very poor category, 14.2 per cent have moved to next higher income group and 114.28 per cent remained in the same bracket. From the very poor group 12.5 per cent succeeded to higher income bracket. However, beneficiaries from other two higher income groups have not shown any substantial gain. It is seen that 12 per cent beneficiaries of the lowest income groups have been benefited adequately from the scheme enabling them to upgrade their income status.

Table 9.2 : Annual Income of Beneficiaries Prior to Participation in Horticulture Scheme

Sl. No.	*Village*	*(In Rs.) Up to 3500*	*3501-6400*	*6401-8500*	*8501-11000*	*11000 and above*	*Total*
Plain Sector							
1.	Oringi	9(18)	6(12)	5(10)	1(2)	1(2)	22(44)
2.	Purunaguma	5(10)	3(6)	1(2)	1(2)	—	10(20)
							32(64)
Hilltop Sector							
3.	Bayapada	2(4)	2(4)	1(2)	—	—	5(10)
4.	Suripada	3(6)	—	—	—	—	3(6)
5.	Gangapada	—	—	—	—	—	—
6.	Badankiaguda	—	—	—	—	—	—
7.	Ghisingbeda	—	—	—	—	—	—
							8(16)
Cut off Sector							
8.	Jantri	2(4)	1(2)	1(2)	—	—	4(8)
9.	Totaguda	2(4)	2(4)	—	—	—	4(8)
10.	Sanyasiguda	2(4)	—	—	—	—	2(4)
11.	Dabuguda	—	—	—	—	—	—
12.	Dishariguda	—	—	—	—	—	—
							10(20)
	Total	25(50)	14(28)	8(16)	2(4)	I(2)	50(100)

Note : Figures in bracket indicate percentage.

Table 9.3 : Annual Additional Income of Beneficiaries in Post Programme Stage (Horticulure)

Sl. No.	*Annual income bracket (In Rs.)*	*No of B. HH*		*Net Growth*
		Pre	*Post .*	
1.	Up to 3,500	25 (100)	22 (88)	–3 (12)
2.	3,501-6,400	14 (100)	16 (114.2)	–2 (14.2)
3.	6,401-8,500	8 (100)	9 (112.5)	–1 (12.5)
4.	8,501-11,000	2(100)	2(100)	—
5.	Above 11,000	1(100)	1 (100)	—
	Total	50 (100)	50 (100)	6 (12)

Note : Figures in bracket indicate percentage.

The vegetable mini-kits being supplied by DDA under *Rabi* and *Kharif* programmes are well received by the plain villagers. However, they have become fully dependant on the DDA aids and assistance and expected to receive all kinds of inputs free of cost from DDA every time. This tendency has made them more dependant than ever and they do not pursue the scheme in subsequent years on their own. Thus, the scheme ultimately becomes non-sustainable. It is certainly not a positive sign in order to make them self-reliant and economically independent. Furthermore, it is found that the DDA has been providing assistance to the same beneficiaries in subsequent years. Looking at the nature of implementation, it is necessary that no beneficiaries may be entitled to benefits/inputs under a particular scheme not more than three times. An overall assessment indicates that the horticultural programme achieved success enabling 12 per cent beneficiaries HH to enhance their economic status.

The supply of HYV seeds, pesticides and supply of vegetable mini-kits, have encouraged the plain cultivator as indicated in Table 9.1. The supply of fruit saplings are found to be not well accepted by the villagers of three sectors as they have stated that already there are perennial fruit bearing trees, namely mango, jackfruit, tamarind, banana, etc. in their areas. The scheme has not been able to create enthusiasm amongst them due to long gestation period and lack of commercial viability. The cause of failure of the scheme, as has been ascertained due to the following reasons :

(a) The supply of seeds and vegetables mini-kits was made during festival and off season periods, when they are in a festive mood. The cultural factor seems to have been over-looked.
(b) They are supplied with seedlings and saplings, in which they do not have interest. Example : turmeric, ginger and fruit tree saplings.
(c) The cut off beneficiaries have to collect the seeds, other inputs and the pesticides from the project office and carry the loads which is found to be uneconomical

and inconvenient as the transportation charges (Bus and ferry) are more than the cost of input received by the HH. The hilltop beneficiaries have to carry these inputs on their heads which is inconvenient and instead they prefer to carry their day-to-day consumable items from Kudumulugumma market.

(d) Lack of knowledge in handling of pesticides and manure seems to be another factor for improper implementation of the scheme.

(e) The free distribution of the saplings, vegetable mini-kits and pesticides, is creating an indifferent attitude amongst them, as these items are found to be in a despondent state.

(f) It is learnt that some of them consume and sell or barter the given seedlings in the local market and get the essential items because it becomes an immediate gain for them. It is seen that turmeric and ginger seedlings are exchanged for their daily needs, viz. salt, edible oil, and kerosene.

(g) Lack of marketing facilities in hilltop and cut off sector villages, discourage the beneficiaries.

The success of any income generating scheme depends on the extent to which the forward and backward linkages of the schemes have been taken care of and depends on the various developmental factors as already been discussed. The following suggestions may be taken into consideration to ensure sustainable economic gains to the Didayi :

(a) People's Participation : People's voluntary participation and priorities are essential in selecting the type of fruit saplings and vegetable seeds. To make the programme more people oriented opinion of the people may be sought from time to time. This implies that people's active involvement in selecting varieties and types of seeds and saplings to suit their requirement is essential for the success of the programme.

(b) Timely Supply : The saplings, vegetable mini-kits and seedlings need to be supplied in right time and not during off seasons. Also care may be taken not to supply the items during the festival periods, when they do not like seriously to carry out the programme. Their cultural and traditional customs and practices have to be taken into account, while implementing the scheme.

(c) Nominal Charges : A nominal amounts to an extent of 10-20 per cent of the cost of the supplied items, may be charged to the beneficiaries instead of giving those free of cost. This would definitely minimize people's callousness and negligence towards the supplied items. On the other hand, it may create a sense of belonging to the given inputs.

(d) Motivation : The villagers may be motivated and educated about the benefit of the scheme. The village headman and the elderly respected persons are necessarily be associated with the development of nursery-*cum*-demonstration farm and activities so as to induce the fellow villagers.

(e) Soil Testing : After soil testing only the horticulturists should recommend required items and procedures to be followed by beneficiaries. An agricultural expert may be appointed and be given responsibilities to look after the agriculture and horticulture related schemes.

(f) Supply in Phased Manner : The items may be supplied in phased manner after assessing the progress on the utility of the previously supplied items.

(g) Marketing Facility : In the absence of assured marketing facilities the fruits and vegetables produced, are subjected to depressed sale. During the field study it has been observed that fruits and vegetables are sold in throwaway price, viz. Rs. 2 per dozen of ripe banana and Re. 1 per kg. papaya. There is no sub-centre of LAMPS of Kudumulugumma operating in hilltop and cut off sector to meet their credit-*cum*-marketing activities. Hence, opening of sub-centres (LAMPS) are needed particularly in inaccessible sectors to facilitate marketing.

Agriculture

Didayis were following traditional backward production technology with the age old agricultural tools and implements. Shifting cultivators used to grow mixed crops with traditional manure for three to four years consecutively. The settled cultivators used to get agriculture produces both during *Khariff* and *Rabi* season, because they were dependant on rain as well as perennial water sources for irrigation.

DDA has now given more emphasis to increase productivity by supplying advanced agricultural implements, HYV seeds, fertilizers and pesticides and improving irrigation facilities. Under the agriculture programme, a total amount of money, i.e. Rs. 13,41,822 has been spent in the last 13 years (Tables 8.4 and 8.5). However, it is seen that the programme has benefited only the plain Didayi. The monitoring of *Khariff* and *Rabi* programmes have been conducted under the guidance of the agricultural staffs and found to be very successful in these villages.

The opinion survey reveals that 97 per cent plain households are aware of the scheme whereas only 13 per cent hilltop and 8 per cent cut off households know about the scheme. Out of 88 (plain) beneficiaries 64.7 per cent are found satisfied and 35.3 per cent dissatisfied. Both hilltop and cut off Didayis are unhappy with the scheme (66.7 and 62.5% respectively).

However, out of 50 beneficiaries HH randomly surveyed for assessing economic impact of the Agriculture scheme, it is found that the beneficiaries constitute as : (1) destitute group (42%), (2) V.V. Poor (26%), (3) V. Poor (22%), and (4) Poor (10%) prior to their participation in the scheme (Table 9.4). Among these beneficiaries maximum are from plain sector (56%). Other two sectors constitute 22 per cent beneficiaries each. The economic status achieved by participating beneficiaries over a decade has been depicted in Table 9.5. It reveals that 76.1 per cent of Destitute beneficiaries have raised their income up to V.V. Poor status and only 24.9 per cent failed to improve. From the beneficiaries of V.V. Poor category, 46.15 per cent have succeeded to next income group of V. Poor. Rest 53.8 per cent remained in the same status line. Beneficiaries from V. poor and Poor group have shown 63.6 and 100 per cent success respectively. It is seen that 6 HH (12%) have been able to cross the poverty line, though 22 HH (44%) have used the scheme successfully to upgrade their financial status. However, maximum successful beneficiaries (90%) belong to plain sector including the HH those crossed the poverty line. Therefore, it seems that the Agriculture scheme has certainly made a positive impact on the beneficiaries.

Table 9.4 : Annual Income of Beneficiaries Prior to the Participation in Agriculture Scheme

Sl. No.	*Village*	*(In Rs.) Up to 3,500*	*3,501- 6,400*	*6,401- 8,500*	*8,501- 11,000*	*11,000 and above*	*Total B.HH*
Plain Sector							
1.	Oringi	7 (14)	5(10)	3(6)	1(2)	—	16(32)
2.	Purunaguma	6(12)	3(6)	2(4)	1(2)	—	12(24)
							28(56)
Hilltop Sector							
3.	Bayapada	3(6)	1(2)	1(2)	1(2)	—	6(12)
4.	Suripada	2(4)	2(4)	1(2)	—	—	5(10)
5.	Gangapada	—	—	—	—	—	—
6.	Badankiyaguda	—	—	—	—	—	—
7.	Ghisingbeda	—	—	—	—	—	—
							11(22)
Cut off Sector							
8.	Jantri	1(2)	1(2)	2(4)	1(2)	—	5(10)
9.	Totaguda	2(4)	1(2)	2(4)	1(2)	—	6(12)
10.	Sanyasiguda	—	—	—	—	—	—
11.	Dabuguda	—	—	—	—	—	—
12.	Disariguda	—	—	—	—	—	—
	Total	21(42)	13(26)	11(22)	5(10)	—	50(100)

Note : Figures indicate percentage in bracket.

Table 9.5 : Annual Additional Income of Beneficiaries in Post-Programme Stage (Agriculture)

Sl. No.	*Annual income bracket (In Rs.)*	*B. HH Pre*	*B. HH Post*	*Net Growth*
1.	Up to 3,500	21(100)	5(24.9)	-16(76.1)
2.	3,501-6,400	13(100)	7(53.3)	-6(46.15)
3.	6,401-8,500	11(100)	18(163.6)	+7(63.6)
4.	8,501-11,000	5(100)	14(280)	+9(180)
5.	Above 11,000	—	6(12)	+6 (12)
	Total	50(100)	50(100)	22(44)

Note : Figures in bracket indicate percentage.

The expenditure sheet of DDA reveals that the benefit given by DDA has been mostly enjoyed by villagers of plain sector. The supply of agriculture implements like crow bar, pick axe, spade and plough and bullocks are made to the villages of three sectors. This has created dissatisfaction among the villagers who have not received the benefit of the programme. Those who are benefited are also expressing their dissatisfaction over the quality of the bullocks and the agricultural implements.

In order to overcome the above shortcomings and to improve the efficacy of the programme, the following points may be taken into consideration :

(a) Supply of agricultural inputs like HYV seeds, pesticides, fertilisers, etc. should be made available to all willing individuals at a nominal price on cash payment and adequate training may be given to use the above items correctly and efficiently.

(b) The provision of the free supply of inputs may be stopped so as to create a sense of belonging to the beneficiaries.

(c) In every step of implementation people's involvement may be considered.

(d) Care may be taken to provide irrigation facilities to benefit the maximum number of villagers, taking into account of the facilities and the resource availability.

(e) It is necessary to provide diesel pumps to evolve irrigation facilities to all possible places and Didayis may be trained to repair these pump sets as and when the same go out of order. This facility has to be continued till electricity is provided to all areas.

(f) Shifting cultivators may be motivated to adopt terrace system of cultivation for which suitable slope lands be identified and permanent *pattas* be given to them, as they have been using these *podu* lands since generations for their livelihood.

(g) Though agro-forestry scheme has been proposed to adopt *podu* lands with the cooperation of the selected persons dividing them into different groups, no such endeavour has been taken up yet in this regard.

(h) At the time of providing the saplings and seedlings, the identification of the composition of the plants and trees, their suitability, compatibility with the present forest growths, requirement of the villagers for their day-to-day use, etc. are to be taken into account. The Didayi leaders of the three sectors may be involved from the very beginning stage : that is the selection of seedlings and saplings. So that, they can motivate their fellow villagers.

(i) Didayis should be motivated, guided and encouraged to adopt various means for improvement of their agricultural produce by establishment of demonstration farms at central locations, so that maximum people could visualize the importance of new schemes.

(j) Provision of free supply of implements, seeds, fertilisers, pesticides etc. may be discontinued as it has been found that the beneficiary households sell or barter these items to the traders for their needs. Some of them also consume the seeds whenever there is scarcity of food.

(k) Proper utilisation of local resources like broom grass, bamboo, lac, etc. be given priority. DWACRA scheme has been giving broom binding training to the Didayi women as there broom grasses are abundantly available in the surrounding forests. This broom cultivation may be taken up in order to reduce soil erosion in the hills. The present practice of planting vetivera grass which do not give much benefit may be replaced by the plantation of broom grass, since it is eco-friendly and economical also. Feasibility of broom cultivation on the old *podu* land which are abandoned after 3-4 crops for a couple of years may be encouraged. The broom grass cultivation will not only enhance their income but also make the degraded *podu* land more fertile.

Animal Husbandry Scheme

Animal husbandry schemes have been implemented to generate additional income for the beneficiary. The scheme which includes supply of plough and bullocks, rabbit rearing, goatary and supply of net and boat, have been launched since 1990. A sum of Rs. 4,86,396 has been spent on the programme, benefiting only 343 beneficiaries (26.69%) out of 1285 households. On an average, on each beneficiary, a sum of Rs. 1,418 has been spent on the scheme.

(a) Plough and Bullock

The beneficiaries of the scheme pointed out that in the beginning they were highly anxious and curious to avail the benefit of the scheme as they never had such opportunity ever before, but at last the scheme failed to fulfil their hopes and aspirations. The beneficiaries of the scheme felt utter dissatisfaction owing to the fact that they all had been supplied with diseased and substandard ones which succumbed to death in no time. So, these animals were required to be sold immediately or to be slaughtered as and when required. At the time of study it was found that 99 per cent of animals supplied through the scheme were not existing. Although the scheme seems to be very promising one, still could not be successful because of the environmental and socio-cultural constraints. Here are some noteworthy constraints, as discussed below.

One of the most interesting case is that Bhudha Angra of Oringi village was given a pair of bullocks and plough. When he found the deteriorating condition of the bullocks, he decided to sacrifice them in the purification ceremony of his diseased son.

Arjun Pangi of Bayapada village stated that he wanted goats as he had already a pair of plough and bullocks. He has only one acre of *beda* (old *podu* patch) land where his own plough and bullocks are serving the purpose. He is dependent mostly on his own agricultural implements for shifting cultivation. When he received the animals he sold them to meet the requirements during a police case as he subsequently got involved in a criminal case and was under police custody for five months.

The inadequate number of Veterinary Dispensaries and the LAC in these areas are also causing inconvenience to the villagers as they are unable to cater to the medical needs of the pet animals. One of the informant Sukra Bisoi of Jantri village states that he lost his one pair of bullocks due to the lack of the veterinary treatment in the cut off sector.

Also the opinion survey reveals that 96 per cent plain, 8 per cent hilltop and 5 per cent cut off Didayis are aware of the scheme (Table 9.1). The table also depicts that out of 89 plain beneficiary HHs only 22 (24.7%) have expressed their happiness whereas 67(76.3%) HHs have found to be not so enthusiastic about the scheme. Hence, it is evident from the above discussion that the supply of bullocks for farming purpose did not produce any desirable result.

(b) Rabbit Rearing and Duck Keeping Scheme

On trial basis, DDA started Rabbit breeding programme in 1990-91 and Duck farm programme in 1994-95 respectively. DDA had spent Rs. 10,348 on Rabbit rearing scheme, benefiting only four beneficiaries of plain sector. Ducks were supplied to 20 beneficiaries of cut off sector on 50 per cent subsidy. DDA had spent Rs. 26,000 on the duck farm programme. However, these schemes have been discontinued from the very next year of its operation because of the lack of positive response from the people.

(c) Goatary

Goatary scheme, has been implemented in 1998-99 in which there are 25 beneficiaries families belong to two plain villages only, viz. Purunaguma and Tikarpada. The beneficiaries have complained about the poor quality of the goats supplied to them. It is learnt that the Didayi prefer to kill the goats in festivals to consume the animal rather than to generate income. Hence, the scheme was also not able to have the positive impact on the beneficiaries.

(d) Fishery

Under Fishery scheme boats and nets have been given to 336 beneficiaries of cut off villages, amounting Rs. 6,03,010 since 1991. However, the scheme is found to be not enthusiastic for these people as it has been indicated in opinion survey (Table 9.1). The table reveals that 90.9 per cent cut off HHs have expressed their unhappiness about the scheme. Only 9.1 per cent beneficiary HHs have been benefited by an average additional amount of Rs. 150 annually. The main reasons, those can be attributed for this failure state are :

(a) Communal fishing is done for self-consumption but not for sale purpose.
(b) They do not relay on the nets supplied to them because of poor quality. They prefer to use their own nets and small dingy boat, made out of a log.
(c) No repair facility for damaged boats are available. Boats are now being used as cots and other household purposes.
(d) Lack of market facility for selling the fish.
(e) Didayis are seen buying fish from the Bengali-refugees of Dandakaranya Project who are found to be better in fishing trade.

Economic Impact

In order to know the economic outcome of the A.H. Scheme, 50 beneficiary HHs have been taken into account for this study. On analysis of 50 beneficiary HHs participating in the scheme on their economic status pertaining to pre- and post-participation it is found that only .2 per cent HHs have derived marginal economic gain from the scheme. Hence, it is obvious to state that A.H. Schemes did not give much gain to the people.

The following suggestions based on the observation in the field, may be considered for continuation or re-orientation of the A.H. Scheme :

(a) The supply of poor quality of indigenous type of animals do not create more enthusiasm among them as they are used to keep all types of animals before the introduction of the scheme.
(b) In case the DDA will decide to supply better quality of animals, it is necessary to examine whether this can survive and adopt to the new environment and whether the necessary veterinary services can be provided to meet the new situation.
(c) Before the continuation of the scheme the beneficiaries need to be properly motivated not to sacrifice the supplied animals during their religious rites and ceremonies.
(d) Fishing nets and boats may be supplied to those Didyis from other part of the cut off villages, namely, Taberu, Nandimanjiri, etc. who are in habit of catching and selling fish in Onkadally and Balimela markets. The items are to be provided in subsidized rates instead of free of cost to develop a sense of belongingness within them.
(e) The cut off Didayis are found to be in knowledge of weaving fishing nets. This potentiality may be exploited by providing them fishing thread. So that this would provide them a sustainable source of economic gain.

Human Resource Development Programmes

The Micro Project under HRD have carried out development programmes on education, skill building training, health-care and provision of drinking water facilities. The evaluation of the ongoing programmes is given below :

Education

The Project area have only 11 Upper Primary Schools and one Girl's High School, thus lacks adequate schooling facilities. Besides these, there are provision of non-formal education (*Gyanmandirs*) in 10 villages. Looking at the areas of DDA the facilities are found to be far from satisfactory. There is no schooling facilities even at a radius of three to four kilometres of 60 per cent villages in the hilltop and the cut off sectors. Therefore, the children of those villages remain away from both formal and non-formal educational institutions.

It would be inappropriate to ignore the financial aspects of the scheme. It has been found that a sum of Rs. 7,86,230 has been spent on education development and skill building training programmes since the year 1986 (Table 8.19). Even though, Micro project is claiming that the literacy rate has been increased up to 40 per cent from 2 per cent (Annual Action Plan, 1998-99, DDA), in reality it is found from the study that the literacy rate is only 15.93 per cent (Table 8.13). Table 8.13 reveals that out of 682 population of plain sector study villages, there are : 149 (21.9%) neo-literate, 84 (12.23%) literate and 477 (65.6%) illiterate. Whereas, out of 1,120 hilltop population, neo-literate 26 (2.32%), literate 33 (2.94%) and illiterate 1,061 (94.7%). In the cut off sector, out of 294 population, there are neo-literate 24 (8.16%), literate 18 (6.12%) and illiterate 252 (85.7%). Overall, out of the total population of 2096 of the 12 study villages literacy rate is : neo-literate 199 (9.49%), literate 135 (6.44%) and illiterate 1790 (85.4%).

Running of non-formal schools (*Gyanmandirs*) have been found to be an appreciable step taken by the DDA considering the increase in number of neo-literate villagers they have produced. It has been observed that there is a positive response in favour of non-formal schools. But it requires dedicated staff and focused attention by the DDA for better results as there has been more number of dropout cases as recorded in the study villages (Table 8.15). Since 1994, six *Gyanmandirs* of hilltop sector have sent 46 children to various Sevashrams/ Government primary schools. Out of which, almost 40 per cent have dropped out at various levels of education in lower primary standard. There are 13 boys and 9 girls presently continuing in schools. This accounts for only 7.78 per cent of the children in the enrolment strength of the *Gyanmandirs*. The dropout cases are very alarming in the context of achieving 100 per cent literacy.

The steps taken by DDA in providing skill building training to Didayi youths for enhancement of their employment opportunity has been well received by the youths of the plain villages. A total of 41 youths have undergone four different types of training and have found jobs as drivers, draftsman, MPEWS and clerks in both government and private sectors. (Table 8.18). The youths of hilltop and cut off sectors could not avail themselves such opportunities. Inaccessibility is the major distressing factor for them as it is causing hindrance to avail such types of skill building training programmes.

The following findings may be taken into consideration for improving education and skill building schemes in future :

(a) The parents as well as the students may be motivated and some incentive or prizes (in cash) be given to them after completion of the academic session.

(b) All students going out of their villages for higher studies may be given scholarship in a meeting organized in the village to encourage the students as well as to motivate the Didayi of the particular sector.

(c) DDA may provide study materials and uniforms to the non-formal schools as uniforms are being given to the students of the Sevashrams. So that, the children will get used to the modest dress pattern.

(d) *Gyanmandir* should be established in all Didayi villages, so that the children can have an access to the basic education and also start learning in their mother tongue before joining the formal educational institutions.

(e) *Gyanmandir* teachers may be given better salaries. DDA may provide incentives to those non-formal school teachers who have been motivating and sending maximum number of pupils for enrolment to the formal schools. Considering workload, more number of teachers are to be appointed.

(f) It has been found that a number of schools are found in those villages which are located on road side and have strategic locations but there is no school in the interior inaccessible pockets of the Project area. In order to avoid such multiplicity of schools in a particular village, they may be decentralized.

(g) To improve further the education activities in the Project area, proper coordination between the welfare department and education department with the DDA is highly necessary.

(h) Proper school buildings, teaching aids and resources should be provided on priority basis to the non-formal schools.

(i) Medium of instruction should be followed both in their mother tongue and Oriya in *Gyanmandirs*.

(j) Periodic supervision and surprise checks should be carried out to ensure better functioning of the *Gyanmadirs*.

(k) Job-oriented skill building training should be provided to more number of youths belonging to three sectors equiproportionally.

(l) Skill building training, viz. repairing of tube-wells, solar lights, bio-gas plant, sewing machine and diesel hand pumps, etc. may be organized in important GP headquarters.

Health, Hygiene and Nutrition

Health-care facilities are practically non-existent in the project area, except in Kudumulugumma of plain sector. Non-accessibility has been the cause of various health problems. Nutritional status of entire Didayi community has been found to be in a very poor state. There are only six sub-centres of ICDS which are inadequate to give the service to widespread 37 villages. Hence, 90 per cent of children are suffering from malnutrition as has been observed during field study. Functioning of ICDS in the project area is found to be less than satisfactory. Under the health programme, the Micro project has spent Rs. 2,74,975 covering 6179 beneficiaries over a period from 1987-1999 (Table 8.21). This expenditure have been incurred on organizing health camps, transport cost of patients, medicines and the dietary expenses. Also during Pulse Polio programme, the MPEWs assisted the health department staff in implementation of the programme in the area. However, the effectiveness of the programme seems to be doubtful because (a) the vaccine is required to be preserved at a temperature between 2-8 degree centigrade to maintain its quality; and (b) Freezing is not possible because there is no electricity in the area. The polio vaccine vials are carried by the staff from the PHCs of Kudumulugumma to the villages of hilltop and cut off sectors. It requires 6-10 hours walk to reach the targeted villages, thus exposure of the vaccine to higher temperature which makes it ineffective. DDA is providing free medicines to the people of the hilltop and the cut off sector through the MPEWs in absence of the health department staffs who do not have any health-care training, that may lead to further deterioration of the health of the patient.

Keeping the above existing health-care facilities in mind a few suggestions are made :

(a) For the improvement of the health programme, the health department should come forward to assist the DDA for better implementation of the programme.
(b) The health sub-centres should function in the hilltop and cut off sectors to look after the immediate medical needs of 32 villages.
(c) Health workers may be stationed at GP headquarters of hilltop and cut off sectors.
(d) Proposed eight (8) ICDS centres by DDA should come up on priority.
(e) Village midwife and village medicine man (*Dishari*) should be given necessary training to enable them to provide their services in a better manner.

(f) Malaria being the predominant disease in the project area, measures must be taken to prevent the same by educating the people. The Didayi do not use mosquito nets, nor do they take preventive care against malaria. This state of affair can be attributed to the illiteracy and lack of awareness of the people. However, during the field survey, a discussion with the people reveals that they are prepared to use the mosquito net if it will be made available by D.D.A. at concession rate. If these nets can be stitched by Didayis under the tailoring (Skill building) programme by DDA, it can serve both the ends better.

(g) Mass awareness programme on personal hygiene be conducted so that rampant skin diseases can be controlled.

Drinking Water

Safe drinking water is a must for healthy life. But it is seen that one of the acute problems is the shortage of safe drinking water in the study area, especially in the villages of hilltop and cut off sectors. Moreover, the streams and wells on which the villagers depend usually dry up in the summer season and whatever the water remains becomes dirty and contaminated. During the months of early monsoon the water becomes more contaminated. The tube-wells are mostly defunct and except the plain villagers, others are reluctant to use the water for drinking purposes. The cisterns are found to be in disused state. The people of hill and cut off villages are seen using the *chua* water from the stream for drinking purpose.

The DDA has spent Rs. 4,51,575 on constructing cisterns (16), open wells (6) and open well and tube-well platforms (9) in plain and hill top villages (Table 8.22). The cut off villages are yet to be benefited of the drinking water programme of the DDA. Therefore, some of plausible suggestions are made below to meet the requirement of drinking water of the tribal people :

(a) According to the advice of UNICEF, the *'chua'* (small water spring) need to be converted into low level well in order to obtain safe drinking water. Each village must have a tube-well. Open well and cisterns are found to be not useful and hence may be discontinued.

(b) The use of iron pipes in the tube-wells may be replaced by PVC pipes since the people do not like the smell of water.

(c) At least one person per village should be trained to repair the tube-wells (under skill building training) as and when they go out of order.

(d) The depth of the tube-wells be adequate so that even during summer they should not get dry as is the cases with many tube-wells at present.

(e) In addition to this, application of disinfectants is necessary.

Infrastructural Development

Infrastructure base is the main component of development of an area. Basically lack of road communication, electricity and institutional buildings are the main attributes for which the area under DDA can be designated as backward. Therefore, DDA has taken initiative to improve the communication by constructing the village roads. However, except plain villages no other villages are linked by motorable roads as we have discussed earlier. Hence, all the developmemal schemes so far implemented by the DDA have shown better results in this accessible plain sector. Under this programme DDA has carried out various construction works and incurred the expenditure (Table 9.6).

Table 9.6 indicates that DDA has given adequate emphasis on infrastructure development incurring 43.29 per cent expenditure of total utilized fund since its inception. 25.8 percentage, a major expenditure used for road and track construction which is an essential facet of development. However, it is sad to report that the construction work has been limited to only plain villages. There is no construction of village roads in other two sectors. They are still connected by tracks from the road heads or ferry points. More efforts are still required to be done in this sector with massive investments.

Table 9.6 : Expenditure on Infrastructure Development

Sl. No.	*Period*	*Scheme*	*Amount Rs.*	*Per cent out of total Expenditure Rs.1,44,04,777 (100%)*
1.	1988-99	Motorable road & track	37,29,184	25.8
2.	1987-99	Gyanmandir	4,45,670	3.09
3.	1993-99	Drinking water	4,51,575	3.1
4.	1992-99	Irrigation	14,11,908	9.8
5.	1998-99	Housing scheme	5,096	0.03
6.	1992-99	Land Development	1,92,560	1.33
	Total		62,35,983	(43.29)

Note : Figures in bracket indicate percentage.
Source : Annual Action Plan, 1988-99, Didayi Development Agency.

It is unfortunate to note that though they have been displaced for construction of the Machkund-Balimela electricity project, they have not received the benefit of energy supply till today. Thus, it is necessary to have road communication and electricity facilities in the area on priority basis.

The following points may be considered by the planners and policy-makers to improve the situation in the area :

(a) On priority basis necessary funds may be placed with DDA to connect the important hilltop villages with DDA office. DDA has already taken up this matter through the official channel but sanction is still awaited.

(b) This road will be the gateway to all villages of hill and cut off sectors with a bridge at Nilapari village.

(c) During field-study, the ferry boat has been found in overcrowded condition and even many villagers noticed to be stranded at various ferry stoppage points as they could not be accommodated. Therefore, frequency of the ferry services between Chitrokonda and Jantri may be increased.

(d) As far as possible, all villages be made accessible by jeep in hilltop and cut off sector.

(e) Construction of *Gyanmandir* buildings in all villages may be given priority.

(f) All works carried out should be of permanent nature instead of temporary nature where wastage rate is high due to perennial maintenance expenditure on temporary nature of works.
(g) Supply of electricity in the area should be given utmost priority.
(h) Solar lights should be provided at important common points of the villages. But to ensure that the solar lights remain serviceable, the MPEWs may be given in charge of it. The additional training for repair of the solar lights should be provided to the MPEWs or to the villagers under skill building training programme.

Office and Establishment

DDA has spent Rs. 35,35,096 on office establishment since its inception in 1986 till 1999. This expenditure includes pay and allowances, office contingency, POL and maintenance of the vehicles (Table 8.25). The staff position of the Micro project is found to be inadequate to cover the 37 villages, spread over 140 sq. km in three sectors, i.e. Plain, Hilltop and Cut off sectors. Even, for a dedicated staff, it is beyond their physical capability to visit all the villages for supervision of the developmental works at least once in six months as has been discussed earlier. Hence, DDA has proposed to increase its staff position from 9 to 20 and the new staff along with the existing members is given in Fig. 9.1. It is clear from the Fig. 9.1 that the Micro project has proposed one additional senior Clerk for Head-quarter and ten field staff for better administration of the project area. Furthermore, the DDA has mentioned about the specification of the additional staff to be stationed at hilltop and cut off sectors respectively (Fig. 9.2). It seems obvious that the staff posted in respective sectors would be responsible for all the developmental works of the people. As a result, there would be a better coordination between people and the officials. Hence, the programme will be more people-oriented.

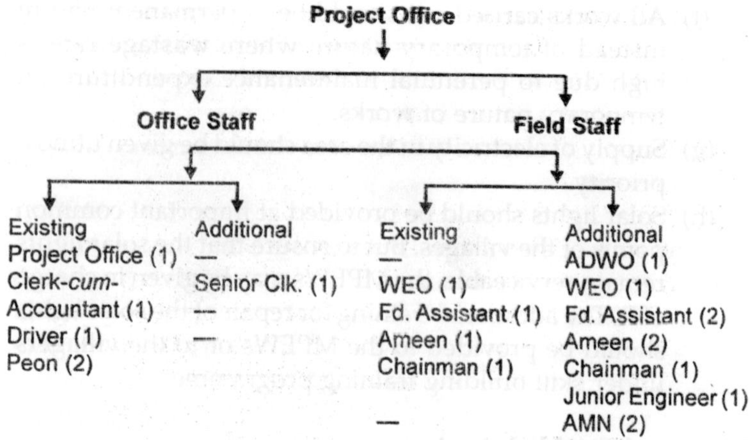

Fig. 9.1 : Restructuring of DDA

Project Officer

Office & Headquarters Staff (Including for Plain Sector)	*Hilltop Sector Staff*	*Cut off Sector Staff*
A.D.W.O.—One	W.E.O.—One	W.E.O.—One
Fd. Asst.—One	Fd. Asst.—One#	Fd. Asst.—One#
Amin—One	A.N.M.—One*	A.N.M.—One*
Chainman—Two	Peon—One	Peon—One
Jr. Engr.—One		
Sr. Clerk—One	# Fd.—Asst. will be trained in all aspects.	
Clk.-*cum*-Acct.—One	* ANM is not authorized to plain sector as a PHC is located.	
Peon—Two		

Fig. 9.2 : Proposed Staff Disposition in Project Area.

Overall Pattern of Expenditure

DDA has spent a total amount of Rs.1,44,04,777 since its inception in 1986 to 1999 on various heads (Table 9.7). It has been found that there is a variation regarding the expenditure amount shown in the Annual expenditure sheet by DDA

(Annexure-I) and statement of utilisation of funds during the period given in Annual Action Plan for DDA 1994-95, published by THRTI, Bhubaneswar. Out of the total expenditure, only 23.15 per cent has been spent on income generation scheme which is not adequate. Whereas, only 7.99 per cent has been given for HRD which is a very meagre amount as regards to socio-economic development of a PTG. Even though, expenditure on education is more than six per cent, still it is higher than the expenditure made for health (1.9%). If the construction of *Gyanmandir* is incorporated under education head, the total expenditure amounts to be 9.11 per cent. Thus, health sector needs more attention. On infrastructure development, though maximum amount of 43.29 per cent has been spent, except the plain villages namely, Oringi, Purunaguma and Muduliguda, rest other 34 villages are found to be still in inaccessible condition. True to the fact that inaccessibility is found to be a major hindrance for them as benefits of various schemes of DDA hardly reach them. However, an adequate amount of 24.54 per cent has been spent on office and establishment besides a miscellaneous expenditure of 1.01 per cent (Fig. 9.3).

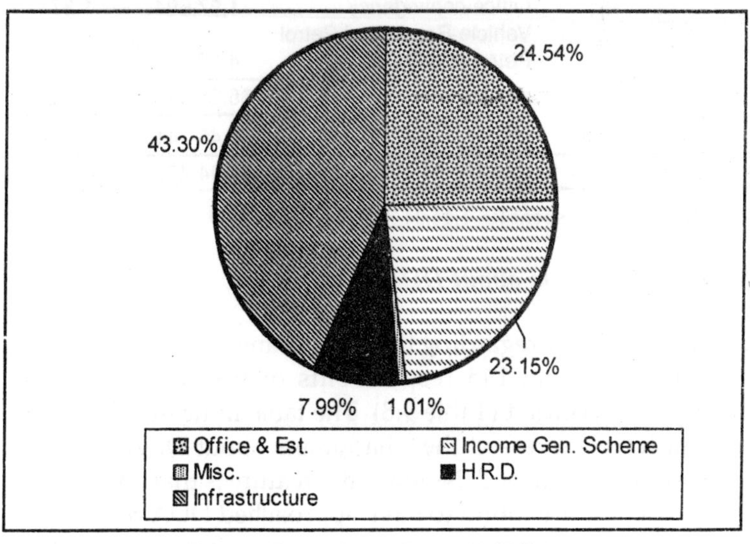

Fig. 9.3 : Expenditure Pattern of DDA.

Table 9.7 : Expenditure Pattern of DDA on Various Heads since its Inception (1986-1999)

Sl. No.	*Heads*	*Sub-Heads*	*Amount in Rs.*	*Percentage (%)*
1.	Income Generation	Horticulture	9,04,514	6.2
		Agriculture	13,41,822	9.3
		Animal Husbandry	4,86,396	3.37
		Fishery	6,03,010	4.1
			3,35,742	23.25
2.	HRD	Education and Skill building	7,86,230	5.45
		Salary of M.P.E.W.	90,000	0.62
		Health	2,74,975	1.9
			11,51,205	7.99
3.	Infrastructure	Road and Track	37,29,184	25.8
		Gyanmandir	4,45,670	3.04
		Drinking water	4,51,575	3.1
		Irrigation	14,11,908	9.8
		Housing	5,096	0.03
		Land development	1,92,560	1.33
			62,35,993	43.29
4.	Office Est.	Pay and Allowance	28,69,582	19.12
		Office contingency	1,97,694	1.37
		Vehicle Repair and Petrol		
		Petrol and Oil for Vehicle	4,67,820	3.24
			35,35,096	24.54
5.	Miscellaneous		1,46,741	1.01
	Total		1,44,04,777	100.00

Note : Total amount spent Rs. 1,44,04,777.

Response of People about DDA

An opinion survey regarding the functioning of DDA, has been carried out among 145 respondents of three sectors and findings are recorded (Table 9.8). The table indicates that 90.3 per cent have expressed their happiness about DDA while a very few are dissatisfied. Noteworthy feature is that about 95.8 per cent people are found to have approached DDA regarding their problems which indicates a good rapport between the

DDA and the Didayi. Out of them, 65.5 per cent have claimed to receive positive response From DDA in solving their problems, whereas 28.27 per cent people have expressed their negative opinion regarding DDA's response.

Almost all of them want DDA to continue and work for them. On asking about their expectation from DDA, all of them have expressed that they want assistance in income-generation, health-care, skill-building training, development of road communication and improvement in ferry service for cut off sector. However, they do not want to take any monetary assistance on loan basis from DDA with an apprehension that they may not able to repay the amount.

Table 9.8 : People's Opinion about DDA (No. of Respondents : 145)

Sl. No.	*Functional aspect*	*Yes*	*No*	*Can't say*
1.	Is DDA beneficial to you?	131 (90.3)	9 (6.2)	5 (3 5)
2.	Have you approached DDA for any problem?	139 (95.8)	4 (2.75)	2 (1.3)
3.	Had DDA responded positively?	95 (65.5)	41 (28.27)	9 (6.2)
4.	Should DDA continue?	141 (97.24)	—	4 (2.75)
5.	Your expectation from DDA?			
	(a) Assistance in Income generating Scheme	143 (98.62)	—	4 (2.75)
	(b) Financial assistance as loans	—	96 (66.2)	49 (33.79)
	(c) Skill building training	143 (98.62)	—	2 (1.3)
	(d) Educational assistance	143 (98.62)	—	2 (1.3)
	(e) Medical care	120 (82.75)	25 (17.24)	—
	(f) Improve road facilities	145 (100)	—	—
	(g) Increase in Ferry service	50 (34.48)	—	—

Note : Figures in bracket indicate percentage.

Overall Impact

In the present study an endeavour has been made to analyze the success and the failure of various programmes and schemes implemented by DDA in the light of seven (parameters) factors affecting development as discussed earlier. It has been realized that before tailoring the developmental schemes, the Micro Project should study their cultural pattern, environmental factors and socio-economic condition, etc. those are based on the built-in mechanism of change and development principle related to the existence of the community. Simultaneously, the 'Top-down' approach has to be substituted with the 'Bottom-up' approach in the planning process. While, analyzing the membership pattern of GB of DDA, it is seen that, Sani Angra (plain village) the president of the Didayi community, is the only tribal representative. Whereas there is no representation from the hilltop and cut off sector villages in the Governing Body. This could be one of the reasons for negligence of these two sectors. The role of the tribal leader is very essential in facilitating their community participation in the development programme. The tribal leaders have to play their role effectively and to involve themselves at all stages of the programme. For this, they need to be made aware of all aspects of the programme to be implemented in their villages. After all, the success of any development activity depends on the collaborative efforts of the planners, implementers and beneficiaries. Therefore, proportionate representation of Didayis from all three sectors in the GB of DDA is essentially desirable.

Although, it is difficult to arrive at a complete and fully reliable estimation, it would not be exaggerated to state that the enhanced socio-economic status of the Didayi has brought about some definite changes in their lifestyle and also in their cultural milieu. From the overall point of view, it can be said that the development process has certain impact on the economic condition of people which in due course of time has indirectly molded their social life. Not only, there is a mere increase in income level but also a rise in the standard of living.

Due to impact of Micro project, Didayis express eagerness for integration into mainstream as evidenced from their changes in traditional attitude of marriage, religious practice and dress pattern, etc. as has been discussed earlier. It has been observed during the study that they have become more conscious about their dress, hair style, mannerism, and have developed some hope and aspirations for themselves as well as for their future generations. They have expressed that they want their children (both son and daughter) to be educated at least up to X standard and find a job of a teacher, police man or as driver, etc.

There are 32 and 19 number of unmarried girls between the age group 20-40 years. This has been recorded from plain and hilltop study villages respectively to show their growing aspirations as a result of developmental impact. They now prefer to marry the boys of plain sector because they are relatively developed in terms of lifestyle and living standard. On the contrary, the plain youths with a little education and exposure to modernity, are seeking alliance with the educated working girls irrespective of tribal classes. It is also observed in the plain sector that the boys hesitate to marry girls of plain sector because they are considered smart and unwilling to do arduous domestic chores. It is because the girls are more exposed to urban way of life and have earning ability through tailoring, broom binding, spice grinding, etc. All these aspirations and capabilities are the contribution of development schemes. Such impact has been often viewed negatively because the girls ultimately do not find the groom from plain area and are bound to remain spinsters.

It is obvious that the plain villagers reflect the greatest socio-economic impact in comparison to the other two sectors. Because maximum (95%) beneficiaries are from plain sector, as a result, only marginal (12%) households have crossed the poverty line (Table 9.5). Not only, income generation scheme but also other developmental schemes such as HRD has benefited the people. Because of the scheme, 41 youths have undergone skill building training and also been employed successfully. In addition to that, the scheme has produced 34.13 per cent literates which is certainly praiseworthy.

The infrastructure facilities have benefited the plain Didayi to a greater extent. Only the plain villages are interconnected with the motorable roads whereas rest 32 villages of the Micro Project are not connected by road.

Except in plain villeges, drinking water facilities are not existing in 50 per cent villages of hilltop and cut off sectors. About 90 per cent of the tube-wells are found in disused state because of poor maintenance and rusty water.

Though, the tribe is displaced for a Hydro-electric Project, it is irony that they are still deprived of electricity. None of the villages in the project area has electricity.

Due to frequent contact with the outsiders as well as the employees of Micro project, the plain villagers are more exposed to the outside world. As a result, there has been a change in their attitude which is indirectly affecting their society and social customs as has been earlier discussed. Even the traditional youth dormitory has lost its significance in the plain villages. A case of religious conversion adopting Christianity by a family has come to notice in one of the plain village, Oringi due to lure of additional pecuniary benefits. This family has been excommunicated. The Plain Didayis are more influenced by Hindu religion and celebrate almost all Hindu festivals in addition to their own traditional worship.

The Hill dwellers show a very negligible state of growth. A portfolio of the socio-economic cultural aspects of the hill Didayis states that despite the sustained planned efforts and introduction of several schemes, the result at the ground level are far from satisfactory. Because of the inaccessibility, lack of conscientization, education and awareness, etc. the desirable kind of development is yet to be achieved in a fullfledged manner.

Cut off Didayis have lost their cultural identity because of the displacement and rehabilitation. Some of them have even forgotten their own dialect as observed during field study. They are following a mixed pattern of rituals viz. Hindu, Bengali refugee, Kondh and own traditional because of their frequent interactions. Due to extreme inaccessibility (8-10 hours journey by ferry from Chitrokonda Reservoir), the Government officials including the Micro Project employees find it very difficult to visit and carry out developmental works. As Phillips states, "The failure of resettlement and rehabilitation programme may push the tribals back to their original line of regression and deprivation from culture etc." (Phillips : 1989 : 251). The statement is as relevant and applicable to the cut off Didayis.

More or less, the Micro Project has brought certain changes in their personal attitude. The Didayi youths have been taking part in various cultural programmes, namely 'Adivasi Mela' held at Koraput and Bhubaneswar and also giving cultural programmes in AIR (Jeypore). It is seen that the DDA office is a common interacting place for the Didayis of three sectors. Not only they interact among themselves but also with the employees of Micro Project. They discuss about various inputs, benefits as well as the lacunae of the supplied items. On top of that, they do not hesitate to complain against the Project employees as has been noticed during the study. This perceptive impact as a guiding factor, is also helping the Project officer in assessing the on-going developmental schemes.

So to say, all that convincing responses the Didayis offered during the opinion survey that they had not rejected development programmes outright but had failed to participate in accordance with the guidelines of the scheme. It is partly due to their ignorance and partly due to the discriminatory dealings of the DDA. However, the plain villagers because of their proximity to the Micro Project office, have been able to derive the greater benefits from the developmental programmes. On the other hand, the hilltop and the cut off Didayis have lagged behind in terms of the targeted socio-economic development and also on account of the number of beneficiaries as they are relatively away from the Micro Project headquarter. Therefore, qualitative road construction has to be taken up immediately as a vital infrastructure development programme by the project authority to bring about rapid changes in the area. So that, it will evoke a sense of movement among the Didayis towards greater participation of the people in specific programmes for generating greater involvement, opportunity and sustainability.

10

Summary and Conclusions

During the post-independence period tribal developmental policies had been consistently modified on the guidelines of the National Planning Commission. The tribal developmental plan took a new turn during the Fifth Five Year Plan (1974-79) to evolve the Tribal Sub-Plan strategy (TSP). The aims of tribal sub-plans are to : (a) focus major thrust on the socio-economic development of the tribal population and strengthen the infrastructure in tribal concentrated areas and (b) protect their rights and eliminate all types of exploitations through legal administrative support.

The Tribal Sub-Plan approach was put into practice through ITDPs, MADA and Micro Projects for the development of areas of tribal concentration with long-term objectives to improve the tribal community particularly the Primitive Tribal Groups (PTGs). Areas having 50 per cent tribal concentration have been delineated as Tribal Sub-Plan area and outside it, tribal pockets have been declared as MADA pockets for the dispersed tribal population. For the PTGs special developmental projects in the name of Micro Projects are in operation for their development. At present TSP operates in 118 block areas of Orissa with a view to alleviating poverty through 21 ITDAs covering area with 50 per cent tribal population, MADA in 46 pockets having more than 80 per cent tribal population and 17 Micro Projects for 12 PTGs with tribal concentration (500-1000 Beneficiary households).

The Ninth Plan acknowledges the need for a National Tribal Policy that gives a special focus on the primitive tribes and displaced tribal groups and their rehabilitation. It adopts a three-pronged strategy of : (i) Social Empowerment; (ii) Economic Empowerment, and (iii) Social Justice, in empowering the disadvantaged groups. It also ensures removal of disparities, eliminate exploitation and suppression and providing protection to the disadvantaged groups. They emphasize to accelerate the on-going process of improving the socio-economic status of the disadvantaged groups through effective implementation of various policies and programmes and thus bring them on par with the rest of the society. The strategy aims at the participation of the socially disadvantaged groups in the process of planning not merely as the beneficiaries but also to take part effectively in the formulation of the need-based programmes, their implementation, supervision and monitoring.

The Didayi Development Agency (DDA), Kudumulugumma, one of the such Micro Project established in August 1986, is providing 100 per cent subsidy for individual family benefit-oriented schemes to the Didayi tribe. The DDA covers 140 sq.km area where the Didayis are inhabiting in 37 revenue villages belonging to four Gram Panchyats of Kudumulugumma and Khairiput Blocks of Malkangiri District, Orissa.

On the basis of geographic features, the total area under Micro Project can be divided into three sectors : (1) the plain, (2) hilltop, and (3) cut off sectors. The plain villages (5 nos.) located at the south-western foothills of the *Kondakamberu* hill range, are approachable by road whereas the hilltop villages (18 nos.) are located on the higher ridges at an average height of 3000 ft on the *Kondakamberu* hill range. There is only a jungle track passing through a Reserve Forest that connects hilltop villages with the plain villages. The cut off sector comprises 14 displaced villages owing to the construction of the Reservoir for Balimela Hydel Project in 1962, located at the bank of the Machkund river. These villages are approachable only through the boat-ferry service from Chitrokonda ferry point.

According to the latest survey conducted by the Micro Project in August-September 1998, the total Didayi population is 5,194, out of which males are 2,531(48.72%) and females 2,663

(51.28%). The female population is 2.54 per cent more than the male population and the sex ratio is 1052.

The villages under plain sector constitute 1297 (24.97%) of the total Didayi population and more than half of the total population 2740 are in hilltop sector (52.76%). The cut off sector has a total population of 1157 (22.27%). Both the plain and the hilltop possess a higher female ratio 1140 and 1074 respectively. The cut off sector has more number of males (52.21%) than the female strength (47.79%) which shows a reverse state of sex ratio 915. However, the overall sex ratio is 1052 with a male population 2531 (48.72%) and female 2663 (51.28%).

Poverty, underdevelopment and unemployment are consequences of the existing social and economic conditions of the area. It is a mere fact that at times, the taking up of different schemes for execution by different departments in an area run at cross purposes as discussed earlier about location and function of various types of schools causing distraction in a particular area. Therefore, DDA is required to implement all the developmental programmes in the designated area for the targeted people. The goal is sought to be achieved through democratic planning and securing the people's involvement and participation in which the programmes are basically culture specific and area specific. The major objectives of the study are to gain an insight into the people's development *vis-à-vis* Micro Project's performance. Much depends upon how much the DDA is people-oriented and responsive to the people's need. Such a study is believed to be helpful in assessing the impact of Micro Project's effort in the area to bring about development for the Didayi community.

In more formal terms, the objectives of the study are : (1) to understand the core elements of the Didayi social identity, defined and redefined over time, (2) to understand the economic life of the Didayi in the context of their society, (3) to study the impact of on-going government sponsored development activities through Block and the Micro Project for the Didayi, (4) to identify the various factors responsible to the cause of failure and success in the development, (5) to understand the hope and aspirations of the Didayi, (6) to find out the alternate strategy to meet the expectations of Didayis and (7) to assess the role of the NGOs (Non-Governmental Organisations) if any, in bringing the Didayi to the mainstream.

The study has been carried out in *Kondakamberu* hill region of Kudumulugumma and Khairiput Blocks in Malkangiri district in order to get the wholesome view of socio-economic status of the Didayi under the impact of programmes being implemented by the Micro Project, namely Didayi Development Agency (DDA). To understand the problems, it is decided to take up the field study in 30 per cent villages in each sector. As a result, the sample villages in all are 12, out of which 2 are in Plain, 5 in Hilltop and 5 in Cut off sector.

During the study, emphasis is given on the collection of primary and secondary sources of data empirically from the people and various official sources including DDA office. The techniques used for collection of data and information from the primary sources through the field study are : (a) Participant and non-participant observations, (b) Interviews, (c) Structured schedules and questionnaires, (d) Case studies and (e) Group Discussion with government and non-government personnels working in the area.

In order to understand the core elements of the Didayi social identity, relevant data on linguistic and socio-cultural life as well as information regarding trends of changes were collected from the respective sectors of Didayi land.

The Didayi society is basically egalitarian. The families are patrilocal, patrilineal and patriarchal. The families which predominate the Didayi society are either nuclear, extended or single member type. Both the nuclear and extended family types are found in majority in all the three sectors. Noteworthy feature is that 44.82 per cent extended families in plain sector constitute 20.5 per cent unmarried girls even beyond 35 years and the hilltop villages are having 23.41 per cent unmarried girls between 20-40 age group as has been earlier described. However, there is no over-aged unmarried girls found in cut off sector. The Didayi family is relatively a self-sufficient unit where all members contribute to their ability. The division of labour on the basis of age and sex is clearly marked.

Since, marriage is one of the most important lifecycle rituals, it embodies multiplicity of rules and regulations. Monogamous is the prevalent form of marriage, although one case of polygamy has been found in a hilltop village. The mean age at effective marriage for girls is 13-18 year, while for boys it is 18-30 year. Besides marriages by capture, marriage by service, love-making, elopement and arranged types are mostly practised. The latter form of marriage earns respectability in the community. Though inter-community marriage is proscribed, such cases are not infrequent now-a-days. The cases of cross-cousin marriage still continue in both hilltop and cut off sectors.

Kinship structure shows equal importance on patri and matri kins and there is a common term referred to both the paternal and maternal kin groups ignoring the gender status apart from denoting a specific term for a specific kin. Thus they exhibit a descriptive-*cum*-classificatory type. Unisexual type of youth dormitory (*Gulisung*) is seen in some villages where boys beyond 10 year attend until they marry. Plain villages do not have the typical youth dormitories. During field study, it was noticed that there are 4 dormitories in hilltop and 2 in cut off villages which still continue to educate and train the hill Didayi boys. The dormitories in other villages have now become communal gathering place (*Gulisung*) owing to relaxation of traditional restrictions. Presence of more number of youth dormitories in the hill sector indicates the prevalence of traditional values but in plain sector the concept has been greatly changed. Hence, it seems that the socio-economic and cultural importance of the dormitory enjoyed in the past is gradually losing its significance.

The Didayis have an elaborate clan organizations that are associated with a cluster of totemic groups. Such groups are identified as Tiger, Cobra, Bear, Vulture (*Gidha*) and Monkey (*Golury*). Each follows clan exogamy. The plain and hilltop Didayis mostly belong to Tiger, Cobra and Bear clan groups whereas the cut off villagers to Monkey (*Golury*) and Vulture (*Gidha*) totemic groups.

Politically, they are fully aware of the modern electoral system and at the same time showing inclination towards traditional village council. Primary sources of data states that about 55 per cent Didayis cast their votes in all elections. It suggests that they are politically active and the voters are divided on political party lines. Among them lady sarpanch and ward members actively participate in the usual activities of the panchayat. The Naik of the traditional village council and the Sarpanch of the Panchayati Raj system are mutually co-existing and cooperating in managing the village affairs. Community meeting is usually held at *Gulisung* generally located at the centre of the village.

Didayis are the worshippers of the Mother Goddess (*Adimata*), the creator (*Mahaprabhu*) and nature (*Biru*). Besides, they also worship many Hindu gods and goddesses like Lord Rama, Lord Shiva, Lord Krishna and Sita, Parvati, Durga, etc. Ancestral form of worship is associated with many domestic rituals. The plain villagers are more influenced towards Hindu religion and celebrate almost all Hindu festivals in association with the caste Hindus of the area. Whereas the cut off Didayis are following a mixed pattern (tribal, Hindu and Bengali refugee) rituals because of regular interaction with the Bengali refugees and Kondh tribal people. However, hilltop dwellers have retained more of their traditional religious identity for adhering to the tribal rites and rituals.

Throughout the year they observe a number of festivals. Chaiti festival or *Chaiti Pandu* is the most important one as the communal ritual hunt practice (*Shikar Bent*) is followed with great joy and enthusiasm. The Didayis of the three sectors observe the ceremonies as per the instructions of their respective village priest (*Palasi* or *Pujari)* with distinct procedures of divinations. They are not in favour of conversion unlike other tribal groups of Malkangiri district. Only one case of conversion to Christianity has been reported from plain village, Oringi. This family has been excommunicated from the village society. Folk dance (*Demsa*) and music is the rhythm of their life, that symbolizes their cultural identity, community consciousness and feeling of broadness among themselves.

The Didayi economic structure traditionally constitute both primary and secondary occupations : (a) practice of settled and shifting agriculture, and (b) collection of forest produces.

The plain villagers are settled agriculturists whereas the hilltop dewellers practise shifting cultivation. The cut off villagers follow both the settled and shifting cultivation. Generally, they are growing mixed crops with their age old cultivation procedure.

On an average a plain Didayi household gets Rs. 8,479 (87.2%), a hilltop Rs. 5,180 (81.6%) and a cut off Rs. 7,424 (87.7%) from agricultural production. Average annual income of a plain Didayi household is Rs. 9,723. Whereas the hilltop and cut off household have lesser income amounting to Rs. 6,347 and Rs. 8,464 respectively. Their source of income constitutes, agriculture (85.93%), wage earning (7.17%), livestock (4.19%) and forest produce (1.91%).

The expenditure pattern states that a plain Didayi household spends an amount of Rs. 9,748 on an average per year. Whereas, a hilltop and cut off household spends Rs. 6,354 and Rs. 8,504 respectively. Of this, consumption expenditure accounts for 91.96 per cent and rest only 8.4 per cent is utilised for agricultural production and acquiring of domestic animals for their income generation.

Based on the national poverty norm (VIII Plan), i.e. income and expenditure status below Rs. 11,000 and calories intake less than 2400 kilo calories (in last 30 days consumption) by the people have been categorised as below poverty line. Owing to the income-expenditure pattern, agriculture produce quantity and the nutritional status, the 98 per cent households come under BPL category. Although, 1.2 per cent Didayis are economically better off (APL), still are found to be in secondary poverty state because of malnutrition.

However, it is seen from the income-expenditure pattern that a Didayi household somehow manages to run in a balanced budget. They do not have any savings in the bank as recorded during the field study. For their own periodic requirement, they keep money in a bamboo hollow. They apprehend to borrow money from outsiders as some of them who have availed the TRYSEM loan have been experienced cheating by the VLW who had demanded Rs. 150 from their loan amount. At times, the outsiders like forest officials and the police persons charge allegation and demand money from them. Within the village though they help each other in socio-cultural functions but cannot get the economic assistance as all of them are in the same economic bracket (BPL). Furthermore, it is revealed from the opinion survey that except Micro Project they do not ask monetary help from others as they are aware of the fact that the Micro Project is only operating for their beneficial sake. Although branches of Mini Bank, State Bank of India and Panchayati Gramya Bank are existing in the project area, no Didayi has been found to avail the loan facility. The ongoing Community Developmental schemes like DWCRA and the income generating schemes of DDA, have been providing economic assistance to the people. The study on beneficiary HHs reveals that 20.63 per cent (DWCRA), 44 per cent (agriculture scheme) and 12 per cent (horticulture scheme) households respectively, have been economically benefited. These income-oriented schemes have helped the people to bridge the household budgetary gaps to some extent. Despite the fact that being in below poverty line, they do not prefer to be indebted as no such case has been recorded.

The Didayi possess meager cultivable lands as per the revenue records. It is estimated that except a few plain Didayis, others in general have less than one acre of land. On an average, 57.6 per cent households are landless. The hilltop villagers cultivate about three to four acres of *podu* lands per household. These *podu* lands are inherited in the patrilineal line of succession though they do not possess the *patta* rights. Whereas, in the cut off villages, cultivation of *podu* land is done by a group of villagers and all of them share the yield. They only possess the *'pattas'* for their low lands which has been submerged. Depending on the water level in the reservoir they reclaim their own land and practise settled cultivation. It is also learnt that every year they demand compensation for the lost crops due to the rise in water level.

Since the inception of the Micro Project (1986), it is expected that the income would increase because of implementation of development programmes. All the developmental programmes can be grouped :

(a) Natural Resource Development and Family Oriented Income Generation Schemes.
(b) Human Resource Development Scheme.
(c) Infrastructure Development Scheme.
(d) Establishment and Administration.

An attempt has been made to find out the extent of success made by each programme and their limitations, in the light of the factors responsible for development. This study has also examined how far each progamme or scheme has been able to bring about sustainable development for Didayis.

Under Natural Resource Development and Family Oriented Income Generation Schemes, various developmental programmes like Horticulture, Agriculture, Irrigation, Animal Husbandry and Fishery have been carried out by DDA. The horticulture and agriculture schemes have been well received by the people. On comparing the pre and post-programme (Horticulture Scheme) income state of the 50 beneficiary HHs, it is revealed that 12 per cent beneficiary households of the lowest income group have been substantially benefited from the scheme and succeeded to higher income bracket. However, more number of beneficiaries (64%) have been selected from the plain villages compared to hilltop (16%) and cut off villages (20%), resulting in unequal economic growth amongst the homogenous community.

On analyzing the pre- and post-programme stage (Agriculture Scheme) of 50 beneficiary HHs, it is found that more number of households are selected from destitute categories (42%) while rest : V.V. Poor (26%), V. Poor (22%) and Poor (10%). Priority has been given to plain sector (56% HHs) whereas only 22 per cent households each, have been selected from other two sectors. Over a decade of participating in the A. Scheme, it is found that 76.1 per cent HHs of destitute category had raised their income up to the V.V. Poor status. Beneficiaries from the V. Poor and Poor group have shown 63.6 and 100 per cent success respectively. From the overall point of view, it is noteworthy to mention that 44 per cent have upgraded their economic status out of which 12 per cent were able to cross the poverty line.

Animal husbandry scheme has failed to derive much success as it is estimated that percentage of failure rate is 75 per cent. There has been a lot of dissatisfaction regarding the selection of beneficiaries and quality of the supplied livestocks. The beneficiaries used the animals not for income generation but for sacrificing the animals during religious ceremonies. Cut off sector people have failed to achieve any benefit from fishery scheme as the opinion survey reveals that 90.9 per cent people have expressed their unhappiness about the scheme. The Veterinary Dispensary at Kudumulugumma and one Livestock Aids Centre located at Jantri, serve the livestocks of the area which are inadequate. The failure of animal husbandry and fishery scheme reflect the lack of people's participation and improper selection of beneficiaries. Due to poor maintenance and non-availability of repair facility in the cut off area, the boats supplied by DDA are found to be in broken state and the wooden planks of the broken boats are used for making cots and stools.

DDA is committed to improve the human resources, because there are 12 primary schools under Education Department and one Kanyashram under TRW Department. These are not adequate. Hence, under Human Resource Development schemes, efforts have been made to enhance their literacy rate by instituting of 10 non-formal schools called *Gyanmandirs*. Another effort is to impart skill building training on driving, tailoring, basket making, carpentry, broom binding, and Health-care facilities, etc. Even after opening of *Gyanmandirs*, it is found that no schooling facilities are available even at a radius of three to four kilometers in villages of hilltop and cut off sectors. To meet the gap more number of formal schools are to be opened by DDA. Recently in 1976 two child labour schools started functioning at Purunaguma and Jantri to cover the dropouts and the working children. It is felt that functioning of schools under various agencies (Education Department, Child Labour and DDA) at one place like village Jantri work at cross purposes.

Opening of the non-formal schools have been found to be an appreciable step taken by DDA because they help to increase the literacy rate as has been recorded : neo-literate

(9.49%), literate (6.44%) and illiterate (85.4%) in 12 study villages. The present study indicates that the literacy rate is only 15.93 per cent which needs more attention. Since 1994, six *Gyanmandirs* of hill sector have sent 46 children to various Sevashrams and primary schools out of which almost 40 per cent are dropouts at various levels of educational standards. There are 13 boys and 9 girls presently continuing education. The dropout case is very alarming and needs to be checked. DDA has spent Rs. 5,35,670 towards construction of *Gyanmandirs* and on the salary head of the teachers. The expenditure appears to be 3.7 per cent of the total expenditure which is inadequate as regards to the educational development.

Health-care facilities are practically non-existent in the project area, except in Kudumulugumma. It is mainly due to lack of road communication, particularly villages of hilltop and cut off area faced innumerable health-care problems. Therefore, the DDA evolved the policy to meet the needs of the people with regard to health, hygiene and sanitation. The Micro Project has organized health camps, immunization programmes and provided first-aid kits to villages through *Gyanmandir* teachers. Nutritional status of entire Didayi community has been found to be in a very poor state. To improve the situation, DDA requested the District authority of ICDS to extend services to the uncovered areas of the project as there are only eight ICDS centres which do not cover all the villages.

Infrastructure is the skeleton that supports a community's economic, social and even its political development. It is the main component of development of an area. Basically, lack of road communication, inaccessible hilly terrain through the reserve forest and isolation by water reservoir are the main attributes for poor status of the Didayi of this area. Any sign of modernity is yet to reach both the hilltop and cut off sector villages. DDA has taken initiative to improve the communication by constructing the village roads. However, hilltop and cut off villages are only connected by foot track and ferry services respectively. Plain villages are linked by motorable roads. Hence, all the developmental schemes so far implemented by DDA, have shown better results in this accessible plain sector. DDA has given adequate emphasis on infrastructure development incurring an expenditure of 41.63 per cent of total utilised funds since its inception. Major percentage (25.8) of expenditure has been on road and track construction, which is an essential facets of development. However, road accessibility has been limited to only plain villages. Hilltop and cut off villages are still connected by tracks from the road heads or ferry points. Much efforts are still desired to be done in these sectors with massive investments.

Where infrastructure need necessarily leads to development of the tribal people, on the contrary, they often face the backlash of development. Therefore, infrastructure development has to be suitably adopted as a part of the bigger package of programmes. It is unfortunate to note that though many of them have been displaced for construction of Balimela Hydro-electric project, they have not yet received the benefit of electricity. As a result of which they are deprived of using TV and other electrical appliances. The major problem is that due to lack of electricity school children waste their study hour especially in the evening. DDA has given utmost priority to undertake electrification scheme soon.

The present strength of the staff of DDA is found to be inadequate to visit and supervise various ongoing developmental programmes within a desirable time-frame in all three sectors. Hence, there is a requirement of additional staff.

Out of total expenditure (Rs. 1,44,04,777), 23.15 per cent has been spent on income generation scheme, which is adequate. However, only 7.99 per cent has been given for HRD, which is found to be inadequate as regards to socio-economic development of a PTG. On infrastructure development, though maximum amount : 43.29 per cent has been spent, other than three plain villages, namely Oringi, Purunaguma and Muduliguda, rest 34 villages are found to be still inaccessible. Inaccessibility is found to be a major hindrance for them and, therefore, benefits of various schemes by DDA have not reached them as desired. The records and the expenditure details given in the Governors Report by DDA, do not give clear particulars of beneficiaries. The statement showing funds received, utilized and utilization certificate submitted to Government (Annexure-I), the Scheme-wise Expenditure Details by DDA and Annual Action Plan (1994-95) by THIRTI (SC & STRTI), the amounts are found to be at variance. The Annual fund utilisation certificate by DDA (Annexure-I), reflects that on an average at least 20-25 per cent of the funds allotted to DDA remains unutilized and being carried forward to the next financial year.

An opinion survey regarding the functioning of DDA, has been carried out among 145 respondents of three sectors to find out the cooperation and coordination between the DDA and the people. Maximum people (90.3%) have expressed their happiness about DDA while 6.2 per cent are dissatisfied. Almost all (95.8%) have approached DDA for their problems which indicate a good rapport. The DDA staff have been able to gain confidence of people which is essential to implement any programme. Only a few of them (28.27%) have expressed their negative opinion regarding response by DDA to their problems. However, all of them want DDA to continue and work for them. On asking about their expectation from DDA all of them want assistance in income generation, health-care, education, skill building training and development of communication.

The Micro project has been utilizing the monetary assistance from ITDA and IRDP. All the CD programmes in the area are carried through the DDA. Didayi people are keenly participating in DWCRA and TRYSEM schemes. About 16.98 per cent plain, 7 per cent hilltop and 14.63 per cent cut off villagers have been benefited through TRYSEM scheme. DWCRA scheme has benefited 105 (20.68%) women operating in seven groups belonging to plain (18.86%), hill top (16.79%) and cut off (36.58%) beneficiary households respectively. The other CD programme, namely NOAP has benefited 34 (6.67%) Didayis of the study villages.

The role of NGOs is very negligible as the Didayis are concerned. There is only one NGO named as 'REACH', has been operating in the cut off sector and the people have been motivated to save the money with a little amount of Re. 1 to Rs. 5 per month. No other NGOs have so far able to reach them.

Lastly, it can be said that no matter how much important development programme may be, if it is not sustained by a continuous events of success and achievements, all endeavour would be futile. Therefore, to ensure sustained development, the efforts should be made in creating the awareness generation, conscientization and sensitization of programmes.

Suggestions for Action

The present study on the impact of DDA on the Didayi and its analysis, has resulted in identifying certain weaknesses because of which the Development of Didayi of the region has not been achieved the desired result in respect of the expenditure. A few findings are enumerated below to ensure better effectiveness of the programmes for the development of Didayi.

NRD and Family Oriented Income Generating Schemes

(a) The proposed Agro-Forestry Scheme based on Slopping Agricultural Land Technology (SALT) as recommended by Prof. K.K. Mohanty for Bondo Development Agency area may also be implemented in Didayi area as both are having similar topography and shifting cultivation practices.

(b) The record of rights (*Patta*) should be given to the shifting cultivators for the *podu* lands which is being cultivated since generations. This will prevent them destroying other adjoining primary forest for the purpose.

(c) Free distribution of the saplings and vegetable mini-kits may be discontinued. These items may be provided to interested villagers at a nominal price on cash payment in order to create a sense of belonging. So that, bartering of these items and loss due to careless handling can be avoided.

(d) As a first step, the people are required to be motivated by establishing demonstration-*cum*-nursery farms and simultaneously be educated about the benefit of the scheme. People's active participation is essential in selecting the type of fruit saplings, HYV seeds and agricultural implements as per their need to make the programme more people-oriented rather than Micro project oriented.

(e) A judicious distribution as well as identification of the beneficiaries may be made from all three sectors to avoid dissatisfaction amongst the villagers and to check unequal economic growth in the sectors.

(f) Care may be taken to supply the items at the right time and not during off season and festival periods. Because, they follow a traditional cultivation procedure and rituals as per their yearly schedule.

(g) Subsequent incentives only may be given to those beneficiaries who have made sincere efforts on the scheme and not to those who sell off/barter the items or misuse it.

(h) Irrigation schemes need be created, at suitable places after due technical appraisals and not just creating something which does not serve their purpose as has been noticed in Bayapada (Hilltop) and Jantri (Cut off) villages.

(i) Manpower has to be trained from the locality to attend to immediate repairs of the diesel pump sets, tube-wells and solar lights in their area.

(j) Instead of planting vetivera grass, the naturally available siali creepers and broom cultivation need to be encouraged to stop the soil erosion and develop fertility of *podu* land. Since, these plants are already part of the ecosystem and Didayis are deriving economic benefits out of these, so further cultivation may be encouraged.

(k) A fresh, *suo moto* verification of the *Patta* records may be carried out in cut off sector villages as a large number of people claim to be Didayis and are getting benefits from DDA, whereas, in the Revenue records held at Chitrokonda Tehsil it shows different tribal status. This will avoid possible future complications on the issue.

(l) Marketing facilities for trading of agricultural and forest produces need to be provided to both the hilltop and the cut off sectors, as the villagers are seen selling their produce at depressed price in the villages because of inaccessibility and lack of marketing avenues. The LAMPS at Kudumulugumma Block headquarters has no sub-center in the project area to accommodate their requirements. Hence, sub-centers of LAMPS are required to be operated in these inaccessible areas to meet their credit-cum-marketing activities.

(m) The study has reflected that animal husbandry scheme did not fair well. The reason is mainly due to the incompatibility of their attitudes. As such, they have domesticated animals and are not happy with the quality of the animals they receive. Instead, they consume or use the animals for ritual sacrifice.

(n) Supply of net and boats have found to be not effective due to lack of people's interest.

A lot has been discussed earlier about the schemes but it needs to emphasize on the basis of shortcomings and lapses of the development programmes for necessary rectification in the future.

Human Resource Development

Adequate attention has not been given to this sector as only 7.99 per cent of total amount (Rs. 1,44,04,777) has been spent on this aspect. More priority is needed to be given to this sector as HRD comprises the major aspect of the socio-economic development of any community.

Education

(a) The literacy growth rate is found to be at a low (15.93%) state which needs adequate attention for its acceleration.

(b) Adult education programme may be continued as a number of neo-literates (9.49) are found among Didayis who can motivate and inspire their children to study.

(c) *Gyanmandirs* or non-formal schools need to cover all the interior villages and teachers should be given the responsibility of the adult education. Other additional work-loads may be reduced to give adequare time to the children. DDA may provide incentives to those teachers who have motivated and also sent more number of pupils to U.P. schools and M.E. schools.

(d) Location of all types of schools in the area are to be coordinated in order to avoid duplication of schools in one village and none in other villages. Villagers are found to be in confused state regarding the purpose and the function of the respective educational institutions, i.e. Government Upper Primary School, Child labour school and *Gyanmandir*.

(e) In the beginning of an academic year DDA may arrange a village meeting and distribute prizes to the students who have successfully completed one academic year. It would not only motivate the children for higher studies but also help to check the drop-out cases as more number (40%) of cases have been recorded.

(f) The inherent and natural skills of the Didayis, namely broom binding, basket making, net weaving, *bidi* making, etc. need further grooming and proper marketing facilities are required to be provided for their economic enhancement.

(g) Skill building training in the activities which are required by them in their villages, viz. repairing of tube-wells, solar lights, bio-gas plant, sewing machine and diesel hand pumps, etc. may be organized to make them self-sufficient.

Health, Nutrition and Sanitation

The health-care system in the Didayi area seems to be poor and inadequate as we have discussed earlier. To improve the health-care certain fundamental issues have been raised for active consideration :

(a) Health sub-centres may be started in hilltop and cut off sectors to cater to the emergency need of the people in these inaccessible areas. Health workers need be stationed at suitable villages.

(b) The Didayi are found to be suffering from nutritional deficiency and the most vulnerable groups are the women and children. Their staple diet (*gruel*) is found to be rich in carbohydrates and proteins but it lacks the fat contents and other vital nutrients. According to the opinion of the local doctors, the following steps may be taken up for improving the nutritional status of the Didayis :

   (i) Regular supplementary feeding through ICDS is required in all the villages.

   (ii) Mini-Anganwadi services are to be accelerated.

   (iii) Women-oriented programmes be conducted to enlighten the people about their nutritional deficiencies, cooking procedure, vitamin contents of food, etc.

(c) Owing to the lack of safe drinking water, sanitary condition and health consciousness, most of the people suffer from diseases, like gastroenteritis, skin disease, Leprosy, Acute Respiratory Infection (A.I.R.), Eye diseases and Malaria. Following preventive steps may be taken into action :

   (i) There is a need to improve health and sanitary conditions through the improvement of KAP (knowledge, attitude and practices), with regards to home environment.

   (ii) Keeping of domestic animals inside the house should be discouraged and the houses need be properly lighted and ventilated.

   (iii) Through audio-visual aids, health, nutrition and sanitation programmes can be shown to the people.

(iv) Malaria precautions and prevention measures may be taken and awareness programmes may be conducted to educate the villagers. Mosquito nets may be provided at concessional rate.

(v) Health camps need to be organized at intervals to detect the T.B. and the Leprosy cases.

(d) The local tribal medicinemen (*Dishari*) and the village mid-wife need be given necessary short-term training on health education, the use of herbal medicines and First-aid, etc. Once these traditional medicinemen are well trained, health-care service work can more effectively function as the people have immense faith in their own traditional medicinemen.

Drinking Water

(a) Each village may be provided with a PVC piped bore well (to avoid rustic and smelly water) for drinking water.

(b) At least one person of a village may be trained to repair the tube-wells as and when required.

(c) Open wells are seen in dry state. The cisterns made by DDA are found in disused state. People are only fetching *'chua'* water for drinking purpose. Hence, further construction of cisterns may be discontinued and open wells are to be made deeper.

Infrastructure Development

Top most priority need to be given to this aspect, without which no other schemes can be effectively implemented and the development of the area as well as the Didayi as a community, will remain as a distant dream even after another decade. Following suggestions may be considered :

(a) The roads must be developed to connect villages of the Hilltop sector as well as the Cut off sectors. Necessary permission to build the road through the Reserve Forest between Oringi and Bayapada be obtained on priority from the competent authority and the road be provided immediately. If need be, additional funds may be diverted by suspending other schemes.

(b) Frequency of ferry services connecting Chitrokonda and Jantri is to be increased.

(c) Under Rural Electrification Scheme, electricity may be given to the villagers as a natural compensation for their displacement because of construction of Balimela Hydel Project.

(d) All types of construction works are to be undertaken permanently rather than temporarily where wastage rate is more as frequent repair and maintenance work of village roads and tracks, has been recorded.

Establishment and Administration

In order to make the establishment of DDA more efficient and responsive to the targeted people, following suggestions may be considered :

(a) Additional staff have to be appointed to meet the requirement of DDA.

(b) Incentives and additional benefits may be given to the staff to make them motivated and committed. Suitable accommodation for the staff, some reservation in hostel accommodation for their school and college going children, reservation in technical education (engineering and medical colleges) for their children and a choice of posting after the completion of tenure may be considered.

(c) They need to interact with the people of three sectors equally and try to educate and motivate them to use better techniques as well as to ensure people's involvement in all the developmental schemes from planning to execution stage.

(d) Since most of the interior villages are generally not visited by the Government officials, the DDA staff are required to go to the villages to understand their grassroots problems before formulating the schemes.

(e) In the Governing Body meeting, tribal members from all three sectors may be asked to participate besides the Didayi leader.

(f) The beneficiaries records and the financial expenditure records need be maintained in proper manner so that effectiveness of a scheme can be assessed. Names of the beneficiaries and villages are to be mentioned.

Last but not the least, it must be kept in mind that all developmental programmes are to be carried out without polluting their natural habitat and socio-cultural identity. Moreover, it would always be kept in mind that the development is for them. Hence everything is to be done by them and they need be trained in the process to take adequate care in tailoring their own future. The people may not be treated as only aid receiving beneficiaries but as development partners of the nation. They need to be involved in the developmental process from planning to all stages of implementation, so that it may incorporate into their own traditional way of life. Gradually, it would provide impetus for further sustainable growth which will bring in the desired level of socio-economic development over a period of time. Major thrust are to be given on communication and education, which are the key elements for the development particularly in the context of Didayi tribe. Other aspects can be achieved in better and effective manner, through these key factors, i.e. health, education and communication.

The present study has made an endeavour to analyze the success and failure of various programmes and schemes implemented by DDA to achieve the objectives. However, a further analysis and extensive study is required to understand the core cultural values relating to land and forest in order to focus on Didayi identity. The refugees in Malkangiri district apparently constitute a dominant society. Therefore, another dimension of study needs be made on the inter-relationship between the Didayi and the rehabilitated Bengali Refugees on the Didayi land because it can provide the future implications of appropriate development strategies.

ANNEXURE-I

Statement showing funds Received, Utilised and Utilisation Certificate submitted to Government (Annual) Didayi Development Agency, Kudumulugumma (1986-1999)

Year	Opening balance as on 1st April.	Amount received directed welfare Department	Total funds available for expr.	Amount utilised during the year	Utilisation certificate.	Balance for expenditure
1	2	3	4	5	6	7
1986-87	—	1,59,050	1,59,050.00	1,31,434.23	—	27,615.77
1987-86	27,615.77	26,85,211	27,17,826.77	4,33,940.73	—	22,78,886.04
1988-89	22,78,886.04	6,70,000	29,40,886.04	6,05,808.63	—	23,43,077.41
1989-90	23,43,077.41	5,50,000	28,93,077.41	23,24,466.78	3,11,654.87	5,68,610.63
1990-91	5,68,610.63	13,00,000	18,68,610.63	10,94,305.30	7,67,534.62	7,74,305.25
1991-92	7,74,305.25	10,67,000	18,41,305.25	15,53,504.60	6,15,070.65	2,87,400.65
1992-93	2,87,408.65	15,67,000	17,94,400.65	14,40,592.00	25,96,511.60	3,53,808.65
1993-94	3,53,808.65	11,21,000	14,74,808.65	12,46,046.00	32,92,6365.34	2,28,672.65
1994-95	2,28,762.65	11,60,000	13,88,762.65	11,61,415.00	14,34,941.00	2,27,347.65
1995-96	2,27,347.65	17,96,000	20,23,347.65	10,99,047.00	10,21,178.00	9,24,250.65
1996-97	9,24,250.65	5,87,000	15,11,250.65	14,70,030.00	23,47,608.37	57,220.65
1997-98	57,220.65	7,23,000	7,80,220.65	3,84,280.00	—	3,95,940.65
Total		1,33,41,261		1,29,457,321.00	1,24,37,261.00	3,95,940.65
1998-99	3,76,534.65	13,69,600	17,45,534.00	14,59,456.00		2,86,078.65

Source : DDA Kudumulugumma.

ANNEXURE-II

Literacy Level

(*Extract taken from the Medicine issue register maintained by DDA*)

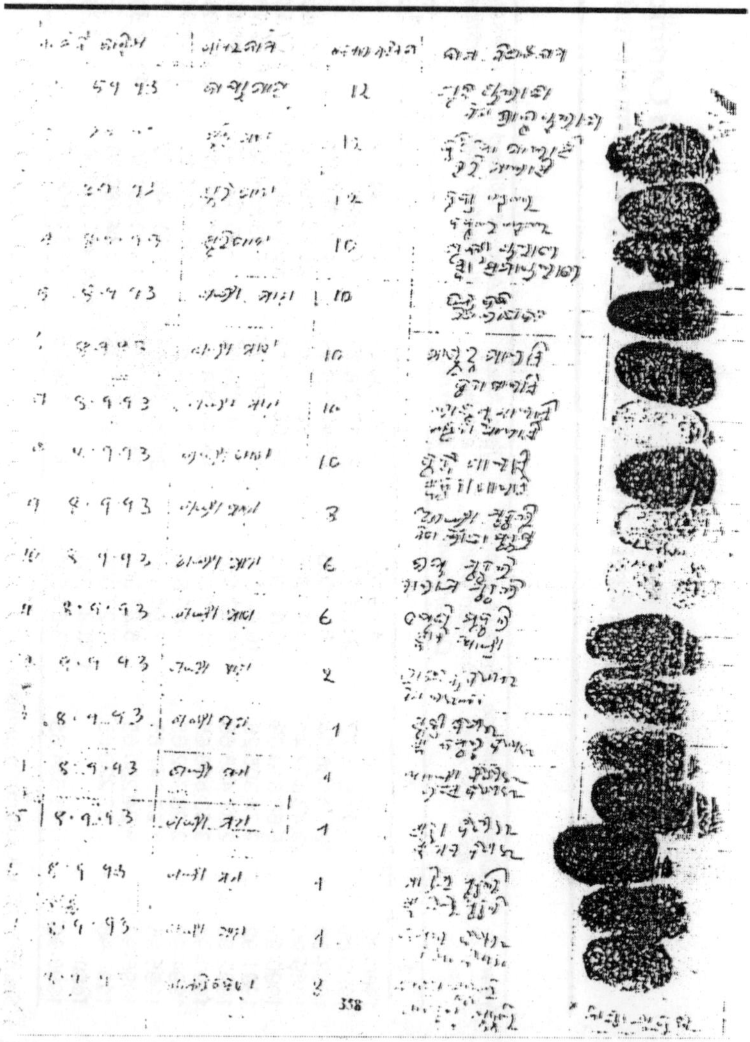

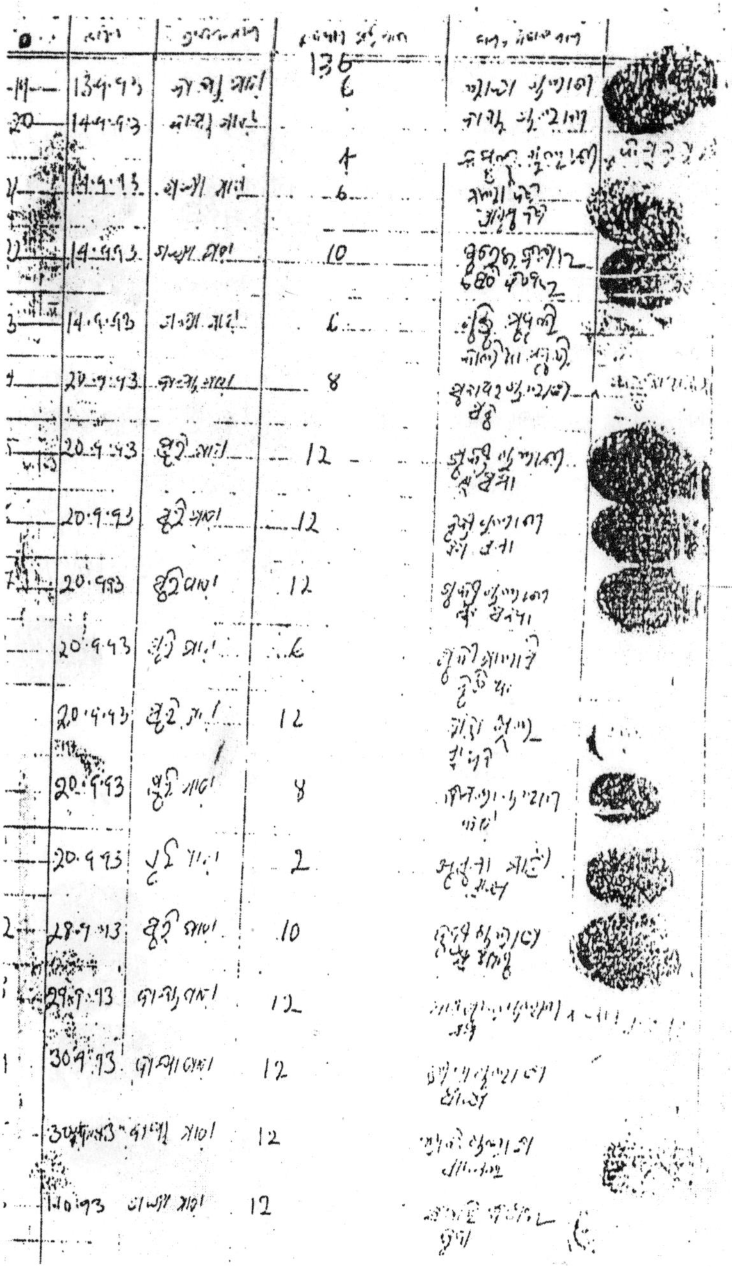

No.	Date	[illegible]	Quantity	Name	Thumb impression
19	13.9.93	[illegible]	6	[illegible]	
20	14.9.93	[illegible]		[illegible]	
			4	[illegible]	
	14.9.93	[illegible]	6	[illegible]	
	14.9.93	[illegible]	10	[illegible]	
3	14.9.93	[illegible]	6	[illegible]	
4	20.9.93	[illegible]	8	[illegible]	
5	20.9.93	[illegible]	12	[illegible]	
	20.9.93	[illegible]	12	[illegible]	
7	20.9.93	[illegible]	12	[illegible]	
	20.9.93	[illegible]	6	[illegible]	
	20.9.93	[illegible]	12	[illegible]	
	20.9.93	[illegible]	8	[illegible]	
	20.9.93	[illegible]	2	[illegible]	
2	28.9.93	[illegible]	10	[illegible]	
	29.9.93	[illegible]	12	[illegible]	
1	30.9.93	[illegible]	12	[illegible]	
	[illegible]	[illegible]	12	[illegible]	
	1.10.93	[illegible]	12	[illegible]	

7

[illegible]	[illegible]	[illegible]	[illegible]	[illegible]	[illegible]
[illegible]	10.10.93	[illegible]	12	[illegible]	× [illegible]
[illegible]	11.10.93	[illegible]	12	[illegible]	
[illegible]	11.10.93	[illegible]	12	[illegible]	
40	11.10.93	[illegible]	10	[illegible]	× [illegible]
41	12.10.93	[illegible]	8	[illegible]	× [illegible]
42	12.10.93	[illegible]	8	[illegible]	× [illegible]
43	12.10.93	[illegible]	6	[illegible]	× [illegible]
44	[illegible].10.93	[illegible]	12	[illegible]	
45	[illegible].10.93	[illegible]	12	[illegible]	
46	[illegible].10.93	[illegible]	12	[illegible]	
47	2.11.93	[illegible]	12	[illegible]	× [illegible]
48	3.11.93	[illegible]	12	[illegible]	
49	4.11.93	[illegible]	12	[illegible]	
50	10.11.93	[illegible]	12	[illegible]	
51	10.11.93	[illegible]	10	[illegible]	
52	10.11.93	[illegible]	12	[illegible]	× [illegible]
53	10.11.93	[illegible]	8	[illegible]	× [illegible]
			360		

[illegible]	[illegible]	[illegible]	[illegible]	[illegible]	
54	12.12.93	[illegible]	12	[illegible]	
55	20.12.93	[illegible]	12	[illegible]	
56	21.12.93	[illegible]	12	[illegible]	
57	[illegible].12.93	[illegible]	6	[illegible]	
58	29.12.93	[illegible]	12	[illegible]	
59	5.1.94	[illegible]	12	[illegible]	
60	18.1.94	[illegible]	12	[illegible]	
61	18.1.94	[illegible]	12	[illegible]	
62	18.1.94	[illegible]	6	[illegible]	
63	18.1.94	[illegible]	12	[illegible]	
64	20.1.94	[illegible]	12	[illegible]	
65	19.8.95	[illegible]	10	[illegible]	
66	19.8.95	[illegible]	10	[illegible]	
67	19.8.95	[illegible]	5	[illegible]	
68	19.8.95	[illegible]	6	[illegible]	
69	19.8.95	[illegible]	[illegible]	[illegible]	
70	19.8.95	[illegible]	10	[illegible]	
71	19.8.95	[illegible]	5	[illegible]	

(*Courtesy* : DDA Kudumulguma—1998)

Bibliography

Ali, Syed. (1998), *"Income and Employment Generation through I.RD.P."* An Analysis, *Kurukshetra*, Vol. 46, No. 10, Ministry of Rural Areas and Employment, Govt. of India, New Delhi.

Anderson Robert S. (1982), *Science, Politics and the Agricultural Revolution in Asia—Rural Poverty for Growth*, Westview Press, Colorado.

Aparajita, Upali. (1994), *Culture and Development, Dongrias Niyamgiri*, Inter-India Publications, New Delhi.

Arora, R.C. (1979), *Integrated Rural Development*, S. Chand Company Ltd., New Delhi.

Bairathi, Shashi. (1991), *Tribal Culture, Economy and Health*, Rawat Publications, Jaipur, Rajasthan.

Bapuji, M. (1993), *Tribal Development and Administration*, Kanishka Publishers, Distributors, New Delhi.

Basu, A.R. and Nijhawan, S. (1994), *Tribal Development Administration in India*, Mittal Publications, New Delhi.

Baviskar, Amita. (1995), *In the Valley of the River : Tribal Conflicts over Development in the Narmada Valley*, Oxford University Press, New Delhi.

Bedi, M.S. ed. (1995), *Tribal Development in Rajasthan, with special reference to Women and Children*, Himanshu Publication, Udaipur, Rajasthan.

Behera, M.C. (1994), *Planning and Socio-Economic Development of the Tribals*, Common Wealth Publication, New Delhi.

Behura, N.K. (1992), *Shifting Cultivation—A Case for Environmental Degradation, Adibasi*, Vol. XXX, No. 4, T.H.R.T.I., Government Press, Orissa.

Bell, R.C.S. (1945), *Gazetteer of Koraput District*, Orissa, Government Press, Calcutta.

Bhowmik, P.K. (1993), *Dynamics of Tribal Development*, Inter-India Publications, New Delhi.

— — — (1994), *Rural and Tribal Development Practices in India*, M.D. Publication, New Delhi.

Bhowmik, P.K. and P. Sahoo (1997), *Tribal indebtedness : A Socio-economic Analysis, Man and Life*, Vol. 23, 727, Lake Town, Calcutta, West Bengal.

Bhusare, M.D. and R.R. Kulkarni. (1990). *Agricultural Technology and Consequent Socio-economic Changes among Tribals*, An Article Published in *Tribal Research Bulletin*, Vol. XII, No. 1, TRTI, Maharashtra, Pune.

Bisoi, Loknath, (1997), "Adima Adivasi—Didayi", Saptahika, Weekly Magazine, *The Samaja*, Cuttack, Orissa.

Bisoi, Loknath. (1998), *Didayi Loka Sanskruti—Eka Alochana*, Oriya Journal, *Mousamee*, Shristi and Shrasta Cultural Organisation, Umarkote, Nawarangapur, Orissa.

Bulletin (1969), The Tribal Research and Development Institute, Government of Madhya Pradesh, Bhopal.

Chambers, Robert and Gujit, Irene. (1995), "Pra Five Years Later : Where are we now?", *Westlands News*, 11(2).

Chandan, Sri and G.K. Prativa Prakasham. (1993), *Tribal Development and Welfare Legislation in Orissa*, Kitab Mahal, New Delhi.

Chaturbedi, H.R and S.K. Mitra. (1982), *Citizen Participation in Rural Development*, Oxford and IBN Publishing Co., New Delhi.

Chaudhuri, Bhuddhadeb. (1990), *Tribal Development in India : Problems and Prospects*, XXXVI, Inter-India Publications, New Delhi.

— — — (1990), *"Didayi" in Tribes in Orissa*, Harijan & Tribal Welfare Department, Government of Orissa, Bhubaneswar.

Chaudhury, S.K. (1993), *Myopic Development and Cultural Lens : An Evaluative Study of Tribal Development Programmes among Kondhs of Orissa*, Inter-India Publications, New Delhi.

Chowdhury, Bhagirathi. (1996), "Tribes and Development", *Orissa Today Annual Survey*, Nayapalli, BBSR, Orissa.

Cohen John, M. and Uphoff Norman, T. (1977), *Rural Development Participation : Concept and Measures for Project*

Design, Implementation and Evaluation, Ithaca, Cornell University, New York.

Danda, A.K. (1991), *Tribal Economy in India*. Inter-India Publication, New Delhi.

Dandekar, V.M. and Nilakantha Rath, (1971), *Poverty in India*, Gokhale Institute of Politics and Economics, Pune, Maharashtra.

Das, G.N. (1957), "The Adibasi of Orissa and their Welfare", *Vanyajati*, 5(2), pp. 74-82.

Das, S.T. (1993), *Tribal Development and Socio-Cultural Matrix*, New Delhi.

Das, Vidhya, (1998), "Human Rights, Inhuman Wrongs : Plights of Tribals in Orissa", *Economic and Political Weekly*, Vol. 33, No. 11, March 14-20, A Sameeksha Trust Publication, Mumbai.

Das Patnaik, P.S. (1990), *Bondo Tribes of Orissa*, T.H.R.T.I., pp. 82-87, Bhubaneswar, Orissa.

Deogaonkar, S.S. (1992), *Tribal Development Plans Implementation and Evaluation*, Concept Publishing Company Pvt. Ltd., New Delhi.

Dubhashi, P.R. (1983), *Grammar of Planning : Concepts and Applications*, Indian Institute of Public Administration, New Delhi.

Elwin, Verrier, (1939), *The Baiga*, Oxford University Press, Bombay .

——— (1950), *Bondo Highlanders*, Oxford Press, Bombay.

Fernandes, Walter (ed). (1985), *"Development and Peoples Participation : An Introduction"*, *Development with People : Experiment with Participation and Non-Formal Education*, Indian Social Institute, New Delhi.

——— (1998), *"Jharkhand or Vananchal : Where are the tribals?"*, *Economic and Political Weekly*, 33(44), A Sameeksha Trust Publication, Mumbai.

Fernandes, Walter, Geeta Menon and Philip Viega. (1988), *Forests, Environment and Tribal Economy : Impoverishment and Marginalisation in Orissa*, Indian Social Institute, New Delhi.

Furer Haimendorf, Von C. (1943), *The Chenchus*, Macmillan Co. Ltd., New York.

Furer Haimendorf, Von C. (1945), *The Reddis of the Bison Hills*, Macmillan Co. Ltd., New York.

George, Jose and S.S. Sreekumar. (1994), *Tribal Development : Legislation & Enforcement*, Commonwealth Publication, New Delhi.

Ghate, Rucha S. (1992), *Forest Policy and Tribal Development : A Study of Maharashtra*, Concept Publishing Company Pvt. Ltd., New Delhi.

Gopalan, M. and V. Kali. (1998), "LAMP": A Micro Study, *Kurukshetra*, Vol. 46, No. 9, Ministry of Rural Areas and Employment, New Delhi.

Guha, Uma and M.K.A. Siddiqui and P.R.G. Mathur. (1968), *The Didayi—A Forgotten Tribe of Orissa* : Memoir, No. 23, Government of India, Publications Branch, Civil Lines, New Delhi.

Gupta, Jai Prakash. (1997), "Emancipation of Tribals : Constitutional Safeguards." *Manpower Journal*, 33(3), pp. 51-58.

Indian Express. (1995), July 23, Begumpet, Hyderabad.

Jadhav, Narendra. (1997), *Economic Thought and Philosophy*, Popular Prakashan, Mumbai.

Jain, S.C. (1998), "Gandhian Approach to Tribal Development : Broaching the Choice," *Kurukshetra*, Vol. XLVI. No. 4, Ministry of Rural Areas and Employment, New Delhi.

Jena, Abhaya Charan (1987), *Citizen Perception and Administrative Performance : A Study in a District of an Indian State*, Ph.D. Dissertation, Berhampur University, Orissa.

Jena, Laxman. (1997), *"Dispossession of the Tribal People from their Agricultural Land : A Case Study of Koras in Midnapur"*, *Man and Life*, 23(1-2), pp. 85-90, 727, Lake Town, Calcutta.

Jhabua Rahul. (1996), "The Unsilenced Valley : The Bhills of Madhya Pradesh.", *Down to Earth*, 5(2), pp. 21-23.

Jha, Veena. (1997), *Tribal, Environment and Sustainable Development : A South Asian Perspective*, Macmillan Press, Hong Kong.

Joshi, G.M. (1997), *Tribal Baster and the British Administration*, Indus Publication, New Delhi.

Joshi, Y.G. (1990), *Development in Overexploited Tribal Regions*, Inter-India Publications, New Delhi.

Journal of the International Association for Impact Assessment. (D-2000), Vol. 18, ISSN 1461-5517, Beech Tree Publishing, G. Britain.

Kabeer, N. (1994), *Reversal Realities : Gender Hierachies in Development Thought,* London.

Kapoor, A.K. (1998), *"Role of NGOs in Human Development : A Domain-Anthropology", Journal of the Indian Anthropological Society,* Vol. 33, Nos. 2 and 3, New Delhi.

Kar, Gourang Kumar. (1998), *Adimanaba Didayi,* A book in Oriya Language, Everest Printers, Jeypore, Orissa.

Kaur, Harpreet. (1995), *Tribal Development Administration,* Shiva Publications, Udaipur.

Khadar, S.K. (1999), *Maximising Allround Productivity, Yojana,* Vol. 43, No. 1, pp. 35-42, Sansad Marg, New Delhi.

Khare, P.K. (1991), *Social Change of Indian Tribes: Impact of Planning and Economic Development,* Deep and Deep Publications, New Delhi.

Kothari, C.R. ed. (1991), *Rural Development,* Volume-1 and Volume-2, Jaipur, Rajasthan.

Kulkarni, R.R and M.D. Bhusare. (1990), "Agricultural Technology and Consequent Socio-economic Changes among Tribals", *Tribal Research Bulletin,* Tribal Research and Training Institute, Vol. XII, No. 1, Mumbai.

Kulkarni, Sharad. (1994), "Tribal Communities in India : Today and Tomorrow", *Tribal Research Bulletin,* Vol. XVI, No. 1, Mumbai.

Kumar, Alok. (1986), *Tribal Culture and Economy : The Mal Paharias of Santal Parganas,* Inter-India Publications, New Delhi.

Kumar, Anil. (1994), *Approaches to Tribal Development,* Sarup and Sons, New Delhi.

Kumaran, K.P. (2000), *Impact of Economic Reforms on SCs and STs,* NIRD, Rajendranagar, Hyderabad.

Mahapatra, L.K. (1994), *Tribal Development in India : Myth and Reality,* Vikash Publications, New Delhi.

Marak, K.R. (1997), *Traditions and Modernity in Matrilineal Tribal Society,* Inter-India Publications, New Delhi.

Mehta, P.C. (1994), *Tribal Development in Rajasthan,* Shiva Publications, Udaipur, Rajasthan.

Menon, P. S.K. (1995), *"Institutional Framework for Social Justice"*, *Yojana*, Vol. 39, No. 6, New Delhi.

Mishra, K.K. (1994), *Tribal Elite and Social Transformation : The Case of Khamti in Arunachal Pradesh*, Inter-India Publications, New Delhi.

Mishra, P.K. (1996), *"Performance of LAMPS in Orissa": Problems and Prospects, Co-operative Movement in India : A Case Study of an Indian State*, A.P.H. Publishing Corporation, New Delhi.

——— (1988-89), "Development Constraints : A Micro-Study of Economy and Polity Among the Bauri of Ganjam District", *MANAVA*, Volume 3, Vision.

Mohanty, M.K. (1990), *Tribal Society Programmes Planning and Economic Change*, Chugh Publications, Allahabad.

——— (1996), *Development Hand Book for the Bond Development Agency Area (An Acion Plan Based on Techno-Economic Survey)*, T.H.R.T.I., Govt. of Orissa, Welfare Department, Bhubaneswar.

Mohanti, K.K. and P.K. Mishra and M.R. Acharya. (1996), *Development Intervention : Study of the Lanjia Saora of Orissa*, Nabakrushna Choudhury Centre for Development Studies, Bhubaneswar, Orissa.

Mohanty, S.C. (1981), "Tribal Development Programmes", *Adibasi*, Vol. XXIX,. No. 3, Tribal Research Bureau, Bhubaneswar, Orissa.

——— (1981), "Didayi : A Picturesque Tribe of Orissa", Adibasi, Vol. XXI, Nos. 1-4, Tribal Research Bureau, pp. 1-10, Bhubaneswar, Orissa.

Mohapatra, P.M. and P.C. Mahapatra. (1997), *Forest Management in Tribal Areas : Forest Policy and Peoples Participation* : Proceedings of the Seminar, Forest Policy and Tribal Development during 15-16 February at Koraput, New Delhi.

Mukherjee, Neela. (1998), "Gandhi's vision and Micro-Level Sustainable Development", *Kurukshetra*, Vol. XLVI, No. 4, pp. 17-18, Ministry of Rural Areas and Employment, New Delhi.

Mukherjee, Bhabananda. (1963), "Socio-Economic and Religious Organization of the Raj Banshi", *Bulletin of the*

Anthropological Survey of India, Vol. XII, No. 384, pp. 66, Calcutta, W.B.

M.P. Jahangir. *Ambedkar Journal of Social Development and Justice*, Volume 2, pp. 32-40.

National Institute of Rural Development. (1994), *Course on Planning and Management of Tribal-Development Programmes in Sithampet Mandal of Srikakulam District : An Evaluation* (Reading-Material), N.I.R.D., Hyderabad.

— — — (1996), *Course on Planning and Management of Tribal-Development Programmes* (Reading Material), N.I.R.D., Hyderabad.

— — — (2001), *Journal of Rural Development*, Special Issue on Welfare of SCs and STs in Independent India, Volume 20, No. 1, N.I.R.D., Hyderabad.

Nalla, Arjuna. (1998), *"Am Malkangiri", An Oriya Booklet*, Printed by Lucky Printers, Berhampur, Orissa.

New Indian Express (1999), 12 August, Begumpet, Hyderabad.

Ogburn,Willam F. and Meyer F., Nink Off. (1966), *A Handbook of Sociology*, Eurasia Publishing House.

Pati, Jagannath. (1999), *Social Welfare Journal*, Vol. 46, No. 3, p. 29, New Delhi.

Patanaik, N. and B. Choudhury and P. S. Das Patnaik. (1984), *The Bondos and their Response to Development*, T.H.R.T.I., Bhubaneswar, Orissa.

Padma Seth. (1995), "Women and Social Development", *Yojana*, Vol. 39, No. 6, New Delhi.

Patnaik, N. (1989), *Tribal Development Administration*, T.H.R.T.I., Bhubaneswar, Orissa.

Patanaik, S.M. (1996), *Displacement Rehabilitation and Social Change: The Case of the Paraja Highlanders*, Inter-India Publications, New Delhi.

Parmar, H.S. (1992), *Tribal Development in Himachal Pradesh*, (*Policy, Programmes and Performances*), Mittal Publications, New Delhi.

Pareek, Vijay Ku. (1992), *Adult Education : Tribal Development, Migration and Inequality*, Himanshu Publications, New Delhi.

Pasayat, Chitrasen. (1998), "Social Forestry and the Tribes of Orissa", *Social Welfare Journal*, Vol. 45, No. 8, pp. 27-31, New Delhi.

Patel, M.L.. (1994), *Tribal Development without Tears*, Inter-India Publications, New Delhi.

Phillips, W.S.K. (1993), *Development of Tribals Effected by the Narmada Project : Tribal Situation in India*, Edited by Vidyut Joshi.

Prasad, R.R. (1988), "Tribal Development in India—Strategies and Programmes", *Journal of Rural Development*, Vol. 7(1), pp. 81-103, NIRD, Hyderabad.

Praharaj, D.M. (1988), *Tribal Movement and Political History in India*, Inter-India Publications, New Delhi.

Pathy, Jaganath. (1984), *Tribal Peasantry : Dynamic of Development*, Inter-India Publications, New Delhi.

Raghvan, Jyoti. (1996), "Tribal Welfare : A New Dimension (Success Story), *Cooperator*, 33(10), pp. 370-372.

Rao, P.V. (1988), *Institutional Framework for Tribal Development : A Micro-Level Study*, Inter-India Publications, New Delhi.

Roy, Burman, B.K. (1985), "Issues in Tribal Development", *Mainstream*, January 5 and 12, New Delhi.

— — — (1995), *Tribal Situation and Approach to Tribal Problem in India : A Preliminary Appraisal, Discussion Paper*, Rajiv Gandhi Institution for Contemporary Studies, New Delhi.

Samal, Prasanta, K. (1996), *Tribal Development : Options, National*, Gyanodaya Prakashan.

Sikidar, Sujit. (1990), *Economic Development of Tribal India*, Ashish Publishing House, New Delhi.

Singh, C.P. (1994), *Tribal Development Administration : A Case Study*, Mittal Publications, New Delhi.

Sahoo, S.C. (1998), "Marketing through Co-operatives : A Study of Working of LAMPS in Orissa"; *Kurukshetra*, Vol. 47, No. 3, pp. 19-23, Ministry of Rural Areas and Employment, New Delhi.

Shrivastava, M.P. and Ruby Dhar (1998), "HRD : Socio-economic Perspective", *Kurukshetra*, Vol. 47, No. 3, pp. 37-41, Ministry of Rural Areas and Employment, New Delhi.

Shroff, Jagannath. (1997), *Forest Policy and Tribal Development in "Forest Management in Tribal Areas—Forest Policy and Peoples Participation"*, Ed. Mahapatra, P.M. and Mahapatra, P.C., Concept Publishing Company Pvt. Ltd., pp. 65-69, New Delhi.

Spardely, J.P. (1980), *Participant Observation*, Holt, Rinehert and Winston, U.S.A.

Social Science Research. (2001), Vol. 30, ISSN 0049-089x, Academic Press, *Online Journal Library*, 525 B Street, Suit 1900, San Diego.

Social Welfare Journal. (2001), ISSN 0037-8038, Vol. 48, No. 1, New Delhi.

WDR. (1990), *World Development Report*, World Bank, Oxford University Press, New York.

World Bank. (1993), *"The East Asian Miracle : Economic Growth and Public Policy, A World Bank Policy Research Report"*, Oxford University Press, New York.

Government of Orissa. (1997), *State's Economy in Figures*, Directorate of Economics and Statistics, Bhubaneswar, Orissa.

— — — (1997), *Statistical Outline of Orissa*, Directorate of Economics and Statistics, Bhubaneswar, Orissa.

— — — (1998-99), *Governor's Report*, Annual Administration of Scheduled Areas in Orissa, Didayi Development Agency, Kudumulugumma, Orissa.

— — — (1994-1998), *Annual Action Plan*, Didayi Development Agency, Kudumulugumma, H and TRW Department, Orissa.

— — — (1998-99), *Annual Action Plan*, Didayi Development Agency, Kudumulugumma, H and TRW Department, Orissa.

— — — (1999-2000), *Annual Action Plan*, Didayi Development Agency, Kudumulugumma, H and TRW Department, Orissa.

Index